WORSHIP
and AWE
in CHRISTIAN
PSYCHOLOGY

"This groundbreaking work challenges psychology's foundations by repositioning God at the center of therapeutic practice. Knabb thoughtfully integrates psychological research with theological wisdom, demonstrating how worshipfulness—not the self-centeredness often unintentionally fostered in traditional clinical practice—enables true human flourishing. Both theoretically sophisticated and practically transformative, this book offers clinicians a radical reorientation toward God-centered care. Essential reading for anyone seeking to practice psychology within a Christian worldview."

—**M. Elizabeth Lewis Hall**, Rosemead School of Psychology, Biola University

"In *Worship and Awe in Christian Psychology*, Joshua Knabb offers a deeply needed vision for Christian psychologists—a vision that calls us back to the heart of our work: reverence for God. This is not just another integration text; it's a soulful, intellectually rich invitation to consider how awe and worship shape us as followers of Christ. With theological depth, clinical insight, and spiritual humility, Knabb helps us reflect on the sacred work of therapy. I found myself pausing, worshiping, and realigning. This book will form you as much as it informs you. A beautiful, essential contribution."

—**Jennifer S. Ripley**, Regent University

"So dominant is secular psychology and therapy in our day that most Christians are unaware that their faith entails a God-centered psychology with a very different model of human flourishing. What a gift, then, is this gem of a book that considers—from many different perspectives—the psychological value of worshipfulness, a worthy alternative to mindfulness, or at least its ultimate fulfillment. After reading this book, one might just wonder if humans were made to worship God and enjoy him forever."

—**Eric L. Johnson**, Christian Psychology Institute

"*Worship and Awe in Christian Psychology* is such a refreshing and practical guide for readers to reorient their lives around a deep, reverential awareness of God. What sets this book apart is its thoughtful integration of empirical psychological research with Scripture and spiritual practices from a wide range of Christian traditions. I especially appreciated the clear framework for intentionally cultivating awe. The journaling and exercises from different Christian traditions help make awe a regular rhythm, not just a fleeting moment. Joshua Knabb's unique expertise shines through, making complex concepts easy to apply in daily life. This is a rich resource for personal growth and for those guiding others, including pastors, counselors, and mentors."

—**Kenneth T. Wang**, Fuller Theological Seminary

WORSHIP and AWE in CHRISTIAN PSYCHOLOGY

HOW CENTERING GOD TRANSFORMS MENTAL AND SPIRITUAL HEALTH

JOSHUA J. KNABB

Baker Academic
a division of Baker Publishing Group
Grand Rapids, Michigan

© 2026 by Joshua James Knabb

Published by Baker Academic
a division of Baker Publishing Group
Grand Rapids, Michigan
BakerAcademic.com

Printed in the United States of America

All rights reserved. No part of this publication may be reproduced, stored in a retrieval system, or transmitted in any form or by any means—for example, electronic, photocopy, recording—without the prior written permission of the publisher. The only exception is brief quotations in printed reviews.

Library of Congress Cataloging-in-Publication Data
Names: Knabb, Joshua J. author
Title: Worship and awe in Christian psychology : how centering God transforms mental and spiritual health / Joshua J. Knabb.
Description: Grand Rapids, Michigan : Baker Academic, a division of Baker Publishing Group, [2026] | Includes bibliographical references and index.
Identifiers: LCCN 2025023644 | ISBN 9781540968562 paperback | ISBN 9781540969194 casebound | ISBN 9781493450152 ebook | ISBN 9781493450169 pdf
Subjects: LCSH: Public worship—Psychology | Mental health—Religious Aspects—Christianity | Psychology, Religious
Classification: LCC BV15 .K63 2026 | DDC 248.301/9—dc23/eng/20250813
LC record available at https://lccn.loc.gov/2025023644

Unless otherwise indicated, Scripture quotations are from the Holy Bible, New International Version®, NIV®. Copyright © 1973, 1978, 1984, 2011 by Biblica, Inc.® Used by permission of Zondervan. All rights reserved worldwide. www.zondervan.com. The "NIV" and "New International Version" are trademarks registered in the United States Patent and Trademark Office by Biblica, Inc.®

Scripture quotations labeled ESV are from The Holy Bible, English Standard Version® (ESV®), copyright © 2001 by Crossway, a publishing ministry of Good News Publishers. Used by permission. All rights reserved. ESV Text Edition: 2016

The names and details of the people and situations described in this book have been changed or presented in composite form in order to ensure the privacy of those with whom the author has worked.

Cover design by Paula Gibson

Baker Publishing Group publications use paper produced from sustainable forestry practices and postconsumer waste whenever possible.

This book is dedicated to my wife, Adrienne,
who displays a life of worshipfulness toward God
on a moment-by-moment basis
in her self-sacrificial, Christlike love.

Contents

List of Exercises xi

Preface xiii

1. An Introduction to Worship and Awe in Christian Mental Health 1
2. Worship and Awe in Christianity 27
3. Worship and Awe in Psychology 55
4. Christian Worship and Awe with Thoughts and Images 95
5. Christian Worship and Awe with Behaviors 127
6. Christian Worship and Awe with Relationships 167

Acknowledgments 201

References 203

Index 221

Exercises

Puritan Meditation   111
Puritan Prayer of Adoration   112
Ignatian Prayer   113
Medieval Contemplation   116
Lectio Divina   118
Classic Hymn   119
Practicing *AWE*   120
Mirror Metaphor   142
Visio Divina   144
Travel a Labyrinth   145
Meditative Walking   148
Practicing the Presence of God   150
Puritan Prayer of Praise   153
Listening to a Hymn with God   155
Participate in Communion   157
Meditating on God's Creation   181
Meditating on God's Providence   182
Meditating on God's Gifts   184
Meditating on Jesus's Love   187
Meditating on Jesus's Resurrection   188
Jesus Prayer   192
Admiring a Human Talent   193

Preface

It is my contention in the pages that follow that optimal Christian mental and spiritual health can be traced back to one powerful, all-encompassing word. This word is threaded across our thoughts and images, emotions, behaviors, and relationships. It comes up in every domain of life, whether family, church, work, community, or leisure. The word is "worshipfulness," as a noun, or "worship," as a verb. It can be succinctly defined as a surrendering, thankful response of reverential awe to an infinitely good, wise, powerful, present, and holy God, who is the Creator, Sustainer, and Redeemer.[1]

Worshipfulness may be the Christian version of mindfulness, which is highly prized in the psychology literature of the twenty-first century. Mindfulness, in fact, has been used in contemporary psychology as a strategy to cultivate a greater sense of awe for all of life.[2] It can be succinctly defined as a present-moment, nonjudgmental, flexible awareness of each unfolding experience.[3] This awareness can be related to the inner world, such as a thought, feeling, or sensation, or outer world, including a sound coming from the environment. Mindfulness has been called "beginner's mind,"[4] given there is a newness and open curiosity, rather than criticism and judgment, applied to each emerging second of the day, like a child having an experience for the very first time.

---

1. Here I offer a definition of healthy Christian worship, which acknowledges God at the center of existence. In subsequent chapters, I'll also discuss unhealthy Christian worship that is directed toward ourselves, others, and things.
2. See, e.g., Thompson (2022).
3. Bishop et al. (2004).
4. Bishop et al. (2004), 233.

In this book, I argue that Christian worshipfulness as a psychological and spiritual discipline is a fitting, worldview-sensitive alternative to mindfulness, given that mindfulness has been derived from the millennia-old Buddhist religious tradition. Like mindfulness, Christian worshipfulness can be applied to all of life for optimal psychological health. Worshipfulness can help you, as a Christian, to better understand the ultimate purpose for the "good life." This purpose is to view all of life with reverential awe because you have a personal relationship with God as Creator, Sustainer, and Redeemer.

If you are a student in a graduate psychology or related training program learning how to work with Christian clients in a professional context, or a mental health professional already providing services in the field, this book can help you in two ways: to pursue mental and spiritual health in your own life, and to better serve your Christian clients by using it as a direct resource with them in psychotherapy or professional counseling. This is especially true if sustained worshipfulness, applied to *all* of the Christian life, is essential for optimal psychological and spiritual functioning. Beyond these two contexts, if you are a Christian who simply desires to better understand your own psychological suffering and improve your mental or spiritual health, this book can also be helpful. It is filled with useful explanations, exercises, and examples to move you toward more purposeful, reverential, worshipful awe of God on a moment-by-moment basis.

Yet, as Christians, we can easily get distracted by the wrong objects of devotion—God's creation, including ourselves, others, and things—without acknowledging and praising the Creator. This ubiquitous human struggle with self, other, and thing worship may be what has led to a sizeable increase in the prevalence of mental disorders in the twenty-first century,[5] with the antidote to this psychological suffering being a loss of the preoccupation with the self.[6] Although being in awe of people and things is inevitable because a perfect, benevolent God is their author, they should invariably point us as Christians back to him. When they don't, and we end up worshiping ourselves, others, and possessions without returning to God, this may add to our psychological and spiritual suffering in a fallen, broken, imperfect world.

My main argument throughout these pages is that what we worship is *the* most important decision we make in life, with profound implications for our mental and spiritual health. Also, our collective, gradual societal shift over the last century or so from God at the center to the self at the center is

---

5. See, e.g., Daly (2022), who has revealed an increase in adolescent depression from 2009 to 2019. See also Twenge (2014, 2018), who makes the case that younger generations in the twenty-first century seem to be increasingly struggling, psychologically speaking.
6. Welsh and Knabb (2009).

making us miserable, psychologically and spiritually speaking, because we were never designed to unilaterally turn inward for psychological and spiritual well-being. Rather, God designed us to worship him, and Christians will not live optimally until we learn to make this important pivot[7] from self to Other on a moment-by-moment basis.

Research in the secular psychology literature over the last few decades has increasingly elucidated this dilemma—overly focusing on the self, not God, for mental and spiritual health may not ultimately contribute to a life of flourishing. The Christian tradition, therefore, can help us better understand why self-preoccupation is leaving us dejected, exhausted, and isolated, both individually and collectively. Overall, contemporary psychological science can give us a granular understanding of *what* is happening, *who* is affected, *when* prevalence rates for mental disorders are increasing or decreasing, and *how* psychological variables (capturing both mental health and disordered functioning) are theoretically and empirically related. Christian theology, on the other hand, can offer us a useful account of *why*—God designed us to worship him, not ourselves. And we will continue to suffer beyond the day-to-day adversities that inevitably exist in a fallen, broken world until we unequivocally return to him.

In terms of my background, I write as a Protestant Christian with professional training as a clinical psychologist. I lead with my Christian identity and do so from a Reformed perspective.[8] This means I believe that the Bible is infallible and God's revelation to humankind. The Bible, from this perspective, is a source of both psychological and spiritual knowledge for optimal Christian living. As a result, I humbly attempt to begin and end with a biblical worldview,[9] wherein God is infinitely good, wise, powerful, present, and holy, among other attributes; God's providence, or good governance and protective care, extends to all of creation; the Bible, not just science, is a source of psychological knowledge to guide life; and a spiritual reality, in addition to a physical reality, exists with God at the center. In my interaction with Scripture, I believe the entire Bible is applicable to daily living, and I attempt to extend an orthodox reading and understanding of God's Word to psychological and spiritual functioning and the "good life." As a Reformed Christian, I operate

---

7. Throughout the book, I use the word "pivot," drawn from acceptance and commitment therapy (ACT) (see Hayes et al., 2012). This word suggests we should, moment by moment, flexibly shift or turn from unhelpful thoughts, feelings, sensations, memories, and images in the inner world to living out a set of values or principles for living in the outer world. As a parallel for Christians, our pivot is from self, other, and thing worship to God worship.

8. See, e.g., Barrett (2017).

9. See, e.g., Knabb et al. (2025).

from the notion that belief in and a personal relationship with Jesus Christ is necessary for salvation and reliant on God's grace (see, e.g., John 3:16; 14:6; Rom. 10:9–10; Eph. 2). Therefore, I draw on Christian theologians and philosophers to make better sense of worship and awe in the good life.

While my foundation is Reformed Christianity, I also believe Christian spiritual writings and practices/disciplines from the far-reaching, centuries-old, diverse Christian tradition can be helpful for psychological and spiritual insights and growth. As a result, I draw from a range of classic Christian spiritual writings. In doing so, I think about and interpret them "evangelically."[10] This means I take the best ingredients from them while also ensuring I am faithful to an orthodox reading and application of Scripture along the way. I have been researching these classic Christian spiritual practices/disciplines as interventions for psychological and spiritual change for the last several years, with some promising results: Christian meditation, prayer, and contemplation can be helpful for Christians suffering from worry,[11] rumination,[12] stress,[13] and trauma-related symptoms,[14] among other types of mental distress. I integrate some of these empirically tested practices to help you cultivate and maintain worshipful awe before God for Christian mental and spiritual health.

What is more, although I begin and end with a biblical worldview, I also believe that God provides a common type of grace to all communities, even secular ones. This means Christians can learn and grow from some of the insights of secular psychology (in this case, theoretical and empirical perspectives on worship and awe and their psychological benefits) just as long as this knowledge does not contradict Scripture.[15] Some have called this approach for attempting to reconcile the Bible and psychology either integration or Christian psychology.[16] In either case, a biblical worldview is foundational in this book, and I attempt to assimilate some content from psychology that aligns with this Christian view of the world to help twenty-first-century Christ followers cultivate and maintain worship and awe for Christian mental and spiritual health.

In terms of content, chapters 2 and 3 serve as the foundation. In them, I attempt to make the case that—both spiritually and psychologically—worship

---

10. Goggin and Strobel (2013).
11. Knabb et al. (2017).
12. Knabb, Vazquez, Pate, Garzon et al. (2022).
13. Knabb and Vazquez (2018); Knabb, Pate, Sullivan et al. (2020).
14. Knabb, Vazquez, Pate, Wang et al. (2022).
15. See, e.g., Mouw (2001).
16. Johnson (2010b).

and awe are key for the good life. Specifically, chapter 2 covers worship and awe from a Christian perspective by drawing on the Bible and theology to better understand the importance of this topic for optimal living. Chapter 3 explores the theory, research, and practice of worship and awe from within the discipline of psychology to offer some of the newest advancements from psychological science. In chapters 4 to 6, I discuss worship and awe in the context of three awe triggers, including thoughts and images (cognitive/conceptual triggers), behaviors (physical/sensory triggers), and relationships (social/relational triggers). In each of these three concluding application chapters, my hope is to help you be more intentional about pursuing worshipful awe before God. I do so with your thinking, physical interactions and sensory experiences in the world, and relational and other social interactions. And my wish is that, with the embedded insights and practices, you will slowly learn to be worshipful across every domain of life (e.g., family, work, church, community, leisure), not just on Sunday mornings at church. As a result, I include definitions, journaling exercises, practices, reflection questions, and biblical and life examples so you can, as a Christian, better understand and apply the material to your Christian faith. Ultimately, my priority is to explore with you, the Christian reader, how worship and awe can be helpful for Christian mental health in the twenty-first century, especially in an age of widespread disenchantment, materialism, and secularism.

Regarding the intended audience, this book is written for Christians who recognize on at least some level that worshiping the things of this world will never truly satisfy and, thus, are looking to improve their relationship with God by developing specific psychological and spiritual strategies to do so. My hope is that along the way, such Christians may move toward improved mental and spiritual health within the context of the Christian faith. Beyond this foundation, my hope is that this book can be used as a supplemental text in graduate-level courses in psychology and related programs (e.g., psychotherapy and professional counseling intervention courses, faith integration courses) to train mental health professionals (e.g., psychologists, psychiatrists, marriage and family therapists, professional counselors, social workers, pastoral counselors) to work with Christian clients in a Christian-sensitive manner, as well as a resource for professionals in the mental health field. Beyond training programs and professional contexts, my hope is that Christian readers simply looking to improve their mental and spiritual health will find this resource useful, because I've intentionally written this for them as well.

Although I interact with sources from both Christianity and psychological theory and research, this book is in no way meant to be a substitution for professional mental health services. If you believe you are struggling with a clinical issue such as depression, anxiety, or trauma-related symptoms, or your daily functioning is impaired because of such symptoms, please reach out to a Christian mental health professional for help.

CHAPTER ONE

An Introduction to Worship and Awe in Christian Mental Health

To be human is to worship.
—Daniel Block, *For the Glory of God*

God made us to worship. That is why we were created. Everything has its reason for being here. We have this reason: that we might worship the Father Almighty, Maker of heaven and earth.
—A. W. Tozer, *Worship*

Introduction

I can still vividly remember the panoramic landscape. I traveled with family and friends up a mountain—some may call it a hill—which included a large, protruding, historic white cross at the top and a 360-degree, far-reaching view of the surrounding cities. As we rested at the base of this enormous landmark, which majestically and effortlessly stretched toward heaven, I looked toward the horizon that enveloped us. I used my God-given senses to immerse myself in God's beautiful creation, with a deep experience of his presence and goodness and vastness. In this moment, I felt small, in a good way. I was able to let go of the mental agitation, stress, and other unpleasant inner experiences that I so often struggle with when I turn inward, unnecessarily focus on myself, and ineffectively ruminate and worry about the pressures of the day. In this instance, it was me and God. He was big, and good, and wise, and powerful, and holy, and the Creator, and I was little and the created. I did not need to protect myself, inflate myself, compulsively try to change myself, be the center of attention, or compete for others' praise. I could let go and feel overwhelmed, in reverential worship and awe before God. During these brief, enchanted minutes, time, paradoxically, seemed to slow down. I could sink into the enormity of the present moment, which God held in the palm of his proverbial hand. As I worshiped God with all my attention, with an attitude of deferential, yielding awe, I felt more connected to him than I had in weeks, maybe even months or years. I just rested in his loving arms. As we got ready to trek back down the hill, I praised him, with a simple, "Thank you, God." I knew that he was far too great to fully contain within my finite human mind, and this moment was far too important for me to be swept away by the ordinariness of the day. I could, in reverence, honor, and praise, just thank him with my mere, less-than-fully-adequate human words—a few imperfect syllables strung together to form a child's sentence. I did not, in this moment, need to be in control. Rather, I could surrender, in reverential worship and awe, to a perfect, benevolent King, who was and is in full control and much more immense than I can ever imagine. Although most of my life may be spent lost in the mundane ordinariness of the day—filled with relational conflicts, work deadlines, and modern-day distractions like sitting in traffic or scrolling through superficial social media posts—on this hilltop I recognized the importance of Christian worship with a big God and a small self.

The "Ordinariness" of Life

In C. S. Lewis's classic twentieth-century Christian writing *The Screwtape Letters*, which is a fictional exchange of letters between two demons, he makes the case that one of the most effective ways to draw humans away from Christianity and a transcendent, worshipful approach to all of life is to entice them with the ordinary day-to-day. This ordinariness is made up of mere human sensory experiences, which are perceived to be "real" at the expense of a truly divine reality. "Keep pressing home on him the ordinariness of things," one demon suggests to another as a strategy to distract a human from spiritual matters.[1] In their very first fictional letter exchange, in fact, the uncle demon confidently writes to his nephew to share his success of distracting a human with the need to eat when the man began to consider a transcendent reality in a public library. As soon as this distraction of hunger was presented, the man

1. Lewis (1996), 4.

walked outside the library and became preoccupied with the ordinariness of life, such as a bus driving by and a kid delivering newspapers.

Contemporary Christians battle the ordinariness of our industrial, technologically enhanced Western life, with far-reaching advancements, increased secularization (and now often atheism), and nearly ubiquitous media advertising we get from moment to moment to consume more and more. This ordinariness constantly pulls us away from a spiritual, transcendent reality, wherein God is at the center of all of life and worthy of our worship and awe. Because of this, Christians can easily forget about God and inevitably start to worship the self (or others or things), believing we are living in a purely material world with only sensory experiences and an isolated, individual human mind, consistent with Lewis's spiritual insights in *The Screwtape Letters*.

With contemporary living in an industrialized, secularized, and technologically saturated society, Christians are now distracted by the ordinariness of things.[2] We struggle to recognize a spiritual reality that extends to all of life, wherein God is at the center and worthy of our worship and awe. With the ordinariness of things, you may have a hard time maintaining an awareness of God's presence and, consequently, your ultimate purpose for the "good life" (in the Greek, *telos*).[3] And this real, ongoing struggle has mental and spiritual health implications.

Since the beginning of recorded history, humankind has wrestled with our telos, or ultimate purpose, for the good life, quite possibly more than anything else. In this timeless pursuit that spans eras, cultures, and continents, we can easily place ourselves, not God, at the center. And this self-centeredness may quickly give rise to narcissism—which involves "excessive self-love or egocentrism"[4] and can be more prevalent in highly individualized, affluent societies—with narcissism positively linked to psychological suffering like depression and anxiety and negatively linked to psychological well-being.[5]

An array of contemporary Western disciplines—philosophy, the arts, the sciences, and so forth—now commonly operate from the assumptions of materialism and atheism (e.g., there is no God, only the physical world exists, the individual is at the center of existence, the individual decides the ultimate purpose for living, the individual is the ultimate source of their own happiness)[6] in an effort to make sense of life's telos. In contrast, Christians believe that the Bible as God's divine revelation tells us who

---

2. Lewis (1996), 4.
3. Anderson et al. (2017); Smith (2009).
4. American Psychological Association (n.d.d).
5. Henttonen et al. (2022).
6. Anderson et al. (2017); Smith (2009).

God is (e.g., as infinitely good, wise, powerful, present, and holy), our position before him (e.g., as finite, dependent, and created by him to be in relationship with him and worship him), our psychological and spiritual vulnerabilities (e.g., wanting to be like God and worship the self, others, or things rather than relying on God and worshiping him), and our ultimate purpose in life for fulfillment (e.g., to be in relationship with, commune with, and worship and glorify God and surrender to his perfect will).[7] This enduring struggle—wanting to be like God (at the center of our own existence) and worship the self rather than relying on God (with him at the center) and worship him—has far-reaching mental health implications in the Christian life that can easily be overlooked, with the Bible providing penetrating insights into this ongoing vulnerability.

Throughout Scripture, we read of a grand narrative that spans from Genesis to Revelation.[8] Although humans were created to be in relationship with God, we wanted to be like God, not dependent on and worshipful toward him, which led to Adam and Eve's banishment from the garden of Eden and our estrangement from God (see Gen. 1–3). In the postfall biblical narrative, we read about humankind's rebellion against God throughout the Old Testament, whether they are complaining to God (see, e.g., Num. 11:1) or engaging in full-blown idolatry (see, e.g., Exod. 32), with the latter involving worshiping someone or something in place of God. Even with humankind's constantly wayward ways, God has offered us a redemptive plan, revealed in the New Testament, which is to reconcile us to him: Because of Jesus's sacrificial, substitutionary death on the cross (i.e., the atonement) in our place, Christians are now friends with God, can commune and fellowship with him, and will eventually be face-to-face with God in heaven.[9]

So, within this biblical narrative, Christians move from justification (to be made right with and reconciled to God through our union with Jesus Christ), to sanctification (being made holy and more like Jesus Christ), to glorification (being with God in heaven, where Christians will have the privilege of worshiping God face-to-face).[10] When Christians are eventually face-to-face with God, we will join in the organic, inevitable worship that is already taking place in heaven[11] and revealed in Revelation 4. So, our ultimate purpose is to

---

7. Knabb et al. (2019, 2025); Morgan and Peterson (2020).
8. This summary is based on Morgan and Peterson (2020) and Wolters (2005).
9. Boersma (2018).
10. Boersma (2018); Morgan and Peterson (2020).
11. Wright (2014).

eventually see God face-to-face in heaven,[12] wherein we will naturally worship him in love to "participate in the life of the Triune God."[13]

Consistent with this biblical understanding, at the beginning of the *Westminster Shorter Catechism* (written in the 1600s by English and Scottish theologians) the authors suggest that "the chief end of man" is to "glorify God and to enjoy him forever."[14] This means that the purpose, or telos, of the Christian life is to praise and worship God. From a Christian perspective, then, optimal psychological and spiritual health in the twenty-first century includes a God-given telos—to worship God in awe by glorifying and enjoying him forever in anticipation of being face-to-face with him for eternity. If we were created to worship, then what or whom we worship is key, especially if humans are always worshiping someone or something.[15]

For Christians, the telos of our existence is to worship in awe an infinitely loving, wise, powerful, and present personal God. When we are distracted from doing so, we may end up worshiping lesser things and, consequently, exacerbate our psychological and spiritual suffering on this side of heaven because these things do not ultimately provide us with the satisfaction and meaning we long for. If this is the case, all of life for the Christian should be an act of "worship" (as a verb) or "worshipfulness" (as a noun) toward God, who is the Creator and Sustainer of all. When Christians worship God in awe, we do so to know him, draw closer to him, and glorify him in our pursuit of the good life.[16] Yet, several developments in contemporary Western living may have made this Christian pursuit of the good life much more difficult.

The Problem: Disenchantment, Atheism, and the Self at the Center

Writing several decades ago in *The Secular Age*, the Christian philosopher Charles Taylor made the case that we have moved from an era of enchantment and theism to disenchantment and atheism in our contemporary, highly industrialized, and technological Western society.[17] For Taylor, the previous age of enchantment consisted of a world in which God, Satan, angels, demons, and a transcendent morality (and corresponding sense that good would be victorious over evil) exist. And meaning, in this world, came from a transcendent source, not the self. Taylor's current age of disenchantment, on the

12. Boersma (2018).
13. Smith (2009), 150.
14. *Westminster Shorter Catechism* (n.d.), question and answer 1.
15. Smith (2016).
16. Peterson (1992).
17. Taylor (2007).

other hand, is made up of the notion of a purely physical, material world, with only human minds, no belief in a transcendent God for meaning, a need to find inspiration and fulfillment outside of a relationship with God, and meaning derived from the self. With this recent seismic shift, we appear to have moved from worshiping God at the center to worshiping the self (and others and things) at the center. In other words, in the twenty-first century, we often worship everyone and everything but God and may end up struggling, psychologically and spiritually speaking, as a result.

Over three hundred years prior to *The Secular Age*, the Puritan Richard Baxter, in his theological work *Walking with God*, suggested that an "abundance" of atheism exists in the world, even among those who identify as Christian.[18] This atheism involves "living as without God in the world" and is in contrast to "walking with God," which is "living as with and to God in the world and in the church,"[19] reminiscent of Taylor's philosophical observations on the movement from enchantment to disenchantment. Of this "walking with God," Baxter further notes,

> [It] includes the practical acknowledgment (that is made by the will as well as the understanding) of the grand attributes of God, and his relations to man; that he is Infinite in his Being, that is, Immense and Eternal; as also in his Power, Wisdom and Goodness: That he is the Creator, Redeemer and Sanctifier: That he is our absolute Lord (or Owner), our most righteous Governor, and most bountiful Benefactor (or Father): That "of him, and through him, and to him, are all things"; That "in him we live, and move, and have our being": That he is the fountain, or first cause, from which all (proper) being, truth and goodness in the creature is but a derived stream. To have the soul unfeignedly resign itself to him, as his own; and subject itself to him as our Governor, walking in the awe of his sovereign power.[20]

Here, we can see that walking with God for the Christian means we know who God is as infinitely good, wise, and powerful and should acknowledge him as the benevolent governor who reigns over and directs all things. On the proverbial roads of life, Christians should walk with God in reverential awe, according to Baxter:

> That our walk with God must be with the greatest reverence: were we ever so much assured of his special love to us, and never so full of faith and joy, our reverence must be nevertheless for this. Though love cast out that guilty fear

18. Baxter (2017).
19. Baxter (2017), 10.
20. Baxter (2017), 9.

which discourages the sinner from hoping and seeking for the mercy which would save him, and which disposes him to hate and fly from God, yet does it not cast out that reverence of God, which we owe him as his creatures, so infinitely below him as we are. It cannot be that God should be known and remembered as God, without some admiring and awful apprehensions of him.[21]

So, whereas Baxter's "atheism" involves "living as without God in the world" (or living in an age of disenchantment, to use Taylor's language), "walking with God" consists of doing so in reverential awe (or returning to enchantment, a re-enchantment, to borrow again from Taylor).

For Christians in a contemporary age of disenchantment and atheism, as we focus less on God and more on the self (and others and things), we may experience more psychological suffering because we are not living in a manner consistent with our God-given purpose and, consequently, are worshiping lesser things. Like eating cheap, convenient, nutrient-deficient, addictive fast food that may offer a quick spike in the neurotransmitter dopamine and corresponding feeling of pleasure that will soon diminish and never truly satisfy, nourish, or sustain us,[22] we are missing out on the five-star cuisine that God has prepared for us, which has profound psychological and spiritual implications.

Empirical findings within the psychology literature may at least partially support this understanding. (Although I unpack the psychology literature in greater detail in chap. 3, for now I would like to briefly share the results of a few important studies.) Research in the last several decades has revealed a negative relationship between intrinsic religiousness (i.e., an authentic, mature religiosity that involves prioritizing God in life as *the* aim, not a means to attain some other perceived benefit) and symptoms of narcissism (e.g., an inflated and entitled sense of self, a fragile self in need of frequent admiration from others).[23] This means that the more authentically Christians report living out their faith, the fewer symptoms of narcissism they disclose. Psychological research has also uncovered a negative link between spirituality (i.e., a perception that life is sacred and has a unique purpose) and symptoms of narcissism.[24] This suggests that as individuals endorse higher levels of healthy religious and spiritual functioning, they report fewer symptoms of narcissism. As another example, researchers have elucidated a positive relationship

21. Baxter (2017), 26.
22. Garber and Lustig (2011).
23. Sandage and Moe (2011); Watson et al. (2004).
24. Doehring et al. (2009); Sandage and Moe (2011).

between symptoms of narcissism and symptoms of depression[25] and anxiety.[26] This means that those who report more symptoms of narcissistic tendencies also report more depressive and anxiety-related symptoms. There may be a sizeable cost, in terms of mental health, associated with the self-centeredness inherent in narcissism.

Theoretically, these studies seem to reveal that religion and spirituality may help to protect against extreme self-preoccupation and an overinvestment in the self.[27] This may be especially since Christianity teaches its practitioners to love God and others (Matt. 22:36–40), deny the self (Matt. 16:24–26), and consider others more important than the self (Phil. 2:3–5). Extreme self-preoccupation fails to deliver on its promise. Rather than improving mental health, the turn inward to worship, celebrate, and overly prioritize, admire, and assert the self may actually bring with it a whole host of additional symptoms, such as low mood, worry, and so forth.

In addition, research has uncovered a negative association between intrinsic religiousness and celebrity worship (e.g., being preoccupied with, identifying with, and prioritizing a perceived relationship with a celebrity as the most important goal in life).[28] This finding makes sense, since Christians are taught to avoid worshiping other gods and to worship only the God of the Bible (Exod. 20:3; 34:14; 2 Kings 17:35–36). To offer another example, researchers have highlighted a positive association between celebrity worship and symptoms of narcissism[29] and depression and anxiety.[30] This result reveals that, at least theoretically, efforts to worship others may fail to improve mental and spiritual health. Instead, worship of others may enhance psychological suffering (e.g., low mood, a loss of interest in things that used to be pleasurable, worry, preoccupations with danger and future catastrophe).

To provide one more example, research has illuminated a negative link between intrinsic religiousness and unhealthy attitudes toward money (e.g., believing that money is the ultimate status symbol in life and will impress others).[31] This finding seems to overlap with teachings in the Bible to avoid being preoccupied with love of money (Matt. 6:24; 1 Tim. 6:10; Heb. 13:5). What is more, researchers have discovered a positive link between materialism (e.g., believing that having material things is central to life and will lead to

---

25. Clarke et al. (2015); Marčinko et al. (2014).
26. Clarke et al. (2015); Schoenleber et al. (2015).
27. Miller and Worthington (2012).
28. Maltby et al. (2002).
29. Ashe et al. (2005).
30. Brooks (2021).
31. Watson et al. (2004).

success and happiness) and symptoms of depression, along with a negative relationship between materialism and well-being.[32] So, at least theoretically, being overly focused on money and material things does not lead to happiness and, rather, brings with it symptoms of low mood and sadness. Yet, also on a theoretical level, for those who endorse higher levels of religion and spirituality, they may be less enticed by materialism, which has beneficial mental health implications.

To summarize and consolidate some of these findings from psychology, although further research is needed to study these ideas in unison, the aforementioned individual studies seem to provide some preliminary support for a pattern—as participants tend to report greater religiosity (which includes God worship), they often report less narcissism (self worship), celebrity worship (other worship), and materialism (thing worship). Moreover, when participants commonly report greater self, other, and thing worship, they also frequently report more symptoms of depression and anxiety. Once more, whom or what we worship is key, which has far-reaching mental health implications for daily life.

Drawing on these insights from philosophy, theology, and psychology, what might the solution be for twenty-first-century Christians struggling with mental health in an age of disillusionment and disenchantment? If we are always worshiping someone or something[33] and we were created to worship God, a return to enchantment, theism, and worshipful awe of God is paramount. This thesis—worship and awe are especially important for Christian mental and spiritual health—is supported by writings, theory, and research across philosophy, theology, and psychology. What follows is a review of what may be the solution for contemporary Christians. This solution draws on introductory biblical, psychological, and integrative perspectives on worship and awe as a response to much of our psychological and spiritual suffering in an age of disenchantment.

The Solution: Enchantment, Theism, and God at the Center

If disenchantment, atheism, and the self at the center is a major problem for contemporary Christians, a return to enchantment, theism, and God at the center may be the solution. This understanding is supported by both Scripture and Christian theology, on the one hand, and recent insights from psychological science and the newer awe literature, on the other. In this introductory

---

32. Muñiz-Velázquez et al. (2017).
33. Smith (2009, 2016).

chapter, thus, I offer an initial presentation of worship and awe in both Christianity and psychology, then an integrative understanding to illuminate worship and awe in Christian mental health.

A Biblical Perspective

The Bible seems to reveal over and over again that God created humans for worship and awe, with awe as the proverbial motor that drives worship.[34] In Scripture, we read across the Old and New Testaments about worship, which is a foundational theme.[35] In Genesis, we learn that everyone and everything was created by God—which means God is our Creator and Sustainer—and we read that humans were created in his image to be in relationship with him.[36] Because of God's sovereignty, God is worthy of our worship and should alone be worshiped,[37] which is eventually revealed in the Ten Commandments (e.g., not worshiping other gods, not worshiping idols of God) (see Exod. 20).

Throughout the Old Testament, the Bible reveals that Israel sought to worship God in specific places and structures (e.g., the temple of Solomon in Jerusalem) with particular practices, including bowing down before God, serving him, and devoting all of life to him.[38] They also displayed certain attitudes and dispositions (e.g., loving God with both the head and heart) with an ultimate goal of fellowshiping with God.[39] This ability to fellowship with God during this time was made possible by the system of animal sacrifice that God put in place, which made God's people holy before him so they could approach him in worship and awe to commune with him.[40]

The Old Testament also elucidates a rich theology of worship in presenting what *not* to do, such as in Judges, where Israel worships other gods, replacing the one true God with false gods.[41] Because Israel struggled to worship God alone, they angered God and did not receive his blessings.[42] The lesson of Judges may be that we are always worshiping someone or something, which can be either an infinitely good and powerful God or a lesser, finite object, with the latter bringing about psychological and spiritual consequences.[43]

---

34. Peterson (1992).
35. Forrest et al. (2021).
36. Osborne (2021).
37. Osborne (2021).
38. Lee (2021).
39. Lee (2021).
40. Lee (2021).
41. Ross (2021).
42. Ross (2021).
43. Ross (2021).

Turning to the New Testament, we find a major theme: Jesus Christ is the Son of God and, thus, deserves our worship as Christ followers, such as praising, surrendering to, serving, and emulating him.[44] Because of Jesus's self-sacrificial, atoning act on the cross to reconcile us to God, we should be eternally grateful via worshiping Jesus in reverential awe.[45] We read in Acts about the types of worship services within the first-century church that began to develop, which included fellowshiping together in unity, teaching, praying, praising, and taking Communion (see, e.g., Acts 2:42–47).[46] Finally, the New Testament concludes with Revelation, which is filled with the theme of worship.[47] In chapter 4, heaven worships God as the Creator of all, whereas all of heaven worships God as the Redeemer in chapter 5.[48] As a central concept throughout the New Testament, Christians are to inevitably and naturally worship God because of who he is as Father, Son, and Holy Spirit and what he has done via his ultimate act of redemption through Jesus's loving, reconciling act on the cross.[49]

Based on what God has revealed in the Old and New Testaments, Christians can draw a few conclusions about how we are to live life, psychologically and spiritually, as we prioritize worship and awe of God as the telos, or ultimate purpose, for our short time on this planet. First, God is the benevolent Creator, Sustainer, and Redeemer and, because of who he is and his perfect plan, ultimately worthy of our worship and awe for his glory. Second, since God created humans in his image and this world and everything in it, there are inevitably many things to be in awe of within God's wonderful creation. We can, therefore, use our God-given senses to experience and appreciate the beauty of creation. Third, when we try to worship the self, other people, or things and these don't point us back to God as the ultimate Source, we may experience added suffering because these things can never truly satisfy our longing for him and God ultimately commands us to worship him only. From a Christian perspective, awe of creation should always point us back to God, whom we worship for who he is (e.g., infinitely good, wise, powerful, present, and holy), his plan, and what he's done for us (e.g., creating us in his image to be in personal relationship, dying for us to reconcile us to him in spite of our wayward ways, inviting us to spend eternity with him in heaven).

44. Blomberg and Crenshaw (2021).
45. Blomberg and Crenshaw (2021).
46. Tabb (2021).
47. Hindson (2021).
48. Hindson (2021).
49. Hindson (2021).

In sum, if Christian worship is captured as thankful, reverential wonder before the God of the Bible,[50] then Christians can purposefully respond with awe to who God is and his perfect plan revealed in both his Word and his creation.[51] And this intentional worship should be threaded across our thoughts and images, emotions, behaviors, and relationships in the context of family, church, work, and other areas of daily living. Interestingly, in the last several decades the psychology literature has also taken notice of some of the benefits of awe.

A Psychological Perspective

Since its formal founding as a scientific discipline some 150 years ago, psychology has often posed similar questions to Christianity, such as, What is the good life? Although many answers have been proposed via both theory and research, one recent line of investigation has revealed the importance of awe as a central component of the good life. "Awe" is defined as a positive emotional response to the inexplainable, transcendent mysteries and immensity of life all around us, with no shortage of awe-inducing moments in the here and now.[52] It can include (1) the experience of bigness, transcending our finite sense of self; (2) the need to adjust, modify, or accommodate previously held beliefs, mental representations, perspectives, and ideas to make room for the new, novel, transcendent experience of wonder and amazement;[53] and (3) gratitude and thankfulness in the here and now in response to the amazement of a thought, physical structure and corresponding sensory experience, or relationship.[54] The *APA Dictionary of Psychology* defines "awe" more succinctly as "the experience of admiration and elevation in response to physical beauty, displays of exceptional ability, or moral goodness."[55]

All of life has the potential for this type of transcendent amazement and wonder, which may have a range of mental health and relational benefits. This may be because we are shifting from a preoccupation with the self, common with many types of mental disorders (e.g., depressive, anxiety related, trauma

---

50. Block (2014).
51. Forrest et al. (2021).
52. Keltner (2023).
53. Keltner and Haidt (2003).
54. In their scale development study, Büssing et al. (2018) found that scale items capturing both gratitude (e.g., "I have a feeling of great gratitude") and awe (e.g., "I have a feeling of wondering awe") loaded onto one factor (i.e., gratitude and awe could be reduced to one variable, not two separate variables), suggesting the construct of awe has the ingredients of both awe/wonder and thankfulness/appreciation.
55. American Psychological Association (n.d.a).

related), to a focus on a bigger, more transcendent, shared perspective on life, which can give meaning and purpose.[56] Awe can also be something we experience in a plethora of unfolding moments, not just rare, occasional awe-inspiring events (e.g., staring out at the Grand Canyon as a child, watching a top athlete perform a near-impossible play in the Super Bowl as an adult).[57] So, much more commonly, awe can be triggered socially/relationally, physically/sensorially, and cognitively/conceptually on a daily basis.[58] These triggers may come from human relationships (e.g., when someone is kind), mystical, religious, and spiritual encounters (e.g., feeling God's presence, worshiping God), viewing art (e.g., staring at a priceless painting in a museum), listening to music (e.g., attending a live symphony orchestra performance), matters of life and death that lead to new insights or perspectives (e.g., the birth of a child, a near-death experience), and breakthroughs and other ideas and insights that are paradigm shifting (e.g., discovering a cure for a disease, meditating on God's omnipresence).[59] And for many, including Christians, awe is especially important in the context of a relationship with and worshipfulness toward God.[60]

Once again, awe can be beneficial for mental health and well-being via helping us relate differently to ourselves, other people, and the world around us. This may be because we are shifting from overly relying on our thinking mind—filled with worries, ruminations, judgments, criticisms, and self-preoccupations—toward a bigger, more transcendent perspective, wherein we are small and the world is large.[61] Awe can also provide meaning in life, which can be beneficial for mental health and well-being.[62] More succinctly put, it helps us to be less preoccupied with ourselves and, in turn, experience how amazing the world around us can be. We can see all of life with a sense of excitement and wonder, like a child playfully skipping along the shoreline of a warm, sunny beach, caught up in the joy of the moment.

And awe can be intentionally cultivated via awe interventions, as recent research has revealed, such as when we take "awe walks" outside to purposefully experience awe when walking for fifteen minutes a day.[63] Awe interventions can also lead to greater life satisfaction, as evidenced by research that has illuminated that imagining ascending the stairs in an extremely tall building

---

56. Chirico and Gaggioli (2021); Monroy and Keltner (2023); Shiota et al. (2007).
57. Keltner (2023).
58. Eagle and Amster (2023); Sundararajan (2002).
59. Keltner (2023).
60. Keltner and Haidt (2003).
61. Keltner (2023).
62. Upenieks and Krause (2024).
63. Sturm et al. (2022).

can lead to enhanced well-being.[64] Overall, when examining a range of ways to intentionally elicit awe in formal lab interventions, psychologists have had positive outcomes by presenting awe-inducing videos, images, and music, asking research participants to imagine a past awe-inducing personal experience, and asking participants to partake in a simulated awe-inducing experience in nature.[65] The results of such laboratory awe interventions suggest that they can lead to an increase in the emotional experience of awe.[66]

Building on some of these successes, a short, skill-based, three-step mindfulness practice for cultivating awe has been recently developed using the fitting acronym *AWE*:[67]

- *Attend:* Being intentional about devoting all our focus to something amazing within the immediate environment.
- *Wait:* Staying present to what we have our attention on, savoring it, and engaging in deep, natural breathing to slow down and appreciate it. Waiting is in contrast to rushing on to the next distraction in our environment.
- *Exhale* and *expand:* Staying fully immersed in the current experience by slowly exhaling to dually remain calm and enhance whatever inner experiences (e.g., physiological sensations, the emotion of awe) occur.

In this short, practical intervention to cultivate and maintain awe throughout the day, we are "microdosing mindfulness"—meaning it's a condensed mindfulness exercise.[68] The goal is to apply *AWE* to all of life so that we can devote our full attention to each unfolding moment by slowing down with the in-breath and out-breath.[69] This approach is certainly a simple, skill-based, meditative strategy for cultivating awe in all of life. However, mindfulness—with its corresponding mental skills of focused attention, awareness of the present moment, and nonjudgmental acceptance of unpleasant thoughts, emotions, sensations, memories, and images[70]—comes from the millennia-old Buddhist religious tradition. In comparison, Christianity has its own meditative heritage that is anchored to the moment-by-moment worship of the personal God of the Bible and a comprehensive biblical worldview.

64. Rudd et al. (2012).
65. Ji et al. (2021); Pérez et al. (2023).
66. Ji et al. (2021); Pérez et al. (2023).
67. Eagle and Amster (2023).
68. Eagle and Amster (2023), 12.
69. Eagle and Amster (2023).
70. Feldman et al. (2007).

For Christians, God as Creator and Sustainer is the lens through which the wonder of and gratitude toward the world is to be experienced and life's meaning is derived. This perspective has been empirically confirmed in recent research that has elucidated a positive link between awe of God and a "religious sense of meaning in life."[71] Research has also revealed that awe of God is linked to fewer depressive symptoms and more life satisfaction, with these links explained by Christians having a perception that life is meaningful, possibly because of the belief that a big God has a transcendent plan.[72] And although this awe of God may not be triggered by directly experiencing the triune God with the senses (e.g., seeing, hearing, touching) because God is immaterial and invisible, Christians' awe of God can be triggered (1) cognitively/conceptually by using thoughts and images to meditate on his attributes (e.g., God is infinitely good, wise, powerful, present, and holy) and actions (e.g., God is the Creator, Sustainer, and Redeemer) to experience grateful amazement, (2) physically/sensorially by behaviorally interacting with and being immersed in his beautiful creation to experience grateful amazement, and (3) socially/relationally by relating to both God and others, who are also created in his image, and spending time with God in solitude and silence to experience grateful amazement.

These three awe triggers—cognitive/conceptual, physical/sensorial, and social/relational[73]—can be intentionally pursued and targeted and lead to more fully experiencing the vastness of and a thankfulness toward God. The triggers can also lead to needing to adjust our smaller, more compartmentalized image of God. This is because he is so much bigger and wiser than we can ever imagine. To pursue these awe triggers, God must be permanently acknowledged and recognized at the center, and we must learn to worship him by standing (or kneeling or bowing) on the periphery. What follows is an integrative perspective on wonder and awe, drawing from both Christianity (as a starting and ending point) and newer theory and research in psychology.

An Integrative Perspective

As Christ followers, what we end up worshiping, prioritizing, and being appreciative of in life—the self, others, and things, on the one hand, or God, on the other—is of paramount importance. If Christians worship the self, others, and things, we are not living out our God-given purpose to glorify him. Yet, if we worship God, we are doing what we were created to do. For

---

71. Krause and Hayward (2015b), 232.
72. Upenieks and Krause (2024).
73. Eagle and Amster (2023); Sundararajan (2002).

Christians, worship includes awe of God, because he is the Creator, Sustainer, and Redeemer. Awe of God involves being overwhelmed by his vastness and mysteriousness to the point that we need to adjust our beliefs about him to make room for this reality. Drawing on an array of diverse sources from both Christianity and psychology,[74] I define Christian worship as follows:

> An adoring, surrendering, meaning-deriving, self-minimizing and Other-maximizing grateful response of reverential awe to the trinitarian God of the Bible. When we worship God, we honor him for who he is as infinitely good, wise, powerful, present, and holy. We adore him for his actions as Creator, Sustainer, and Redeemer, especially his ultimate act of redemption via the birth, life, death, resurrection, and ascension of Jesus Christ. Finally, we honor him for his providential care, or his perfect, loving, and guiding governance that is personally and intimately extended to all creation. Christian worship is carried out via intentional and purposeful psychological and spiritual disciplines with all our being, including our thoughts and images, emotions, and actions. By regularly acknowledging and worshiping God at the center of existence, we can celebrate all of life across the areas of family, church, work, school, community, and leisure.

More plainly worded, worshipfulness is about recognizing and being overwhelmed with gratitude for a big and perfect God in the foreground and relocating a small and imperfect self to the background. Christian worshipful awe is really, to be as succinct as possible, grateful amazement or thankful wonder toward the triune God as Creator, Sustainer, and Redeemer. And this awe of God includes experiencing God's vastness and mysteriousness to the point of needing to let go of our erroneously small and limiting images of and beliefs about him.

A wide variety of classic Christian spiritual practices, such as worship, meditation, prayer, and singing hymns, can cultivate awe of God (again, as an alternative to Buddhist-derived mindfulness meditation[75]). This is because we are opening ourselves up to who God is with gratefulness and a sense of mystery, not who we imagine him to be with our finite human mind.[76]

For Christians, worship of God is the primary vehicle through which awe of God is cultivated and maintained, not the mindfulness that comes from

---

74. American Psychological Association (n.d.a); Block (2014); Büssing et al. (2018); Calhoun (2015); Forrest et al. (2021); Foster (2008); Holman (2004); Keltner (2023); Monroy and Keltner (2023); Peterson (1992); Schneider (2004); *Upper Room Dictionary of Christian Spiritual Formation* (2003b); Whitney (2014); Yaden et al. (2019).
75. Knabb and Vazquez (2023).
76. Van Cappellen et al. (2021).

another religious tradition and has a different ultimate aim. (Mindfulness is an insight meditation to gain a greater awareness of the three marks of existence, which include the ideas that all of life is suffering, there is no individual self, and everything is impermanent.)[77] The emotion of awe is a God-given relational signal that tells us that we are small, he is big, and we need to regularly adjust our finite and limited understanding of the world to make room for the reality that God is at the center of all of creation. And because God is infinitely good, wise, powerful, present, and holy, we can celebrate this reality with gratitude and thanksgiving.

This unique Christian worshipful awe is different from secular awe for at least one major reason. If secular gratitude is defined as being thankful upon getting a gift from someone else[78] and Christian gratitude has an added active ingredient of praise toward God for the undeserved blessings he has generously given,[79] Christian worshipful awe is about recognizing that an amazing God is the Creator, Sustainer, and Redeemer. This means that all that is good can be traced back to God's gifts and blessings. With this understanding in mind, all of life can be an act of worship via standing in awe in wonder, amazement, and mystery because God is the Source. For Christians, again, worship of God is the primary vehicle that delivers awe. And awe fuels worship, to continue with an engine metaphor, bringing it to life and giving it movement and a trajectory traced back to God. Fascinatingly, worship and awe seem to influence one another in a bidirectional manner.

With the above in mind, there may be major mental health implications for Christians, since God created us to worship him—not the self, others, and things, which can never truly fulfill or satisfy us—with thankful wonder, and we are shifting from preoccupations with our own inner struggles (e.g., worry and catastrophizing about the future with anxiety; ruminating about a guilt-ridden past or anticipating a hopeless and meaningless future with depression) to a transcendent God. Along the way, we are cultivating amazement, mystery, and, ultimately, reverential awe. This can help us to experience all of life in new and exciting ways and provide meaning and purpose. In other words, when Christians prioritize worshiping God, we can more fully appreciate his creation and be a part of his perfect plan. This is because we are focusing on, and building and maintaining, a deeper relationship with *the* Creator, Sustainer, and Redeemer as we anticipate being face-to-face with him in heaven for eternity.

---

77. Knabb and Vazquez (2023).
78. American Psychological Association (n.d.b).
79. Knabb et al. (2021).

In support of this theoretical perspective, recent research has revealed that greater religious worship service attendance among Christians was positively correlated with awe of God.[80] In this same study, positive links emerged between awe of God and life satisfaction and awe of God and personal health, and a negative link was uncovered between awe of God and depressive symptoms.[81] In several other studies, a greater frequency of religious worship practices, such as prayer and meditation, were positively linked to awe.[82] Finally, in an experimental study, religious participants (which included Christians) were asked to remember an event that included "strong feelings of spirituality and connection to the divine," which ended up predicting awe, with a diminished focus on the self as a likely explanation for the spirituality-induced awe.[83]

An Integrative Model

To cultivate awe via Christian worship (not Buddhist mindfulness), three shifts may be helpful for twenty-first-century Christ followers: self to Other, others to Other, and things to Other. When these key shifts take place, all of life, whether relating to the self, others, or things, can be filtered through the lens of worshipful awe before God. This is what we were created for and what Christians will eventually be doing in heaven. For a visual model of this shift from creation worship to Creator worship and awe that may lead to greater meaning in life and Christian mental health, see the accompanying figure.

In this figure, notice we start with worship, which is inevitable with both types—worshiping creation or the Creator.[84] Yet, for Christians, we are shifting from merely worshiping creation, which can lead to the pursuit of a lesser type of creation awe and lesser meaning and purpose in life and more unnecessary suffering, to worshiping the Creator, which can lead to better appreciating God's creation and, consequently, a greater type of Creator awe and corresponding meaning and purpose and less unnecessary suffering. So, from a Christian perspective, we might simply say we are shifting from creation to Creator worship, creation to Creator awe, and self-derived to God-derived meaning and purpose. Creation worship can result in less meaning and purpose and Creator worship can lead to more meaning and purpose, since we directly go to the Source of all that is beautiful and good. In agreement,

---

80. Upenieks and Krause (2024).
81. Upenieks and Krause (2024).
82. Büssing et al. (2018, 2021); Kearns and Tyler (2022).
83. Preston and Shin (2017).
84. See, e.g., Smith (2009, 2016).

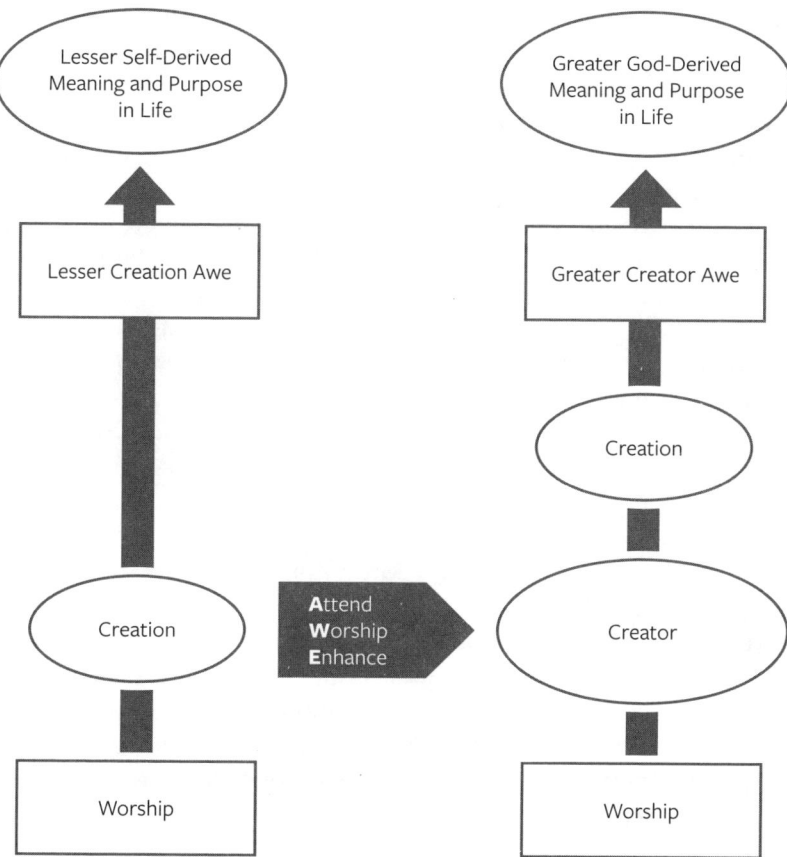

Moving from Worshiping Creation and Creation Awe to Worshiping the Creator and Creator Awe in the Christian Life

Lewis fittingly declared, "There is but one good; that is God. Everything else is good when it looks to Him and bad when it turns from Him."[85]

An Integrative Practice

Practice-wise, I draw from Christianity, including the Bible (e.g., songs of worship in the Psalms), theological works (e.g., texts on the theology of worship), and writings on Christian spiritual practices/disciplines (e.g., *Sayings of the Desert Fathers*, the *Philokalia*, the *Cloud of Unknowing*, Brother Lawrence's

85. Lewis (1994), 106.

Practice of the Presence of God, Ignatian spirituality, Puritan spirituality). I also draw from psychology, such as the most recent theory and research on awe and the *AWE* technique (i.e., "microdosing mindfulness")[86] previously mentioned for attempting to grow and maintain worshipful awe applied to all of life. Yet, I modify this practical *AWE* technique (which originally employed Buddhist-derived mindfulness) to offer a distinctly Christian form of reverential awe via a uniquely Christian form of worship, applying this approach to your thoughts and images, emotions, behaviors, and relationships. My hope is that you will gradually learn to apply, with the insights and practices in this book, worshipful awe across *every* area of life (e.g., family, church, work, community, leisure) as you practice shifting from self to Other, others to Other, and things to Other.

If God is at the center of reality, offering life if we remain tethered to him (see, e.g., John 15; Col. 1:17), then directly focusing on and worshiping him may indirectly lead to improvement, psychologically and spiritually, in each of these domains of life. This is because we are living our God-given telos and ameliorating gratuitous self-preoccupations that leave us miserable.

I especially derive inspiration and content from two main Christian spiritual writings. First, I build upon Brother Lawrence's work, *The Practice of the Presence of God*, given his emphasis on recognizing that God is at the center of life even with what seem like the most mundane of activities (e.g., washing the dishes). According to Brother Lawrence, a humble seventeenth-century French monk who developed a reputation for practicing God's presence in all of life, "The holiest, most ordinary, and most necessary practice of the spiritual life is that of the presence of God. It is to take delight in and become accustomed to his divine company, speaking humbly and conversing lovingly with him all the time, at every moment, without rule or measure."[87] For Brother Lawrence, each unfolding moment of the day can be devoted to worshiping God in reverential awe: "Since you are aware that God is present to you during your actions, that he is in the depths and center of your heart, stop your activities and even your vocal prayers, at least from time to time, to adore him within, to praise him, to ask his help, to offer him your heart, and thank him."[88] To do so, we can simply pair whatever activity is before us, which is done slowly and intentionally to glorify God, and a simple phrase, such as "God of love, I love you with all my heart."[89] Any activity, whether large or small, or significant or insignificant, can be practiced with God in

---

86. Eagle and Amster (2023), 12.
87. Lawrence (1993), 38.
88. Lawrence (1993), 38.
89. Lawrence (1993), 43.

mind. We can engage in the task across all domains of life (e.g., work, family, community, church) in reverential awe before God. This practice, anchored to the Christian tradition, can be used in place of Buddhist-derived mindfulness meditation. By practicing God's presence, Christians are cultivating the mental skills of attention, present-moment awareness, and acceptance,[90] doing so with God at the center.

Second, I draw from the larger, rich heritage of published works on Christian spiritual disciplines within the centuries-old Christian religious tradition.[91] These specific practices are anchored to God's Word, the Bible, and have been developed for daily use in Christian communities over the last several hundred years and beyond. They are defined as "a rule of life or a set pattern of living intended to facilitate spiritual growth and community."[92] Many such practices focus on inner growth with our thoughts, feelings, sensations, images, and memories (e.g., meditation, prayer, contemplation), outer growth and our behaviors (e.g., virtuous acts), or interpersonal growth in Christian and other communities (e.g., corporate Christian worship as the collective body of Christ).[93] According to the contemporary Christian spiritual director and author Adele Calhoun, "Worship is every [spiritual] discipline's end game."[94] Calhoun further explains: "In worship we live into the reality that the first and best thing in life is nothing less than a transforming relationship with the God who made us, named us and called into being. Worship ignites and attaches us to this truest and best-of-all desire—the desire to let God have his way with us." Christian writer Donald Whitney succinctly describes worship in terms of a Christian discipline as "focusing on and responding to God."[95]

Christian spiritual disciplines are intentional inner, outer, and relational/communal practices that help Christians to grow psychologically and spiritually and become more like Christ.[96] We can practice them by, foundationally, worshiping a God who resides at the center of existence and holds everything together (Col. 1:17). We are simply and directly acknowledging via purposeful practices what is already a reality. In the process, we are indirectly cultivating mental and spiritual health because we are aligning our will with God's will and our purpose with God's purpose on the proverbial roads of this short, fleeting, embodied human life.

90. Feldman et al. (2007).
91. Calhoun (2015); Foster (2008); Whitney (2014).
92. *Upper Room Dictionary of Christian Spiritual Formation* (2003a), 85.
93. Foster (2008).
94. Calhoun (2015), 32.
95. Whitney (2014), 106.
96. Calhoun (2015); Foster (2008); Whitney (2014).

> **AWE STEPS**
>
> - *Attend:* Attend to God as Creator and Sustainer by focusing on and prioritizing an awareness of him, not yourself, others, or things.
> - *Worship:* Worship God as Creator and Sustainer in wonder in the immediacy of the moment by slowly breathing in to symbolize filling yourself up with his amazing presence.
> - *Enhance:* Enhance your worship of God as Creator and Sustainer to include a larger appreciation for all of his amazing creation by slowly breathing out to symbolize resting in him with reverential and worshipful awe.

See the accompanying sidebar for the three modified *AWE* steps[97] to help you develop and maintain Christian awe by way of the intentional and purposeful Christian psychological and spiritual discipline of worship. For Christians, the *A* stands for *attending* to God, not the self, others, or things; the *W* stands for *worshiping* God in the here and now by being present to his infinite goodness, wisdom, power, presence, and holiness as Creator, Sustainer, and Redeemer (not attempting to worship the self, others, or things, which will inevitably fail to satisfy); and the *E* stands for *enhancing*, extending, and enlarging an awareness of God's beautiful presence within both the inner and outer world to include an appreciation and gratitude for all of God's creation.

Along the way, attention, present-moment awareness, and a nonjudgmental, open, and accepting curiosity are key skills that are developed.[98] We also utilize the practice of slowly breathing in to practice God's presence symbolically and worshipfully and slowly breathing out to rest in him in reverential awe, amazement, and wonder. In this process, a short phrase that is consistent with Brother Lawrence's teaching can be paired with the breath. For instance, we may say, "My God" with the in-breath and "thank you" with the out-breath, or "God" with the in-breath and "you are good" with the out-breath. Or, we may recite specific and short passages in Scripture (e.g., the Psalms) that are aligned with the full breath cycle to capture amazement and awe before our Creator, Sustainer, and Redeemer God. To further capture the need for this shift from worshiping the self, others, or things to God, I'd like to share

---

97. Eagle and Amster (2023); Feldman et al. (2007); Lawrence (1993).
98. Feldman et al. (2007).

a metaphor that may help to illuminate the dilemma of the self as a barrier to Christian worship and awe.

A Metaphor

Living on my new street in my new home, I'm once again miserable—resentful, lonely, anxious, and depressed. I'm waiting for others to come to *my* party to celebrate and be in awe of *me*. Yet, I can hear the loud and booming party next door with sounds of joy effortlessly traveling through the walls. There, my neighbor is the one being cherished and revered. In fact, he has been telling me about his big, grand party—which everyone in the neighborhood has been invited to—ever since I moved in next door.

Over the last few months, I have gotten to know this neighbor quite well. He is the most generous, friendly, loving, self-sacrificial, and likable person I've ever known. He has a stellar reputation, and the whole neighborhood invariably wants to hang out with him. He's the best athlete on the block and most talented, creative musician and artist in town. Frankly, I've been in awe of him ever since our first handshake.

Yet, because I desire to be held in such esteem by my neighbors as well, sometimes I can't bring myself to appreciate his amazing talents. As I once again sit alone this evening, a thought hits me: There's no such thing as a party of one. And in this very moment, I can simply walk next door to join in the celebration of this impressive neighbor. To do so, though, I need to leave my own house and abandon the cake, balloons, and other decorations that have my name proudly and prominently displayed on them. I also must recognize that no one's coming to celebrate *me*, at least not for very long, and the perfect amalgam of celebrating, singing, dancing, and praising are happening next door and directed toward *him*. A huge shift, thus, is needed for me to fully experience the amazement and wonder I crave—I need to celebrate my neighbor, not me.

For Christians, Jesus is the talented, awe-inspiring neighbor, and the person sitting alone is the fallen, prideful self, inevitably prone to being self-focused because of the fall of humankind. Fittingly captured in this metaphor, from moment to moment Christians have a decision to make. We can wait around for others to celebrate us, or we can join the party that Jesus has welcomed us to. To join the celebration, we need to recognize that Jesus is worthy of praise, not us, and we can find true fulfillment in fully immersing ourselves in this reality. This book, therefore, is about shifting from wanting to be at the center and worthy of worship and praise to focusing on the Other—the trinitarian God as Father, Son, and Holy Spirit. Before ending the chapter, I'd like to offer a short tale of worship and awe.

A Life Example

Seth, a twenty-three-year-old Christian college student, was raised in a conservative Christian home, with vivid memories of being taught by his parents that God is the creator of all. In particular, he can remember going on camping trips with his family, wherein they would sit around the campfire, sing worship songs, and watch the stars. During such trips, his father would often comment, "God made each and every one of the stars in the sky, Seth." These types of childhood experiences had a profound impact on him, since he often organically experienced God's wonder. Although he did not know it at the time, he commonly felt awe. He struggled in a good way to come up with the words to describe just how big and majestic God is.

Yet, in his adolescence several things changed, leading to the tragic perception that this big and majestic God was actually small and ineffective. First, Seth's father began to struggle with anxiety, so much so that he would have a hard time leaving the house to complete even basic tasks, such as getting the mail, shopping for groceries, attending church, and driving to work. As Seth observed his dad's ongoing suffering, he couldn't help but conclude that God wasn't sovereign after all. As fear overwhelmed his father, Seth also started seeing the world as a place of catastrophe and doom. He saw God as a distant, apathetic, and ineffective deity passively watching it all unfold. Rather than looking up to heaven and feeling overwhelmed by an infinitely good, powerful, and present God, Seth simply felt anxious and out of control.

As Seth moved into adulthood, his anxiety followed him. He had a general sense that the uncertainties of life were not tolerable. Seth needed to be big and in control because God was small and weak. Rather than being in awe of God in a good way with a sense that the benevolent Creator and Sustainer of the universe was beyond his comprehension and, thus, he could just marvel at God's mystery and vastness, Seth was quick to become anxious. When this happened, he tried to control his environment by constantly seeking reassurance from others. Gradually, he developed an anxiety disorder, generalized anxiety, which involved worrying from one topic to the next to try to predict his future and seemingly control his environment. For Seth, though, his worry ended up making life worse because he could not enjoy each day, and his mind was exhausted.

Still, on one summer afternoon, he was driving down Pacific Coast Highway in sunny Southern California. During this drive, Seth was caught in a cycle of worry, anxiety, and compulsive behaviors to try to control his world. As he drove alone with the windows rolled down—because his car's air conditioner was broken—he began to feel the wind brushing against his face, which caught his attention. As he looked to the right, he could see the enormity of the ocean, with the sun reflecting on the water. Instantly, he felt overwhelmed in a good way, experiencing God's presence and vastness and power and the sense that a benevolent Creator was sustaining all things. Although he had no adequate words to describe this experience, he knew he felt reverential awe, reminiscent of his earlier childhood, and he spent the next few minutes of his drive just savoring this powerful emotional encounter with God. As tears rolled down his face, he was relieved to be able to focus on God, not himself. He had a profound awareness that God was in control, which meant he did not need to worry or compulsively (and ineffectively) try to control his own life. This experience, for the next hour or so, left him feeling overwhelmed by and thankful for God's greatness as he continued to drive down the highway of life. It served as a much-needed catalyst for beginning to actively worship God in reverential awe.

Conclusion

Christian worship and awe are integral to Christian mental and spiritual health in the twenty-first century, especially since we are now living in an age of disenchantment. Although the ordinariness of life can certainly be a distraction to worshiping God in reverential awe, as Christians we have the opportunity to, from moment to moment, pivot from worshiping the self, others, and things to worshiping God as Creator, Sustainer, and Redeemer. In doing so, we can live out our God-given purpose to worship him with our thoughts and images, emotions, behaviors, and relationships across every domain of life, whether family, church, community, work, or leisure.

Whether you are a graduate student attempting to better understand how to integrate the latest psychological science on awe and mindfulness with a Christian worldview, a clinician working with Christian clients in psychotherapy or professional counseling, or a Christian simply looking to better understand how worshipful awe of God can be extended to all of life for your own mental and spiritual health, my hope is that this book can be a useful guide. As we get started, my prayer is that you will consider the possibility that optimal Christian living involves regularly pivoting from self to Other, others to Other, and things to Other on the roads of life, doing so in reverential awe before God.

CHAPTER TWO

Worship and Awe in Christianity

What people revere, they resemble, either for ruin or restoration.
—G. K. Beale, *We Become What We Worship*

Fully to enjoy is to glorify. In commanding us to glorify Him, God is inviting us to enjoy Him.
—C. S. Lewis, *Reflections on the Psalms*

Fall on your knees, oh, hear the angel voices.
O night divine, O night when Christ was born.
—Placide Cappeau, "O Holy Night"

Introduction

In this second chapter, we explore a distinctly Christian perspective on worship and awe by drawing on the Bible and Christian theology. In particular, I present the importance of worship and awe in the Christian life, including definitions of "worship" and "awe," how worship includes awe, and how Christian worship and awe need to include God—not the self, others, or things—at the center. Starting with Christianity, not psychology, is essential. This is because God is sovereign over all of life (Col. 1:16–17), even the (secular) psychology literature. Examples from the Old and New Testaments of the Bible are illuminated, along with an instance of worship and awe in psychotherapy for mental and spiritual health. Essentially, this chapter serves as the foundation for the remainder of the book. When combined with chapter 3's emphasis on theoretical and empirical perspectives on awe and worship in psychology, it can help you as a contemporary Christian to cultivate and maintain worshipful awe of God with thoughts and images (chap. 4), behaviors (chap. 5), and relationships (chap. 6).

In the context of Christian mental health, we may be collectively miserable—with unnecessary and added psychological suffering—in contemporary living because we often futilely try to be our own creator, sustainer, and redeemer. We also ineffectively try to be infinite and independent, with our own self-generated power and wisdom, which is simply not possible. We may be mentally unhealthy (with frequent symptoms of depression, anxiety, and stress), frustrated, and exhausted because we are not authentically living out who or what we were formed to be. Teleologically, we were designed by God as finite and dependent to worship him as *the* infinite and independent, yet personally loving, redeeming, and reconciling, God of the universe.

This understanding of our ultimate purpose and meaning for existence has far-reaching implications for Christian mental and spiritual health, flowing from our worldview. This worldview may be secular and consist of the widespread assumptions of the day that attempt to (1) exclude religion from influencing our outward-facing social interactions in the public square; (2) overemphasize autonomy, independence, and personal happiness; and (3) place a heavy emphasis on the compulsive acquisition and consumption of material possessions for happiness. Or, we may embrace a biblically tethered Christian worldview that acknowledges the trinitarian God as Father, Son, and Holy Spirit at the center of existence.[1] With the above in mind, we begin this chapter with a short exploration of worldview, teleology, and worship and awe in the Christian life, given their prominence in Christian mental and spiritual health.

Worldview, Teleology, and Christian Worship and Awe

All humans have a particular view of the world, whether explicit, implicit, or partly explicit and partly implicit. This view is referred to in theology,[2] philosophy,[3] and psychology[4] as a "worldview." Simply put, a worldview is "the conceptual lens through which we see, understand, and interpret the

1. Chandler (2014).
2. Anderson et al. (2017).
3. DeWitt (2018).
4. Koltko-Rivera (2004).

world and our place within it."[5] As one important ingredient of worldview, "teleology" refers to the ultimate goal, purpose, meaning, or end for life, whether it is viewed as external and imposed on humans from a deity or seen as internal and innate within nature itself and not imposed on humans via a higher power.[6] Many Christians, of course, believe in an external teleology—that is, God created humankind with a specific purpose and unique value. For Christians our telos, or purpose, is to worship God in reverential, grateful, humble awe and wonder,[7] which has profound mental and spiritual health-related implications. Paraphrasing the God of the Bible in capturing his purpose and motivation for creating humankind, the twentieth-century Christian spiritual writer A. W. Tozer offers, "That is your end, that is why you were created, that you might worship Me and enjoy Me and glorify Me and have Me as yours forever."[8]

Unfortunately, although our desire to worship is innate, we may end up worshiping the self, others, and things, not God. Within the Christian tradition, this is called "idolatry"[9] and pointedly captured in the first two of God's Ten Commandments (see Exod. 20). Drawing on the Protestant Reformer Martin Luther for inspiration, the biblical scholar G. K. Beale defines idolatry as "whatever your heart clings to or relies on for ultimate security."[10] In its most basic form, idolatry is either worshiping God in inappropriate ways or worshiping anything or anyone other than God, which God does not approve of.[11] According to the Puritan John Knox, "All worship invented by man is idolatry," which has significant psychological and spiritual impacts.[12] This is because prioritizing, pursuing, and worshiping the wrong things will not bring lasting meaning, happiness, and well-being in Christian living.

In Genesis 1:27, we learn that God is the Creator and Sustainer and we are the created, with God creating Adam and Eve in his own image. Because of this, we are "imaging creatures,"[13] meaning we end up becoming like the person or thing we worship, for better or for worse. "Adam and Eve's unique purpose [or telos] in the garden was to bring pleasure, joy and fellowship to God, which is the foundation of all genuine worship."[14] Yet, tragically, Adam

5. Anderson et al. (2017), 12.
6. Cordero (2009); King et al. (2013); Knabb et al. (2025); Olsen (2022).
7. Beale (2008); Calhoun (2015); Tozer (2009).
8. Tozer (2009), 22.
9. Beale (2008).
10. Beale (2008), 17.
11. Knox (2018).
12. Knox (2018), 53.
13. Beale (2008), 16.
14. Tozer (2009), 23.

and Eve rebelled against God by famously eating from the forbidden tree in the garden and placing themselves, not God, at the center.[15] This decision resulted in their banishment from the garden and estrangement from God (see Gen. 3).

As a result, Adam and Eve experienced profound psychological and spiritual suffering and disorientation. They lost their ultimate purpose, which is to worship and "glorify God, and to enjoy God forever"[16] and recognize that God, not the self, is at the center.[17] To this day, we continue to suffer from these psychological and spiritual reverberations. We strive to worship the self, others, and things in place of God, which prevents us from carrying out our ultimate purpose to worship God and reflect his likeness and image. Instead, we commonly choose to reflect the inherently limiting and unsatisfying image of the finite, isolated, and imperfect self; finite and imperfect others; and finite, temporary, and fleeting material things. Still, fast-forward to Revelation, and we see that creation inevitably worships God in heaven as Creator and Redeemer, and this worship will continue forever (see Rev. 4 and 5).[18] So, from Genesis to Revelation, the ultimate meaning and purpose of the Christian life is to worship God, the Creator, not the created. We can do so in reverential awe and wonder, which is the focus of this second chapter.

General and Special Revelation and Christian Worship and Awe

From a Christian perspective, God has revealed to all humankind that he is worthy of our worshipful awe (Rom. 1:19–23), through creation and the beauty and vastness of the natural world, human creativity and intelligence, and cultural diversity and advancements.[19] This is referred to in Protestant Christianity as "general revelation." This concept explains why there is so much in life that is awe inducing and worth celebrating (e.g., Van Gogh's paintings, the Grand Canyon, Mozart's music, the pyramids of Giza). For Christians and non-Christians alike, standing in awe of what exists outside the proverbial walls of the Christian church can help us to better understand the Creator's glory, infinite power, wisdom, goodness, and presence, and, ultimately, providential care (i.e., loving and benevolent governance and guidance over all creation).[20]

---

15. Bonhoeffer (1959).
16. *Westminster Shorter Catechism* (n.d.), question and answer 1.
17. Beale (2008); Tozer (2009).
18. Hindson (2021).
19. Johnston (2014).
20. Ryrie (1999).

Yet, this general form of God's revelation available to all humans only gets us so far, given we also need to know both the Source, personally, and the Source's ultimate purpose for those who believe in him. This special information comes to us via God's divine revelation, the Bible.[21] Specifically, we need to know who we are worshiping (e.g., God's attributes), the past actions this deity has taken and future actions this deity will take (e.g., God's grand narrative spanning from Genesis to Revelation), our relational standing with this deity (e.g., we are the created, finite and dependent, and this deity is the infinite and independent Creator), and our ultimate purpose in life (i.e., to worship God, not the self, others, or things, at the center of existence).

So, to begin this chapter, I review the Bible and key works on the theology of Christian worship to elucidate whom we are to worship, how we are to worship, our role and God's role in the worship process, and, ultimately, the primacy of Christian worship as our telos for the Christian life. These details can help us in our pursuit of optimal Christian mental and spiritual health. Since theology is the study of God revealed in God's special revelation, the Bible, it is only fitting that we begin with this source. Then, I explore key writings on Christian awe and wonder, drawing from Christian theology, given that awe and wonder are inevitably part of and flow from authentic Christian worship. From there, I offer an integrative perspective on Christian worship and awe to combine and synthesize these sources, before concluding with an example of Christian worship and awe in both a church setting and psychotherapy. Ultimately, my hope is that this chapter, when combined with chapter 3 on a psychological perspective on Christian worship and awe, can serve as the foundation for the three remaining chapters on the role that Christian worship and awe play in Christian mental health.

Christian Worship

Definitions

Within the Christian religious tradition, worship is foundational, with Christians tasked with worshiping God, the Creator, not the created (whether the self, others, or material things). As revealed in the *Westminster Shorter Catechism*, a set of biblically linked, Protestant doctrinal statements written in the mid-seventeenth century, the ultimate purpose for humankind is

---

21. Ryrie (1999).

to glorify and worship God and "enjoy him forever."[22] Upon drafting this powerful and poignant statement, which serves as the opening line for this popular Protestant doctrinal work, the authors cited, among other verses, Psalm 86:9: "All the nations you have made will come and worship before you, Lord; they will bring glory to your name." They also cited Revelation 4:11: "You are worthy, our Lord and God, to receive glory and honor and power, for you created all things, and by your will they were created and have their being."

Definition-wise, there are a wide variety of components of Christian worship. The *Holman Bible Dictionary* defines "worship" as "The act or action associated with attributing honor, reverence, or worth to that which is considered to be divine by religious adherents."[23] This dictionary entry further notes that Christian worship involves the following ingredients: (1) devotion to the triune Christian God, with God initiating the process by revealing himself via his special revelation; (2) a personal relationship with Jesus Christ, which restores humankind's broken relationship with God; and (3) acts of adoration toward the triune Christian God as Father, Son, and Holy Spirit. Another contemporary definition of worship is "A specific mode of Godward acknowledgment of God's distinctive and unsurpassable excellence," with an "attitudinal stance toward God [that] is awed, reverential, and grateful."[24]

In a similar vein, the biblical scholar Daniel Block defines worship as "reverential human acts of submission and homage before the divine Sovereign in response to his gracious revelation of himself and in accord with his will."[25] Yet another contemporary biblical scholar, David Peterson, suggests it is a "life orientation or total relationship with the true and living God."[26] Adding to these definitions, one more current biblical scholar, N. T. Wright, puts forth that God created humans to worship him in reverential awe, with his amazing and awe-inducing creation pointing us to the God of love who made us to inevitably love beauty.[27]

Writing several decades before these authors, A. W. Tozer defined worship as follows: "To feel in your heart and express in some appropriate manner a humbling but delightful sense of admiring awe and astonished wonder and overpowering love in the presence of that most ancient Mystery, that majesty

---

22. *Westminster Shorter Catechism* (n.d.), question and answer 1.
23. Holman (2004d), 1051.
24. Williams and Lamport (2021), 6.
25. Block (2014), 23.
26. Peterson (1992), 18.
27. Wright (2014).

which philosophers call the First Cause but which we call Our Father Which Art in Heaven."[28]

In addition to these contemporary definitions, I would like us to also explore other theological descriptions, drawing on the Puritans, a group of English Protestant Christians who wrote prolifically in the seventeenth and eighteenth centuries and humbly attempted to apply Scripture to all of life. For the seventeenth-century English Puritan John Wilson, worship is "devout behavior towards God, by which we acknowledge his sovereignty over us, and the due obedience we owe to him, appearing before him, and waiting on him, in the way he has appointed in his word."[29] For Jeremiah Burroughs, another seventeenth-century English Puritan, "We must all be willing worshipers, but not will-worshipers. We must come freely to worship God, but we must not worship God according to our own wills."[30] Instead, the focus needs to be on God and his holiness, as revealed by Burroughs: "When we come to worship God, if we would sanctify God's name, we must have high thoughts of God. We must look on God as he is on his throne, in majesty, and in glory."[31] So, for Burroughs, we need to focus on God and who he is, not ourselves, when we worship him. John Owen, yet one more seventeenth-century English Puritan, emphasizes that worshiping God is a privilege, which comes from Christians' union with Christ: "By the blood of Christ, believers enjoy the privileges of the excellent, glorious, spiritual worship of God in Christ, revealed and required in the gospel."[32]

To integrate these definitions, Christian worship involves an innate, yielding, reverential, humble, grateful, heartfelt, and freely chosen response to the trinitarian God that is extended to all of life based on God's unequaled greatness. So, rather than being confined to a few worship songs on Sunday morning within a local church setting, worshipful awe before God is a comprehensive approach to all of life with the God of the universe at the center of existence.

Old Testament Examples

Turning from abstract definitions to concrete examples in the Bible, in the Old Testament "worship is at the very heart."[33] It is captured in different Hebrew words (and their variations): worship involves a journey, meaning the Israelites were to seek and prioritize God; worship includes a structure, such as

---

28. Tozer (2009), 8.
29. Wilson (2018), no. 488.
30. Burroughs (2018), 56.
31. Burroughs (2018), 124.
32. Owen (2018), 30.
33. Lee (2021), 28.

when the Israelites built the tabernacle so the holy God could dwell within it and meet them there; worship is made up of a practice, capturing the behavior of bowing down before God to honor and worship him and acknowledge his sovereignty; worship involves an attitude, meaning a heartfelt fear of God in reverential submission; and, finally, worship involves a goal, reflecting the need to offer sacrifices to God to be forgiven of sins and, consequently, be viewed by God as acceptable and able to approach him for communion.[34]

In fact, the Old Testament reveals quite a bit about worship, captured in God's unique covenantal relationship with Israel and a variety of other particular features: Israel's sacrificial system (to be acceptable before a holy God), temple (to meet this holy God in a particular location), and line of priests (to approach this holy God by acting as a representative or liaison of the people).[35] During these Old Testament times, a key theme across a range of nations and cultures involved trying to elucidate who and where this God (or gods) is so that a formal relationship could be developed between God (or gods) and particular societies.[36] Therefore, temples, shrines, and sanctuaries were built within such societies, which priests utilized to try to meet and communicate on a more personal level with this God (or gods).[37]

For Israelites, a people who worshiped only one God, Yahweh revealed himself to them as the Creator and Sustainer of all. God began a relationship with a variety of biblical figures in pursuit of an ongoing covenant with the Israelites, from Abraham, to Isaac, to Jacob, to Moses, to David.[38] In this Old Testament era, God promised the Israelites that he would make them "a great nation," offering land and blessings (Gen. 12:2, 7–8).[39] In return, they built altars to acknowledge God.[40] Then, in Exodus, God revealed himself to Moses on Mount Sinai, telling Moses to lead the Israelites out of their enslavement and suffering in Egypt and toward the new land God has promised them, a land of "milk and honey" (Exod. 3:8).[41] In this famous biblical encounter, God told Moses that the Israelites will be able to "worship [him] on this mountain," revealing his name to Moses (Exod. 3:12–15). In these exchanges, the Old Testament captures the unique and personal relationship that God had with the Israelites.[42] He revealed his name to them, a specific location to worship him, a future land

---

34. Lee (2021).
35. Peterson (1992).
36. Peterson (1992).
37. Peterson (1992).
38. Peterson (1992).
39. Peterson (1992).
40. Peterson (1992).
41. Peterson (1992).
42. Peterson (1992).

that they would possess, and the blessings he would bestow on them.⁴³ Further along, in Exodus 25–31, Moses is given instructions for building a temporary and portable tabernacle. This would be a dwelling place for God, wherein God would interact with the Israelites and the ark of the covenant could be housed, until the first temple would later be built in Jerusalem.⁴⁴ In the ark, the Ten Commandments were stored, which were particular, well-defined religious rules for living revealed earlier to Moses on Mount Sinai.⁴⁵

By setting up this system, which continued when Solomon's temple was later built in Jerusalem (see 1 and 2 Kings), God intended for the Israelites to position worship as central to their lives. So, the tabernacle (and later temple) contained an outer court, wherein priests washed themselves for purification and sacrificed animals as a penalty and atonement for the forgiveness of sins; an inner court (or Holy Place), wherein a table, lampstand, and incense altar were placed; and Holy of Holies, wherein only the high priest could enter once per year to bring incense and blood from sacrificed animals to meet and worship God (see Exod. 25–31; Lev. 16).⁴⁶

Pivoting to the Psalms of the Old Testament, which are a collection of poetic songs of praise that capture "worship postures, languages, and practices that are pleasing to God" and authentically elucidate the full spectrum of the human condition,⁴⁷ the psalmists worshiped God in all of life, whether seasons of orientation, disorientation, or new orientation.⁴⁸ Psalms of orientation and well-being capture periods of gratefulness toward God, worshiping God because he is infinitely good.⁴⁹ Psalms of disorientation and lament illuminate periods of hurt, suffering, and despair, among other ubiquitous human struggles, reflected in the two-step process of complaining to God and praising God even in the midst of pain.⁵⁰ Finally, psalms of new orientation and surprise capture periods of transformation, joy, and restored gratitude, worshiping God as sovereign because he has led the psalmist out of a season of disorientation and despair.⁵¹ With this period of new orientation, there is a newfound sense of hope, new beginnings, and, consequently, new blessings from God.⁵²

---

43. Peterson (1992).
44. Peterson (1992).
45. Peterson (1992).
46. Peterson (1992).
47. Kaiser et al. (2021), 156.
48. Brueggemann (1984).
49. Brueggemann (1984).
50. Brueggemann (1984).
51. Brueggemann (1984).
52. Brueggemann (1984).

As these seasons reveal, psalms of orientation and new orientation commonly offer thanksgiving, praise, and worship to God and are depicted in a plethora of vivid passages: for example, "I will exalt you, my God the King; I will praise your name for ever and ever" (Ps. 145:1); and "I will exalt you, LORD, for you lifted me out of the depths and did not let my enemies gloat over me. LORD my God, I called to you for help, and you healed me" (Ps. 30:1–2).

However, even the psalms of disorientation offer praise to God, illuminated in the two-step process of (1) complaining to him and focusing on the state of the self, then, even in the midst of pain, (2) praising him and focusing on him:

> How long, LORD? Will you forget me forever? . . .
> How long must I wrestle with my thoughts
>   and day after day have sorrow in my heart? . . .
> But I trust in your unfailing love;
>   my heart rejoices in your salvation.
> I will sing the LORD's praise,
>   for he has been good to me. (Ps. 13:1–2, 5–6)

Although we do not know if the psalmist's complaints were ever fully responded to and/or addressed by God, a shift is evident. This shift involves the psalmist praising God, thanking God, and worshiping God, either in the midst of or coming out of a state of disorientation.[53]

Ultimately, the psalmists seem to have captured the inevitable psychological highs and lows of life, doing so while praising God and finding enjoyment in all of life because of who he is. In agreement, in *Reflections on the Psalms*, the twentieth-century Christian writer C. S. Lewis says: "I think we delight to praise what we enjoy because the praise not merely expresses but completes the enjoyment; it is its appointed consummation."[54] So, as Christians, we sing songs of praise, thanksgiving, and adoration to God because we enjoy him, even in the midst of pain and suffering, and recognize who he is as Creator, Sustainer, and Redeemer.

To summarize, within the Old Testament, the Israelites worship God via specific rituals, locations, attitudes, and sacrifices, whether in seasons of gratitude and blessing or pain and suffering. To do so, they focus on who God is as infinitely loving, wise, powerful, present, and holy and Creator, Sustainer, and Redeemer, with God at the center of community life. Let us now turn

---

53. Brueggemann (1984).
54. Lewis (1958), 95.

to New Testament examples of worship to better understand the salience of worship across the entire Bible.

New Testament Examples

Transitioning to the New Testament, we have an array of examples of Christian worship captured in two Greek words (and their variations): *proskyneō*, meaning the visible act or behavior of bending, kneeling, or bowing down to worship and serving as a display of humble reverence toward the worshiped; and *latreuō*, reflecting an authentic, worshipful service coming from the heart that is displayed toward God.[55]

With the first word, *proskyneō*, an example is found in Matthew 8:2: "A man with leprosy came and *knelt* before [Jesus] and said, 'Lord, if you are willing, you can make me clean.'" For the second word, *latreuō*, Romans 1:9 depicts this authentic service toward God. Writing to the newly formed church in Rome, the apostle Paul declares, "God, whom I *serve* in my spirit in preaching the gospel of his Son, is my witness how constantly I remember you." So, with these two words, we can see the outer, behavioral act of bowing or kneeling down to worship God. We can also see the inner, heartfelt act of serving the trinitarian God—Father, Son, and Holy Spirit—authentically and reverentially.

Of course, to conclude the New Testament, Revelation 4 and 5 portray the inevitable worship that takes place in heaven. Revelation 4 focuses on the Father as Creator, and Revelation 5 emphasizes the Son as Redeemer.[56] For instance, in Revelation 4:11, we read of the Father, "You are worthy, our Lord and God, to receive glory and honor and power, for you created all things, and by your will they were created and have their being." On the other hand, Revelation 5:9 illuminates of the Son, "You are worthy to take the scroll and to open its seals, because you were slain, and with your blood you purchased for God persons from every tribe and language and people and nation."

From these Christian definitions spanning the last several centuries and biblical examples, we can see that the most important ingredients of trinitarian Christian worship include a recognition that our ultimate purpose in life is to worship God as Father, Son, and Holy Spirit; an inner and outer posture of submission toward God, who is sovereign and holy; a confident and joyous access to God, who now accepts us and our worship via our union with Christ; a focus on God as the object of worship, not the self (or others or things)

---

55. Blomberg and Crenshaw (2021).
56. Hindson (2021).

in an act of idolatry; a real relationship with a personal God, not a tenuous bond with a distant or removed, impersonal deity; practicing the presence of God in the immediacy of the moment; an attitude of awe, adoration, and gratitude; a recognition that worship is a privilege, not a mere duty, based on Christians' union with Christ; intentional behaviors that celebrate who God is as special and set apart; and the application of worshipfulness to all of life, not merely during certain seasons or periods of time. As mentioned in this array of definitions, authentic Christian worship inevitably includes awe and wonder, which we explore with more precision next.

Christian Awe

Definitions

Within the Christian tradition, worship inevitably includes awe, given that Christians' source of worship is the trinitarian God as Father, Son, and Holy Spirit and Creator, Sustainer, and Redeemer. For instance, the *Holman Bible Dictionary* succinctly defines "awe" as "an emotion combining honor, fear, and respect before someone of superior office or actions," noting that it "most appropriately applies to God."[57] As another example, the *Upper Room Dictionary of Christian Spiritual Formation* defines "awe" as "the gasping of the body, mind, spirit, and soul in wonder and reverence at the mystery and greatness of God."[58] This same entry goes on to note that awe is a "profoundly deep experience of God that leads us to unify all thought, emotion, and experience in rapt attention to God's presence, works, and wonders" and that it is captured via a "continual awareness of God's omnipresence and omnipotence—of God's grace being everywhere at once so that in everything we do we sense God in awe."[59]

Beyond these more mechanical and precise dictionary definitions, almost a decade ago the Christian author and pastor Paul Tripp wrote a popular book succinctly titled *Awe*.[60] In it, he suggests that all humans look for awe to fill the emptiness experienced in the inevitable low points of life, with God creating both a world of awe and the human ability to experience awe. For Tripp, the source we draw on for awe is key, given that only God can truly satisfy our desire to be awed in daily life. More recently, in his popular book *The Awe of God*, the Christian author and minister John Bevere highlights that awe of God is a healthy, humble, worshipful fear, respect, and reverence

---

57. Holman (2004a), 63.
58. Upper Room (2003a), 28.
59. Upper Room (2003a), 28.
60. Tripp (2015).

for God, which inevitably draws us to him via a relationship of intimacy and trust.[61] This is because God is infinitely good and the true source of all that is wonderful, amazing, and awesome.[62]

Turning to more theologically driven understandings of awe, the Christian theologian Frank Macchia suggests that "theology is 'God talk'" and, essentially, "speech about the wonders of God" and the "wonders of God's love poured out into the world."[63] This awesome wonder has recently been depicted by the Christian theologian Emily Hunter McGowin as "amazement elicited by something unexpected and mysterious."[64] For McGowin, "If theology is the study of God and God's world, then sustained contemplation and comprehension of God is simply impossible without wonder."[65] So, awe and wonder, housed within the discipline of theology, is an enduring amazement of the works of God.[66] Awe is coupled with humility and the surrender of human control to him because humans are finite and dependent with limited knowledge and power, whereas God is infinite and independent with unlimited knowledge and power.[67]

Old Testament Examples

Moving on to more concrete examples of awe and wonder experienced by key biblical figures in the Old Testament, the Hebrew word *yare* is often used. It means to honor, respect, be astonished by or afraid of, or revere, often in the context of God.[68] In Genesis 28:16–17, we read that, upon waking from a vivid dream in which God revealed himself to the biblical patriarch Jacob, Jacob proclaims, "'Surely the Lord is in this place, and I was not aware of it.' He was *afraid* and said, 'How *awesome* is this place! This is none other than the house of God; this is the gate of heaven.'" Then, in 1 Samuel 12:18, we learn that the biblical prophet "Samuel called on the Lord, and that same day the Lord sent thunder and rain. So all the people *stood in awe* of the Lord and of Samuel." There are also many examples of awe and wonder in the Psalms, although these verses utilize other Hebrew words. In Psalm 33:8, the psalmist declares, "Let all of the earth *fear* the Lord; let all the inhabitants of the world stand in awe of him!" (ESV). And in Psalm 119:161, the psalmist proclaims, "Princes persecute me without cause, but my heart stands in awe of your words" (ESV).

---

61. Bevere (2023).
62. Bevere (2023).
63. Macchia (2023), 1, 183.
64. McGowin (2022), 18.
65. McGowin (2022), 20.
66. McGowin (2022).
67. McGowin (2022).
68. *Strong's Lexicon* (n.d.c).

New Testament Examples

In the New Testament, the verb *phobeō* (used many times) and the noun *deos* (used once) capture awe, meaning to be in fear or reverence of.[69] In Matthew 9:6 Jesus forgives a paralyzed individual, telling him, "Get up, take your mat and go home." This leads the crowd around him to be "filled with awe" (*phobeō*) and praising God (9:8). In addition, speaking of God's reign and our reconciliation to him through Christ,[70] the author of Hebrews explicates, "Therefore, since we are receiving a kingdom that cannot be shaken, let us be thankful, and so worship God acceptably with reverence and awe [*deos*], for our 'God is a consuming fire'" (Heb. 12:28–29).

Kataphatic and Apophatic Approaches

As another way to theologically make sense of the God of awe and wonder within the Christian religious tradition, Christians throughout the ages have contrasted kataphatic and apophatic theological approaches to understand and experience God. God is knowable through the general (God's works in nature) and special (God's Word, the Bible) revelation he has chosen to reveal to us. He is also unknowable because his greatness is so much bigger than our human minds can comprehend.

On one hand, the kataphatic (from Greek for the "positive way" of knowing God, such as "God *is* love") tradition involves making rational, abstract, and cognitive statements about God. We draw on human language to do so, with words that depict his attributes, actions, and promises. From this perspective, we can confidently turn to both the language of the Bible (God's special revelation) and evidence through his creation (his general revelation) to understand God. This, again, is because God has purposefully chosen to reveal to humans at least part of who he is.[71] Meditation—or mental prayer that involves a cognitive pondering and thinking deeply about God's Word with words and images—is an example of a spiritual practice within this theological tradition.[72]

In the context of awe and wonder, across the Old and New Testaments, we may meditate on God's infinite goodness (Exod. 34:6), wisdom (Rom. 11:33), power (1 Chron. 29:11), presence (Ps. 139:7–8), and holiness (Exod. 15:11), as well as be overwhelmed with amazement at God's actions (Ps. 77) or promises (Prov. 3:5–6). Finally, we may stand in thankful wonder of God

---

69. *Strong's Lexicon* (n.d.a).
70. Hagner (1990).
71. Boa (2020); Bowe (2003); McGrath (2011); Upper Room (2003g).
72. Knabb (2021); Upper Room (2003e).

as Trinity (John 1:1–5), doing so by turning to the pages of the Bible to elucidate these three persons.

On the other hand, the apophatic (Greek for the "negative way" of knowing God, such as "God *is not* reduced to mere love") tradition relies on directly experiencing the living God, not abstract categories about him.[73] Here, we downplay language and images that confine God, given that mere words and images fail to fully capture who God is as ultimately an ineffable and unknowable mystery beyond our comprehension with finite human minds.[74] From this perspective, our reliance on human-constructed, abstract, rationally based theology, built with letters, words, and language as building blocks, is a futile attempt to reduce and limit God to reified, imperfect, imprecise human categories that he cannot and will not be forced into.[75] Language, from an apophatic viewpoint, can sometimes undermine the mystery, vastness, independence, infiniteness, transcendence, and otherness of God.[76] Simply put, God is ultimately ineffable, which means he is too big and vast for us to fully comprehend with our limited, finite, imperfect human minds. This is revealed in the Old Testament when God tells Moses that his name is "I AM WHO I AM" and to tell the Israelites that "I AM" has sent Moses to them (Exod. 3:11–14). Contemplation—or a present-moment loving awareness of God that downplays the use of cognition, words, and images in favor of a loving reaching toward God—is an example of a spiritual practice within this theological tradition.[77]

In the context of awe and wonder, we may contemplate the love of God in solitude, silence, and stillness by slowly, gently, and internally repeating the word "love." We do so without turning to additional thoughts or images to know about God. With this process, we long to experience God's love in solitude and silence.[78] And we downplay overly abstract, cognitive, indirect attempts to know about God in favor of directly experiencing him.

Ultimately, within both the kataphatic and apophatic theological traditions, human awe and wonder are directed toward God, not the self, others, or things, since God is the Creator and Sustainer of all. With God at the center as both knowable and unknowable, we can pursue a deeper intimacy and communion with the God of the universe, recognizing that nothing short of God will induce the awe and wonder we long for. Now, we turn to an

---

73. Boa (2020); Bowe (2003); McGrath (2011).
74. Boa (2020); Bowe (2003); McGrath (2011).
75. Boa (2020); Bowe (2003); McGrath (2011).
76. Boa (2020); Bowe (2003); McGrath (2011); Upper Room (2003f).
77. Knabb (2021); Upper Room (2003b).
78. Knabb (2021).

integrative view of Christian worship and awe by drawing on the Bible, Christian theology, and other Christian writings on the topic.

An Integrative Perspective of Christian Worship and Awe

To offer an integrative understanding of the primacy of Christian worshipful awe in contemporary daily life for mental and spiritual health, the telos of the Christian life is Christian worship. This worship includes our thoughts, feelings, and behaviors that reflect awe and wonder before the trinitarian God as infinitely good, wise, powerful, present, and holy and Creator, Sustainer, and Redeemer. Since we were created by God to worship, whom or what we choose to worship is of paramount importance, whether it is God or the self (or others or things) at the center. And the emotion of awe is a God-given relational signal that elucidates that we are small, God is big, and we need to adjust our limited, finite understanding to make room for this reality again and again on a moment-by-moment basis. When God is not at the center, we end up engaging in what the Christian tradition has historically called "idolatry." This involves worshiping someone or something other than God, which God abhors and forbids, and it will end up failing to truly satiate us. Unfortunately, as fallen, imperfect humans, we often turn to the wrong people and things to direct our worshipful awe.

Beginning in Genesis, humans futilely chose to try to be like God, erroneously attempting to place ourselves, not God, at the center of our own existence. As a result, psychological and spiritual suffering entered the world, and we have been struggling ever since to realize and live out our God-given telos to worship him and him alone.

Fortunately, for Christians, we have both God's general and special revelation to remind us of our need for God as *the* Source to experience genuine, authentic awe as we direct our worship to him as Creator, Sustainer, and Redeemer. Therefore, we can worship the Creator and Sustainer God in awe and wonder by appreciating, with humble gratitude, his creation. This can take the form of being amazed by a vast natural landscape, the intricacies of the human cell, the specialization and localization of brain functioning, a human-made work of art, or a finely tuned orchestra playing Mozart or Beethoven.

Yet, God's general revelation can illuminate only so much, given that we also need God to personally reveal himself to us. With God's special revelation, we can better understand who he is as Redeemer. He is infinitely good, wise, powerful, present, and holy. We can also learn of his past actions and future promises, which are all found in his grand narrative of the Bible that spans from Genesis to Revelation. Fast-forwarding to Revelation 4 and 5, we read that we will inevitably worship God as Creator and Redeemer in heaven, which is what we were designed to do.

Within the Christian tradition, writers have often distinguished kataphatic (using words and images) and apophatic (downplaying the use of words and images) theology to better understand how we can know (or unknow) and relate to God, with both approaches needed in the Christian life. To draw on a fitting metaphor to better understand how these two approaches may relate to one another, when getting to know a good friend, we might first share facts and details through the medium of language to better understand this person's background, characteristics, preferences, passions, and values in a more abstract, cognitive manner. Yet, at a certain point, as we get to know our friend on a deeper level, we may have a more experiential sense that we know them. Here, the words will inevitably fail to fully capture what it is like to spend time with them. Thus, although words are certainly needed to know *about* them, the words themselves are not *the* person. Rather, our preference is to be with them experientially, not just know about them abstractly.

In a similar vein, with God, the language of the Bible certainly captures God's attributes, actions, promises, and ultimate plan spanning the past, present, and future. Still, this language is not God himself, which requires an experiential, personal, real relationship with him as Creator, Sustainer, and Redeemer in our own life. In other words, Scripture points Christians to the living triune God as Father, Son, and Holy Spirit, but it should not be confused with a personal, experiential, intimate, worshipful, and awe-inducing relationship with God himself. In support of this understanding, the Protestant Reformer Martin Luther says, "[In Scripture] you will find the swaddling clothes and the manger in which Christ lies. . . . Simple and lowly are these swaddling clothes, but dear is the treasure, Christ, who lies in them."[79] So, Scripture is the manger, but it should not be confused with the living Jesus himself, which the manger merely holds.

Of course, this ability to both kataphatically know and apophatically experience the triune God is certainly a challenge, given we are distracted, wandering, imperfect human beings who often worship the wrong people and things, traced back to the fall in Genesis. As a result, let us now turn to what Christian writers have referred to as the consequences of worshiping the wrong people and things, both psychologically in the form of wayward thoughts, feelings, and behaviors and spiritually via struggling to maintain a

---

79. Janz (2008), 118.

transcendent perspective and recognize that we were created to worship God at the center of existence.

The Consequences of Non-Christian Worship and Awe

Returning to Tozer, the most important question in life is, "What is my purpose in life?"[80] with the answer being to worship God in reverential and thankful awe and wonder. Yet, according to Tozer, we may tragically come up with the wrong answer. We may futilely try to find meaning and purpose in—and ultimately worship—education, work, pleasure, or thrills and excitement.

Because we were created to reflect God's image (not our own image) through the display of love in our relationships and qualities and characteristics in our personhood,[81] when we worship someone or something else, we end up tragically reflecting the image of the lesser person or thing we are worshiping. And, consequently, this person or thing fails to truly satisfy psychologically or spiritually.[82] This is tragic because finite, imperfect human beings and finite, impersonal things inevitably fall short of who we were designed to be as image bearers who reflect the character, albeit imperfectly, of a perfect and holy God.[83]

Simply put, like Adam and Eve in Genesis 3, when we end up worshiping ourselves (or imperfect others or impermanent things), this inevitably leads to idol worship and, as a result, our estrangement from God, whom we were created to worship. Worshiping ourselves (or others, such as Hollywood celebrities, YouTube influencers, dynamic and charismatic megachurch pastors, or wealthy professional athletes; or things, like money, real estate investments, or sports cars) fails to produce the awe and wonder we long for. And this lesser worship leads to continued suffering, disappointment, loss, frustration, and insatiable cravings.

Over four centuries ago, John Knox astutely defined idolatry as "all worshiping, honoring, or service invented by the brain of man in the religion of God, without his own express commandment."[84] For Knox, we may even "defend" these human-constructed "inventions" as "righteous" before God, since we somehow convince ourselves they are "good, laudable, and pleasant."[85] For Christians, there are an array of possible consequences when we attempt to attain awe and wonder by worshiping the wrong people (the self or others)

---

80. Tozer (2009), 37.
81. See McKim (1996).
82. Beale (2008).
83. Beale (2008).
84. Knox (2018), 72.
85. Knox (2018), 58.

or things (like money or material possessions). These may include pursuing the wrong purpose in life by deceiving ourselves into thinking what we are worshiping is good and, because of this, bearing the image of the person or thing we are worshiping, not God.

This can also have far-reaching psychological and spiritual consequences, since we may be confused about the ultimate meaning and purpose in life. As a result, we may never experience true happiness, well-being, contentment, and joy by worshiping, in reverential gratitude, humility, and amazement, the one true God who is perfect in every way and the only one who can offer the wonder we long for on this side of heaven. But what, exactly, might distinct practices to pivot from self, other, or thing worship to worshipful awe before God look like within the Christian tradition? Now, we turn to several practices and examples of Christian worship and awe for moving toward mental and spiritual health in contemporary Christian living, beginning with *lectio divina*.

Lectio Divina for Christian Worship and Awe

Within the centuries-old monastic Christian psychological and spiritual practice/discipline of *lectio divina* (Latin for "divine reading"), we work toward pivoting from worshiping the self, others, and things (idol/creation worship), which never truly satisfies, to worshiping God (God/Creator worship). This particular spiritual discipline slowly began to develop in Christian monasteries from the fifth century onward.[86] It consists of reading Scripture, meditating on Scripture, praying to God, and contemplating God, likened to the process of eating food.[87]

These four steps, captured with the metaphor of biting, chewing, tasting, and savoring, were solidified by Guigo II,[88] a twelfth-century Carthusian monk who wrote the spiritual classic *The Ladder of Monks*. This work is a widely read manual of sorts for the four-step monastic practice that has since been popularized across Christian communities.

With the first step, *reading*, which is an "outer exercise,"[89] we take an initial bite out of Scripture. We begin to interact with a chosen passage in a slow, deliberate, focused manner. Then, with the second step, *meditating*, which is an "inner act of the mind,"[90] we chew Scripture. We ponder and think deeply about the content with focused, sustained attention. Following

---

86. Robertson (2011).
87. Guigo II (2012).
88. Guigo II (2012).
89. Guigo II (2012), 15.
90. Guigo II (2012), 16.

meditating, we *pray* to God—that is, we taste Scripture and "direct all our strength to the Lord."[91] We ask him to reveal himself and his will to us as we continue to interact with his Word and the chosen passage and move toward the final step. To conclude, we *contemplate* the God of love, or savor God as "heavenly dew," with the "soul thirsting for God."[92] With this last step, we do so by sitting with God in stillness, silence, and solitude, "beyond all feeling and knowledge."[93] We wait upon God with a yielding, surrendering inner attitude and outer posture.

So, as a quick example, if we select Psalm 65:8, we would first slowly and intentionally read the passage, "The whole earth is filled with awe at your wonders; where morning dawns, where evening fades, you call forth songs of joy." We would begin to take a bite out of this verse with intentionality as we spend the next several minutes interacting with it and, through it, the one and only Almighty God.

Second, we would begin to meditate, or chew, on the verse. We would possibly condense the verse to a shorter, more select portion: "The whole earth is filled with awe at your wonders." Upon doing so, we would slowly, gently, and internally repeat and ponder the words in worshipful awe before the Sovereign Lord. Again and again, we would repeat, "The whole earth is filled with awe at your wonders." We would chew on the words as we reverentially thank God for his wonderful works displayed for the world to see by way of his vast creation.

Third, we would pray to God. We would taste his power and goodness by asking him to fill us with awe and wonder as we spend this time with him as Creator, Sustainer, and Redeemer in grateful, adoring worship.

Finally, we would sit with God in loving silence and solitude. We would remain still with focused attention in the here and now by repeating the short, powerful word "awe." We would recognize that God is the only true source of awe, wonder, amazement, and joy and all other awe-inducing moments invariably emanate from him.

As we conclude, we would remain ultimately speechless before him, since words fail to adequately capture his vastness, goodness, and holiness. Rather than filling up the remaining time with words, we would just sit in appreciative, loving silence before our King, who is seated on his throne.

In chapter 4, we will review this practice in much more detail with more precise directions and the opportunity to engage in the practice more fully

---

91. Guigo II (2012), 20.
92. Guigo II (2012), 21.
93. Guigo II (2012), 32.

and intentionally. For now, however, my goal is simply to plant a proverbial seed because this discipline can help you to pivot from worshiping self, others, and things to worshiping God on a daily basis. It can also help you grow psychologically and spiritually in the process.

Before moving on to real-world examples of Christian worship and awe in both church and psychotherapy, I would like to offer a few additional examples of possible practices to cultivate and maintain worshipful awe before God. To do so, I'll be drawing on three Christian books published in the last decade or so.

Other Practices for Christian Worship and Awe

In 2019, the Christian physician and author Christine Aroney-Sine wrote *The Gift of Wonder: Creative Practices for Delighting in God*.[94] In this important work, she makes the case that the "childlike qualities" of awe and wonder are essential for the kingdom of God. Unfortunately, though, many Christians struggle with "play deprivation."[95] This means that we no longer know how to deepen our intimacy with God through a childlike, grateful, present-moment joy in the presence of God. When this happens, we may miss out on glorifying God and reflecting his image by basking in the mystery and vastness of our Sovereign Lord.[96] Therefore, for Aroney-Sine, cultivating and maintaining a childlike joy before the greatness and majesty of God is key. We can do so by, among other strategies, (1) practicing silence in the presence of God to allow our inner world to settle and our attention to be placed on the vastness of God and his creation; (2) spending time outdoors to appreciate, with an adorning gratitude and reverence, God's creation; (3) appreciating, through our God-given sense of sight, the rich, colorful, creative images and works of art all around us, which God has so generously blessed us with; and (4) noticing God's many miracles in daily living by intentionally identifying ten particular ways that God has blessed us with being alive (e.g., the joy of eating a flavorful dessert; playing a game with a child; the shape, contours, and colors of a small rock that God has created).[97]

Writing a few years later in *God of Wonders: 40 Days of Awe in the Presence of God*, the Christian pastoral counselor Faith Blatchford offered a roughly six-week journey to cultivate and maintain awe and wonder before God. In this work, she draws her readers' attention to what it may have been

94. Aroney-Sine (2019).
95. Aroney-Sine (2019), 2.
96. Aroney-Sine (2019).
97. Aroney-Sine (2019).

like for Adam and Eve to experience the garden of Eden and the awe and wonder that naturally emanated from a close, intimate relationship with God as Creator and Sustainer.[98] For Blatchford, even Adam and Eve's first few breaths with a newly formed autonomic nervous system may have produced a profound sense of awe, given everything for them was new and a gift from God.

With this perspective in mind, our God-given breath, which we do not need to forcefully control or manipulate in any way, can be a source of worshipful awe. It can naturally lead to a "Thank you, Lord, for giving me the 'breath of life'" (see Gen. 2:7) mantra throughout the day. In simplicity and adoring reverence for our King, throughout the day we can (1) notice our natural breathing, which is a gift from God as Creator and Sustainer; and (2) thank God for the "breath of life." We can worship God by acknowledging that he has created us and is sustaining us with our God-given autonomic nervous system. Our breath captures this reality from moment to moment on this mysterious trek called life.

To offer one more recent example of wonder and awe in practice, in her popular book *Spiritual Disciplines Handbook: Practices That Transform Us*, the Christian spiritual director Adele Calhoun offers an entire section on worship as a spiritual discipline.[99] Like the many other Christian writers mentioned in this chapter, she notes that God designed human beings to worship. Yet, tragically, we often worship the wrong people or things in life. For Christians, we must regularly pivot from creation worship to Creator worship via surrendering to our Lord with an attitude of "Have your way with me."[100]

Through intentional and simple psychological and spiritual disciplines, we can engage in this moment-by-moment shift. Such disciplines include (1) celebrating God by identifying and acknowledging God's many blessings in our life, such as by writing a letter to or song for God that captures this reality; (2) thanking God with an enduring, heartfelt, genuine gratitude by keeping a daily gratitude journal of all the people, places, and things we are thankful for, both big and small, that come from God; and (3) calling on the many names of God found in the Bible throughout the day to acknowledge in awe and wonder who he is, such as *El Shaddai* (God Almighty) in Genesis 17:1 or *El Olam* (Eternal God) in Genesis 21:33.[101]

In each of these examples, popular Christian authors, whether physicians, pastoral counselors, or spiritual directors, have moved away from an abstract, esoteric Christian understanding of worshipful awe before God. Instead, they

---

98. Blatchford (2021).
99. Calhoun (2015).
100. Calhoun (2015), 40.
101. Calhoun (2015).

advocate for a concrete application and intentional, purposeful, daily psychological and spiritual practice/discipline of grateful, adoring wonder in daily life. They have done so with simple, childlike, humble practices to nourish the soul and improve our mental and spiritual life by acknowledging God at the center of everything. Although many more exercises are offered in chapters 4 to 6 below, for now we are simply recognizing that all of life is a gift from God. Like a child experiencing life's simple (and often underappreciated) moments for the first time, we can approach the day with a newness and amazement that dually enriches ourselves and enriches our relationship with God. Before we end the chapter on a Christian perspective on worship and awe and turn to a psychological perspective in the next chapter, I would like us to explore two examples—one in a church setting and the other in psychotherapy—of worship and awe in daily life to move from abstract to concrete in the immediacy of the moment.

Christian Worship and Awe in Church: "O Holy Night"

For Devon, a twenty-one-year-old African American male, as far back as he could remember, Christmastime was a season of sadness and loneliness. Growing up as an only child with divorced parents, he often remembered playing alone with his Christmas toys and being shuffled back and forth between parents. Although for many families Christmas is a time of celebration, closeness, connection, and ritual, he never really experienced these joys. Now, as a junior in college living on a large college campus roughly two hours from his hometown, he was experiencing suffering on top of suffering as he struggled to make friends.

Yet, on one Wednesday afternoon, a classmate invited him to a local college church group, which met down the road from their school at a small Baptist church he had never noticed prior. Eager to simply make some friends, he enthusiastically agreed to attend, recognizing he had no other opportunities to socialize that evening. Although his parents occasionally brought him to church in his childhood years, over time they stopped attending. This led to Devon struggling to understand what he believed about God and Christianity.

Driving to the little church building that evening, he felt a sense of worthlessness, emptiness, and depression like never before. He ruminated about the weeks and months prior, filled with lonely meals and quiet, invisible strolls around campus. As his new friend greeted him and escorted him into the ordinary church building, he was immediately overwhelmed with awe and wonder. He looked around to see the many Christmas decorations and church band playing Christmas music, which seemed to envelop him and effortlessly invite him in.

As he walked toward the stage, "O Holy Night" began to play. Although he had heard this song many times before on the radio, in person and with fellow college students around him he began to feel God's overwhelming presence in the immediacy of the moment. As the worship leader sang, "Fall on your knees! O hear the angel voices!" he instantly began to weep, feeling God's presence like never before. Then, when the words "Christ is the Lord, O praise his name forever!" rang out within the walls of the humble church, he felt so very small and insignificant in a good way.

In this very instance, he was not preoccupied with loneliness, ruminating about the day, or struggling with sadness or worthlessness. Rather, in worshipful awe he fell on his knees with tears strolling down his cheeks because of who God was and is. Singing the words in unison with those around him, he felt the majesty of God for the first time in his life. He allowed the experience to permeate his inner world like never before.

For Devon, in the here and now, he was extremely grateful to experience God in that small Baptist church, which helped him to pivot from self-preoccupation to a newfound childlike wonder toward the Creator and Sustainer of the universe. And although it would take some time—months that turned into years—for him to more fully deepen his relationship with God and become a devoted follower of Jesus Christ, in this moment he was able to transcend himself to recognize that God was at the center. Consequently, he could surrender to God's holy presence. Building on this example, let us now turn to a more clinical illustration of awe and wonder in Christian mental and spiritual health.

Christian Worship and Awe in Psychotherapy: *Lectio Divina*

For Evelyn, life was always hard. Growing up in a large family of two parents and six kids, she seldom felt seen, heard, supported, or validated. She constantly fought with her siblings for her parents' attention. In her house, Evelyn's mother stayed at home with the kids, whereas her father often worked long hours, which meant he was seldom around. During these years, Evelyn's mother struggled with a diagnosed panic disorder and often experienced multiple panic attacks per week, which her father dismissed as "all in her head." Because of this, Evelyn constantly worried about her mother's mental health, commonly believing that she, Evelyn, needed to be the parent in the house because her mother was barely getting by.

Eventually, Evelyn developed generalized anxiety, another type of anxiety disorder. Her symptoms included chronic worry from one topic to the next, as well as the struggle to academically perform at school or enjoy family or other close relationships because of her frequent worry. Constantly asking "What if" questions—such as "What if my mom gets worse?" "What if I start getting panic attacks myself?" and "What if I never get married because I'm defective?"—Evelyn was often lost in her own head throughout the day. She struggled to be fully engaged in her relationships or daily tasks. As a Christian, she also frequently questioned God. She asked him why she did not have a stronger mom to support her, along with why God gave her a "broken brain" that could not stop worrying or find even brief moments of peace and calm.

In her late teens, she entered psychotherapy, since she felt her worry had become unmanageable. With her psychotherapist, she began to work on her chronic worry, among other goals, by noticing it and shifting her attention to something else, such as her breath. Her psychotherapist also introduced her to the topic of awe. With Evelyn's consent, they discussed her relationships with both God and her mother. Evelyn had always longed to trust in a God who was sovereign and could protect her from the many struggles of the day because her mother was often unavailable to meet this childhood need. With the psychotherapist's help, they explored what the Bible had to say about God. Gradually, Evelyn identified simple tasks that could help her pivot from her own worry and self-preoccupations to God, including *lectio divina*. With this practice, she could meditate on Scripture, then sit in loving silence with God. One particular psalm, Psalm 131, seemed to be especially helpful. This psalm allowed her to surrender her worry to God in worshipful awe, recognizing that God was infinitely powerful and wise, and she was not:

> My heart is not proud, LORD,
>   my eyes are not haughty;
> I do not concern myself with great matters
>   or things too wonderful for me.
> But I have calmed and quieted myself,
>   I am like a weaned child with its mother;
>   like a weaned child I am content.
> Israel, put your hope in the LORD
>   both now and forevermore.

For Evelyn in these moments, God was so much bigger than her human worry housed within her overactive, fallen human mind. It was God who was great and wonderful, which meant she could be calm, quiet, and content. She imagined resting in his loving arms.

Although the change by no means came suddenly, noticing her worry and then pivoting to passages like Psalm 131 assisted her in worshiping God in reverential, thankful, adoring awe. She did not need to inevitably get lost in her inner world with "What if" questions and chronic worry. Despite the reality that her biological parents did not provide the safety and support she needed, God as her Creator, Sustainer, and Redeemer was at the center of her world to meet this need.

Conclusion

To conclude this chapter on a Christian perspective on worship and awe for mental and spiritual health, all humans have a worldview, which is a view of reality that is a blend of both explicit and implicit assumptions.[102] Embedded within this worldview is a telos, or ultimate meaning or purpose for life.[103] For Christians, our purpose is to worship God, with God at the center of all of life as the Creator, Sustainer, and Redeemer.[104] As revealed throughout the pages of the Bible from Genesis to Revelation, we were designed by God to worship him in reverential awe, with self, other, and thing worship never truly satisfying us as human beings.[105] When we attempt to worship idols, which is inevitable because of the fall, we may end up miserable. This is because only God can satiate our need for wonder and awe.[106] When we do not live according to our God-given design, we might pursue idols that influence for the worse who we are.[107]

From a Christian perspective, worship can include prioritizing God, celebrating him in particular locations, particular behaviors like bowing or lifting our hands to him, and specific attitudes such as a yielding surrender to him.[108] Emanating from this worship, awe captures the reverential, thankful wonder that is inevitable because God is great and mysterious, with awe influencing our thoughts, feelings, and behaviors.[109]

Historically, Christians have employed kataphatic (using words and images) and apophatic (downplaying words and images) approaches to worship God, with both working together because God is both knowable (via his general and special revelation) and unknowable (via his ineffability in that he is too big for us to fully comprehend his vastness and greatness). As one historical spiritual practice in Christianity, *lectio divina* involves the combination of both kataphatic (meditating) and apophatic (contemplating)

---

102. Anderson et al. (2017).
103. Knabb et al. (2025).
104. Tozer (2009).
105. Forrest et al. (2021).
106. Beale (2008).
107. Beale (2008).
108. Lee (2021).
109. Upper Room (2003a).

strategies, which makes it a useful discipline to cultivate worshipful awe before God. With this Christian understanding in mind, let us now turn to chapter 3 to focus on a psychological perspective on worship and awe, doing so with a special emphasis on the Christian mental and spiritual health implications.

CHAPTER THREE

Worship and Awe in Psychology

There are two ways to live: you can live as if nothing is a miracle; you can live as if everything is a miracle. The most beautiful thing we can experience is the mysterious. It is the source of all true art and all science. He to whom this emotion is a stranger, who can no longer pause to wonder and stand rapt in awe, is as good as dead: his eyes are closed.

—Albert Einstein, *Einstein Wisdom*

While the nature of humankind is entirely depraved and nothing but weeds could grow out of that depravity—no one doing good from his own impulse, not even one (see Rom. 3:12)—the life of humanity, its history, and our experiences among humanity nevertheless display much that is rich and glorious that we are driven to worship. What grows from our race is never anything but divine gifts of creation—not made by us but sovereignly given to us.

—Abraham Kuyper, *Common Grace*

Introduction

In chapter 3, we begin by exploring the burgeoning awe literature in psychology, including both a theoretical and empirical understanding of awe and the mental health implications. A definition of awe is offered, coupled with common awe triggers and awe interventions to increase this unique emotion. Along the way, current research on the relationship between awe and mental health is presented, as are studies on awe interventions to improve meaning in life and life satisfaction. Although certainly not as popular as awe, worship as a psychological variable is also discussed, since worship is arguably the mechanism through which awe is pursued and maintained whether we realize it or not as inevitable daily worshipers. Included in this discussion is the role that worshiping the self, others, and things plays in psychological functioning, especially psychopathology and other forms of mental suffering. Finally, a metaphor for understanding worship and awe and examples in both daily life and psychotherapy are discussed to reveal the salience of worshipful awe—including its main ingredients of vastness, the need to adjust previous understandings, and gratitude—for all of life,[1] whether experienced in larger events or the seemingly mundane activities of the day. We begin this chapter with a review of a theoretical understanding of awe in psychology.

Awe in Psychology: Theoretical Considerations

History

According to PsycINFO, a popular online database of journal articles within the psychology literature, works that were devoted exclusively to the topic of awe began to emerge over a half-century ago. Writing in the 1950s, the American psychoanalyst Phyllis Greenacre suggested that awe is first experienced in childhood, possibly around the age of four or five years old, and includes the ingredients of fear and admiration.[2] In this work, which may be one of the first devoted exclusively to awe in the psychology literature, the author argues for further study of this important emotion throughout the lifespan. Some two decades later, the psychoanalytic author Irvin Harrison referenced Greenacre's writing on the topic to suggest that the experience of awe is important within the context of the mother-child dyad.[3] Following these two writings, the psychoanalytic author Jeffry Andresen explained that awe is the "discovery of generative goodness within the otherness of the other." He further noted it is bound up in gratitude and emerges when children have a sense that others exist independent of themselves.[4] Although not empirical, these psychoanalytic writings that span four decades seem to be the first of their kind to reference and focus on awe as a psychological experience within the psychology literature.

---

1. Büssing et al. (2018); Keltner and Haidt (2003); Yaden et al. (2019).
2. Greenacre (1956).
3. Harrison (1975).
4. Andresen (1999), 507.

Yet, not until the psychologists Dacher Keltner and Jonathan Haidt came along was awe properly operationalized for further theoretical and empirical inquiries within the psychology literature.[5] Writing a theoretical article on the topic by drawing on works from religion, philosophy, sociology, and psychology, these two authors popularized awe. They suggested it is a "moral, spiritual, and aesthetic" emotion worthy of empirical investigation. At the time of this writing, their theoretical article has been cited over 2,200 times according to Google Scholar. Since Keltner and Haidt's pioneering manuscript, awe has been written on theoretically,[6] including as a religious experience,[7] and studied empirically,[8] with a plethora of books published on the topic.[9]

Definitions

As a key component of this burgeoning literature, to date, there have been several definitions of awe in circulation. According to the *APA Dictionary of Psychology*, "awe" is "the [emotional] experience of admiration and elevation in response to physical beauty, displays of exceptional ability, or moral goodness. The awe-inspiring stimulus is experienced as 'vast' and difficult to comprehend."[10] Individuals may experience awe as a one-time occurrence or dispositionally, meaning they are more prone to experience awe when compared to others. So, according to this dictionary entry, awe is a human emotion that is experienced as a response, whether as a one-time event or more regularly, to a variety of awe triggers, such as beauty in nature and human talents, skills, and virtues.

As an emotion, awe includes a sense of vastness of what is being experienced.[11] What is encountered is perceived as powerful, big, great, huge, grand, or enormous.[12] This is in contrast with a small, insignificant (often in a good way) self.[13] With awe, we also struggle to fully understand or comprehend with a limited and finite human mind what is being experienced with the senses.[14] This leads to the need to adjust or accommodate one's understanding of what is perceived to make room for the new reality.[15]

5. Keltner and Haidt (2003).
6. Schneider (2017).
7. Sundarajan (2002).
8. Piff et al. (2015).
9. For example, Schneider (2009).
10. American Psychological Association (n.d.a).
11. American Psychological Association (n.d.a).
12. American Psychological Association (n.d.a).
13. American Psychological Association (n.d.a).
14. American Psychological Association (n.d.a).
15. American Psychological Association (n.d.a).

Ingredients

Beyond definitions, there are a variety of more specific ingredients experienced with the emotion of awe. First, awe includes the perception that time is slowing down in the present moment.[16] This means that individuals in a state of awe may feel like they have more time on their hands. Second, those experiencing awe might view the self as small, commonly in a good way, in contrast with how large, big, or amazing the awe-inducing trigger may be.[17] An example may include standing at the base of Mount Everest and futilely attempting to locate and stare at the summit. Third, the emotion of awe may elucidate a greater sense of connection with others, as well as the surrounding world.[18] An example may be when someone stares into the sky with friends at a mountain resort to see the vastness of the Milky Way and seemingly limitless number of stars. Fourth, and relatedly, there is an experience of vastness,[19] such as seeing the awe-inducing trigger (e.g., the power of a natural disaster) as too great and immense to fully comprehend with the finite human mind. Fifth, along with vastness, awe dually includes a sense of incomprehensibility and mystery and need to accommodate the trigger.[20] In other words, there is an attempt to adjust current ideas, mental structures, and so on, to make room for the new information, which might or might not be ultimately successful.[21] This may be the case when a tourist stands at the base of the Great Pyramid of Giza and cannot fully understand how humans could have built such an amazing, time-enduring structure thousands of years ago, without advanced technology or equipment (e.g., cranes, bulldozers). Upon staring up at its vastness, the mesmerized traveler must adjust their previous understanding of what constitutes a "big structure," given their limited exposure to business buildings that are only several stories high in their local town, to make room for the new information in the immediacy of the moment. Sixth, unique sensations such as "goosebumps" or "the chills" may be experienced.[22] Finally, in a state of awe, the individual may feel a sense of gratitude and appreciation for getting to take in the new experience.[23] This might be the case when, returning to the Great Pyramid of Giza example, a US tourist is appreciative and thankful for being able to

---

16. Yaden et al. (2019).
17. Yaden et al. (2019).
18. Yaden et al. (2019).
19. Keltner and Haidt (2003); Yaden et al. (2019).
20. Keltner and Haidt (2003); Yaden et al. (2019).
21. Keltner and Haidt (2003); Yaden et al. (2019).
22. Yaden et al. (2019), 476.
23. Büssing et al. (2018).

travel across the world to stand in front of such an overwhelmingly grand stone structure.

Triggers

In addition to the definitions and key ingredients of awe, awe theorists and researchers have attempted to illuminate a variety of potential awe triggers—or the deities, people, places, and things that may give rise to the emotional experience of awe.[24] These are organized around at least three major categories. First, there are social triggers,[25] such as interacting with or experiencing God or a gifted human leader, observing someone performing a set of unordinary talents or skills (e.g., an athlete, a performer), or being in the presence of an individual carrying out a human virtue (e.g., an altruistic act of kindness, such as watching Mother Teresa live among and care for underserved communities). Second, awe may be triggered by experiences in the physical world,[26] including staring at a large human-made structure (e.g., the Eiffel Tower) or structure in nature (e.g., an Alaskan glacier), observing the power of a natural disaster (e.g., a hurricane, a tornado), listening to music (e.g., attending an in-person symphony orchestra performance), or staring at a priceless work of art in a museum (e.g., appreciating Vincent van Gogh's *The Starry Night*). Third, and finally, awe may be induced, or triggered, by cognitions or thoughts,[27] such as attempting to comprehend a scientific theory that has bettered society or meditating on God's attributes/characteristics, like his infinite love or wisdom revealed in the timeless psalms of the Old Testament.

To summarize this theoretical literature, awe is a human emotion that includes the two main experiences of "vastness" and "a need for accommodation,"[28] accompanied by a sense that the self is small and the experience is big, gratitude toward the experience, a sense of connection with the world, a sense that time is slowing down, and sensory experiences like getting chills or goosebumps.[29] Common awe triggers include those that are social, physical, and cognitive. This means there is a range of experiences that can induce (or lead to or

---

24. Keltner and Haidt (2003).
25. Keltner and Haidt (2003).
26. Keltner and Haidt (2003).
27. Keltner and Haidt (2003).
28. Keltner and Haidt (2003), 297.
29. American Psychological Association (n.d.a); Büssing et al. (2018); Keltner and Haidt (2003).

conjure up) the psychological experience of awe.[30] With these definitions, ingredients, and triggers in mind, let us now turn to awe research in psychology

Awe in Psychology: Empirical Considerations

In terms of research on awe, it has been examined in the psychology literature as both a construct for measurement in correlational research (to examine its relationship to other psychological variables) and an intervention in experimental research (to induce awe and examine its psychological effects or outcomes). This research will be described in detail in the next few sections of the chapter.

Awe as a Construct

Several years ago, the Awe Experience Scale (AWE-S) was developed.[31] It includes six main ingredients: time slowing down, small self, a sense of connection with the world, vastness, sensory experiences, and the struggle to fully comprehend, make sense of, or understand the experience.[32] Employing online samples of US adults, the AWE-S developers and researchers found that awe was positively linked to positive emotions and negatively linked to negative emotions. Among this same sample of participants, the most common awe triggers, or event-related themes that resulted in the emotional experience of awe, reported when they were asked to document such encounters in writing were experiencing beauty in the world such as in nature; observing a talent, ability, skill, or virtue in other people; and perceiving the presence of a supernatural deity. Other studies have revealed that awe is positively related to the perception that people have more time in the present moment,[33] well-being,[34] including life satisfaction,[35] prosocial behaviors (e.g., altruism), empathy for others, and a greater sense of connection with others.[36] We now examine these studies in greater detail below.

Because awe is about experiencing vastness in the immediacy of the moment, people may be more connected to the present. They may have a sense that they have more time at their disposal, which might protect against

---

30. American Psychological Association (n.d.a); Büssing et al. (2018); Keltner and Haidt (2003).
31. Yaden et al. (2019).
32. Yaden et al. (2019).
33. Rudd et al. (2012).
34. Zhao et al. (2019).
35. Liu et al. (2023).
36. Jiao and Luo (2022).

symptoms of depression (with preoccupations about a guilt-ridden past or hopeless future) and anxiety (with preoccupations about a future filled with danger and catastrophe). In support of this perspective, in a study among US college students, Melanie Rudd and colleagues investigated whether experiencing awe can increase students' "perceived time availability," meaning the sense that the present moment is "enhanced" and "boundless" and they have more time at their disposal in the here and now.[37] Consistent with their hypotheses, results revealed that awe was positively linked to "perceived time availability." This finding suggests that inducing awe with images such as scenes in nature or outer space may lead to greater present-moment awareness and the experience of having more time to interact with others, carry out important tasks, and, ultimately, live life.

In terms of awe and well-being, well-being includes both life satisfaction (a cognitive component) and happiness (an affective component).[38] With awe, individuals may experience well-being because awe expands their view of the world and offers meaning and purpose in life, with life seen as valuable and significant. In support of this theory, among a sample of Chinese adults, Huanhuan Zhao and colleagues found that awe was positively related to well-being and meaning in life.[39] They also found that meaning in life mediated the link between awe and well-being. This suggests that meaning in life may help to explain the positive relationship between awe and well-being. To offer an example for Christians, experiencing the awe-inducing immenseness and mysteriousness of God may offer meaning, significance, and value in life, which, in turn, positively influences the two components of well-being—life satisfaction and happiness.

When considering awe and altruism (and other prosocial behaviors), those who are more dispositionally prone to awe may also report displaying a greater number of prosocial behaviors, such as altruistic or selfless acts toward others. Among a sample of Chinese college students, researchers found that awe was positively linked to prosocial behaviors, including altruism.[40] This positive relationship was mediated or explained by a perceived sense of connectivity (belonging to a community and humanity) and empathy (an effort to understand the psychological experiences of other people). In other words, as participants reported a higher level of awe, they indicated they experienced greater empathy for and connectivity with others. And as they reported more empathy and connection, they endorsed engaging in more prosocial behaviors,

37. Rudd et al. (2012), 1131–32.
38. Diener et al. (2002).
39. Zhao et al. (2019).
40. Jiao and Luo (2022).

like altruistic and selfless acts. So, ultimately, when we are in awe, we might feel more connected to the people around us and, as a result, strive more frequently to understand them. This may lead to a greater willingness to display positive, helpful, selfless behaviors toward the people in our life.

Moving on to awe and connection, when people experience awe, they may have a greater sense that they are connected to the world around them, including other people, nature, society, and the universe.[41] This may be because awe helps us to shift the focus from the self, which is perceived to be small and insignificant in a good way, to the world around us, which is vast and mysterious and difficult to fully wrap our mind around or comprehend. In other words, there is something beneficial about the world being unexplainable and much bigger than we could ever fully know with our finite human mind. This ability to surrender to something larger and outside of the self may bring with it a sense of peace, given that we do not need to futilely try to control the world around us. Instead, we can simply marvel, with gratitude, appreciation, and adoration, at the mysteries, blessings, and goodness of creation, which Christians believe God created for us to enjoy (Ps. 96:11–12). In support of this understanding, in a study among Chinese college students, Li Luo and colleagues found a positive relationship between awe and connectedness.[42]

In each of these studies, it may be that awe helps us to experience greater "self-transcendence."[43] We may move from self-preoccupation (with constant rumination, brooding, and worry that can often individually and collectively enhance psychological suffering) to a focus on the people, places, things, and spiritual reality around us. Given the ingredients of vastness and mystery,[44] when we experience the emotion of awe dispositionally on a regular basis, we are opening up to the reality that the world is much bigger than any one individual self. In turn, the mysteries of life can be embraced and enjoyed, without the finite human mind futilely striving to be all-knowing and all-powerful. This futile striving is exhausting and ruins and cheapens the experience of being a small self in a grand, amazing world, which Christians believe God made as Creator and Sustainer.

Awe as an Intervention

Moving beyond correlation research, which simply attempts to measure awe as a variable and examine its relationship with other psychological variables

---

41. Luo et al. (2021).
42. Luo et al. (2023).
43. Luo et al. (2021).
44. Keltner and Haidt (2003).

at the same point in time (e.g., well-being, prosocial behaviors), researchers have attempted to experimentally induce awe to examine its outcomes, such as trying to increase awe and other positive psychological experiences. So, researchers may ask participants to write or read about a prior awe-inducing event (e.g., traveling to the Grand Canyon) or watch an awe-inducing video (e.g., someone hiking to a waterfall in Yosemite National Park),[45] and then they hypothesize the participants' awe will increase pre- to postintervention.

For instance, in a study among Italian college students, researchers assigned participants to either an awe-inducing virtual reality (VR) condition or neutral (not awe-inducing) VR condition. With the former, they were exposed to either a beautiful green forest, vast mountain landscape, or view of a distant Earth from outer space. With the latter, they were exposed to yellow and green grass, trees, and flowers.[46] Results revealed that participants who entered the awe-inducing VR environment reported a greater increase in awe, pre- to postintervention, than those who experienced the neutral environment. To offer one more example, researchers investigated the influence of awe-inducing music on US college students.[47] They assigned participants to either an orchestra/crescendo music condition without lyrics (which attempted to elicit awe among the listeners) or silence condition (involving no sound at all). Results revealed that the awe-inducing music group reported a greater increase in positive affect (e.g., feeling excited, enthusiastic, and inspired), pre- to postintervention, than did the silence group.

To summarize, researchers in recent years seem to have successfully designed experiments to increase awe and other related positive emotions when delivering VR and musical interventions. This suggests that awe is by no means an emotion that only some people experience. Rather, awe can successfully be induced, especially when intentionally offering experiences that conjure up the experience of vastness, mystery, and gratitude. We now turn to a more in-depth review of some of the potential mental health benefits of awe as a positive human emotion that is experienced dispositionally along the proverbial roads of life, not as a one-time, fleeting experience.

Awe and Mental Health

Theoretically, there may be many overlapping reasons regarding how awe promotes mental health. To begin, awe might protect against self-rumination

---

45. Luo et al. (2021).
46. Chirico et al. (2018).
47. Ji et al. (2021).

in depression,[48] which is often a central feature of this disorder. With negative self-rumination, we end up thinking about the self in a repetitive, perseverative manner. We may get stuck going over different (and often negative) aspects of the self in an unhelpful, unproductive, rigid manner. In a longitudinal study among German community participants who were 16 to 62 years old, researchers gave them measures of self-esteem, rumination, and symptoms of depression five times over eight months.[49] Results revealed that low self-esteem influenced self-rumination, with self-rumination having an impact on depressive symptoms. With these results in mind, given the prominent role that self-rumination plays in depression, awe may help depressed individuals to transcend the self. Consequently, they may get unstuck from perseverative patterns of negative self-rumination (e.g., self-criticism; believing the self is useless, worthless, or unlovable).

Relatedly, awe may provide a sense of meaning to protect against the perceived meaninglessness that often emanates from episodes of depression.[50] This self-transcendent emotion might allow us to better realize the bigness and vastness of the world and our connection to it. In fact, having a sense of awe-induced meaning in life may help with a wide range of psychiatric symptoms.[51] This may be because the individual has purpose in the midst of suffering, which can help them persevere and press on in the face of inner and outer challenges. When one is experiencing awe, there is a need to accommodate the new incoming information by modifying previously established ideas and mental structures.[52] This can help the individual to generate novel perspectives about life's meaning and their purpose on this planet.[53] As a quick illustration, awe may offer religious individuals the ability to cultivate and maintain an awareness of a more spiritual, permanent reality. Such an awareness can help them to transcend the small self and, in the process, endure the temporary earthly experience of suffering and accept the uncertainty of life.[54]

As another example, awe may promote the widening, rather than narrowing, of attention.[55] This widening can help those with (1) depression to get unstuck from more restrictive, perseverative patterns of rumination; (2) anxiety to get disentangled from rigid, repetitive patterns of worry; and

48. Chirico and Gaggioli (2021).
49. Kuster et al. (2012).
50. Chirico and Gaggioli (2021).
51. Monroy and Keltner (2023).
52. Monroy and Keltner (2023).
53. Monroy and Keltner (2023).
54. Luo et al. (2021).
55. Luo et al. (2021).

(3) trauma-related disorders to ameliorate recurrent thoughts of danger, among other symptoms and disorders.[56]

Relatedly, depressive, anxiety-related, and trauma-related symptoms and disorders often place a proverbial spotlight on the struggling self. Depression focuses on negative thoughts about the self, anxiety is made up of thoughts about a self unable to handle future catastrophes, and trauma imagines the self re-experiencing traumatic events all over again.[57] With this in mind, awe may help us to shift our focus from the self to other people, things, and God (for religious individuals).[58] The wider the world around us, the more we are able to be "other-focused."[59] In other words, the self-transcendent experience of awe might shift our attention away from the suffering self and self-preoccupation,[60] which is commonly needed when attempting to ameliorate many symptoms of emotional disorders.

Continuing with a few more possible mental health benefits of awe, this self-transcendent emotion may allow for a greater openness to new experiences.[61] This openness may be cultivated because we are dispositionally aware of just how vast and mysterious[62] the world actually is, which promotes a sense of mystery and wonder in daily life. This shift in perspective can be helpful for those with depressive, anxiety-related, and trauma-related disorders because such disorders all tend to involve some form of social isolation and avoidance in a futile effort to get rid of unpleasant and distressing symptoms.[63] What is more, awe might promote humility,[64] since a small self is regularly contrasted with a big world (in a good way). And this humility can help us to have a balanced perspective on the strengths and limitations of the self within the world. Gratitude,[65] too, may be experienced with dispositional awe, since we recognize and are thankful for the never-ending awe-inducing experiences that enrich life. As a quick example, in a recent review of sixty-two studies, researchers found a negative link between gratitude and depression, suggesting striving to find the good in life, which resides outside of the self, may be helpful for common mental disorders like depression.[66] More broadly, awe might

---

56. Luo et al. (2021).
57. American Psychiatric Association (2022). See especially the chapters "Depressive Disorders," "Anxiety Disorders," and "Trauma- and Stressor-Related Disorders."
58. Sung and Yih (2016).
59. Sung and Yih (2016).
60. Monroy and Keltner (2023).
61. Luo et al. (2021).
62. Keltner and Haidt (2003).
63. Hayes et al. (1996).
64. Stellar et al. (2018).
65. Büssing et al. (2021).
66. Iodice et al. (2021).

promote a cascade of prosocial behaviors, such as sharing and cooperating, which may improve relationships and, consequently, mental health.[67]

Overall, theoretically, having a more dispositional and enduring emotional experience and stance of awe toward the world around us may help us to regularly pivot from the self, which is small (in a good way), to God, others, and things that bring us a greater appreciation for the many blessings in life. In other words, one possible solution to psychological suffering may be the regular recognition that the self is small and the world around us is big as we surrender to this reality. Rather than ruminating about the past, brooding about the present, or worrying about the future in a futile effort to control and confine the uncontrollable and unconfinable, with awe we are engaged in present-moment appreciation for the vastness and mystery of what is already and always will be around us. To shift from attempting to be all-knowing and all-powerful to embracing a world that is positively puzzling and, at the end of the day, not fully knowable with finite human minds can bring us needed peace in embracing our role as observers of the amazing wonders of life. This shift can be likened to a child spending extended time appreciating the intricacies of a seashell on a seashore for the very first time with newness and open curiosity. Not getting caught up in themselves or allowing the critical, ruminative, and worrying mind to pull them away from the immediacy of their novel sensory experience, this child is simply getting lost in the moment in a good way. They are able to apply uncertainty and freshness to the here and now.

To theoretically dig a bit deeper in explicating why awe may promote mental health, the ideas of "beginner's mind" and "no-self" may be important to consider.[68] They come to us from Buddhist psychology and mindfulness meditative practice, which are quite popular in the psychology literature right now.[69] Although Buddhism and Christianity certainly have more differences than similarities, these two concepts, which have at least some parallels within a biblical worldview, can help us to better elucidate the benefits of moment-by-moment awe for psychological health and flourishing in a fallen, broken world.

With beginner's mind, we are approaching each unfolding moment with an open curiosity.[70] We are embracing awe and wonder and accepting whatever emerges as exciting and new.[71] In other words, we are letting go of the

---

67. Monroy and Keltner (2023).
68. Mathers et al. (2009); Seaward (2023); Tirch et al. (2016).
69. Mathers et al. (2009); Seaward (2023); Tirch et al. (2016).
70. Seaward (2023).
71. Seaward (2023).

tendency to overly rely on the judgmental, critical human mind.[72] This mind constantly tells us the present moment is not quite right in some way and needs to be changed.[73] Instead, with nonjudgmental acceptance, we fully accept, and even compassionately embrace, the here and now,[74] like a child experiencing something simple (and, for adults, often overlooked) for the first time (e.g., eating an ice cream cone, finger painting, skipping rocks on a lake, sensorily taking in the thunder and lightning of a rain storm). In the process, the world opens. We are guided by our curiosity and wonder, not our finite and verbal human mind, which often, and erroneously, believes it is infinitely powerful and knowing. When our environment expands, it gets bigger, and we get smaller in a good way. Each unfolding moment of the day becomes special. Something to cherish, slow down to absorb, and savor. Overall, with beginner's mind, we possess a present-moment, childlike wonder, guided by acceptance, nonjudgment, and reverential awe.

To summarize the ingredients of beginner's mind,[75] it is easy to see how it may assist in facilitating dispositional awe, experienced and directed to all of life. Among other components, beginner's mind includes an open curiosity and attention to inner (e.g., thoughts, feelings, sensations, memories, images) and outer (e.g., people, places, things) experiences.[76] It is coupled with present-moment awareness, a loss of the preoccupation with the self (what Buddhists call "no-self"), and acceptance of whatever unfolds internally/psychologically, whether pleasant or unpleasant.[77]

Indeed, a key aspect of beginner's mind may be no-self. Within Buddhist psychology, this self is not static but dynamic, a process rather than content.[78] When we rigidly try to hold on to or cling to a narrative that we have created about the self, we may end up suffering beyond the ubiquitous pain that is inevitable in this world. So, with mindfulness meditation, practitioners are learning to recognize that the self is impermanent. Also, everything is one, not separate or isolated. As an example, mindfulness of breathing involves following the breath cycle with present-moment, nonjudgmental, open curiosity, concluding that each breath is new and different and exciting. This perspective, that there is an observing sense of self that can simply watch the verbal, language-based self, which is impermanent, is popular among contemporary

---

72. Seaward (2023).
73. Seaward (2023).
74. Seaward (2023).
75. Kabat-Zinn (2016).
76. Kabat-Zinn (2016).
77. Kabat-Zinn (2016).
78. Mathers et al. (2009); Tirch et al. (2016).

cognitive behavioral therapies, such as acceptance and commitment therapy (ACT).[79] Ultimately, no-self is similar to the small self in the awe literature, given that we are moving from being preoccupied with the self to being more connected in awe and wonder and with a beginner's mind to the people and greater world around us.

Of course, given that the popular psychological concepts of beginner's mind and no-self come from one religious tradition, Buddhism, other religious traditions, like Christianity, have sometimes overlapping, although mostly different, perspectives. Yet, such alternative concepts and perspectives are not as frequently mentioned in the psychology literature. For Christians, for instance, having a childlike, humble, trusting faith before God is key (Matt. 18:1–4), as is self-renunciation or denial (Matt. 16:24), not necessarily beginner's mind and no-self.

Awe and Religion/Spirituality

Turning to the relationship between awe and religion/spirituality, researchers have examined these variables together in a variety of studies. To date, despite the fact that a range of authors have identified religious and spiritual experiences as potential awe triggers, with some even referring to awe as a spiritual emotion,[80] researchers within the psychology of religion literature—which focuses on the study of the human mind and behavior embedded within religious and spiritual life—have more narrowly prioritized the theoretical and empirical relationship between awe and religion/spirituality.

In particular, awe may be a correlate of religion and spirituality.[81] For instance, among samples of US community adults and college students, P. O. Kearns and J. M. Tyler found a positive relationship between both a temporary state of awe and enduring dispositional awe, on the one hand, and both religion (e.g., the salience of religious beliefs and practices in participants' lives) and spirituality (e.g., sensing God's presence in daily spiritual experiences), on the other. Awe may even trigger religious and spiritual feelings.[82] In a study among Belgian adults, Van Cappellen and Saroglou asked participants to recall either a prior awe-inducing event in nature, a pride-inducing event (e.g., a public speech, a particular act), or a neutral (no awe or pride induction) event (i.e., details of a recent trip to the movies). These participants were then asked to complete items related to religion and spirituality

---

79. Hayes et al. (2012).
80. Keltner and Haidt (2003).
81. Kearns and Tyler (2022).
82. Van Cappellen and Saroglou (2012).

(e.g., a sense of connection to life, the salience of religion and God in life) and preferences/motivations for traveling to either a spiritual location (e.g., Tibet) or vacation location (e.g., Haiti). Results revealed that, in the awe condition but not the neutral condition, a positive link between religion and spirituality and willingness to visit a spiritual (but not vacation) location emerged. This suggests that as participants experienced the emotion of awe, there was a stronger relationship between religion/spirituality and desiring to go to a spiritual place. In other words, the spiritual and self-transcendent emotion of awe may play a role in explaining the strength of the relationship between religious/spiritual beliefs and behavior-based motivations. So, for self-described religious/spiritual adults, awe might function as a motivator to live out their spirituality with behavioral action, rather than merely endorse religious/spiritual beliefs in an abstract manner.

What is more, being asked to remember a spiritual experience might increase awe, mediated by the "small self."[83] In a study among online US adults, Jesse Preston and Faith Shin assigned participants to either a spiritual group, wherein they were asked to remember a particular occurrence that involved feeling close to a higher power, or a humor group as the control group, which involved being asked to remember a prior humorous or amusing event. After this request, both groups filled out an awe questionnaire. Results revealed that the spiritual group reported greater awe. This same study was carried out again with a similar sample of online US adults, this time with both a measure of awe (similar to the first study) and measure of small self (e.g., feeling insignificant, forgetting daily concerns). Results revealed that the spiritual group reported a greater experience of awe and the small self. Overall, this study lends support to the notion that daily spiritual experiences may result in the emotional experience of awe, along with a diminished sense of self, which involves feeling insignificant (in a good way) and focusing one's attention on the larger surrounding world.

In addition, awe may be positively correlated with a variety of concrete daily spiritual experiences (e.g., perceiving the presence and love of God in daily life) and practices (e.g., meditating, praying),[84] not just abstract notions of religion and spirituality in general. In a study among a combined sample of German college students and community adults, Arndt Büssing investigated the relationship between awe and spiritual experiences and practices, with results revealing a positive link between awe and daily spiritual experiences (e.g., sensing God's love or comfort) and practices (e.g., daily/weekly/monthly

---

83. Preston and Shin (2017).
84. Büssing (2021).

meditation and/or prayer). Therefore, theoretically, the spiritual emotion of awe may be a key component of concrete, real-world daily spiritual experiences and practices among religious adults. In other words, awe might serve as a motivator to behaviorally pursue a deeper relationship with God and experience his presence.

Finally, within a religious context, awe of God (not just secular awe) might be related to life satisfaction.[85] In a study among community US adults, N. Krause and R. D. Hayward examined the relationship between awe of God (captured with ingredients such as seeing beauty in God's creation, feeling small in comparison to the universe that God has made, feeling overwhelmed and amazed with wonder in response to God's infinite power and wisdom) and life satisfaction (which included the experience of reflecting on life and feeling satisfied, seeing the present day as the "best years" of life, and being unwilling to change the past if given the opportunity), mediated by a sense of connection with others (reflected in experiencing a bond with others, as well as a sense that others offer strength). Results revealed that the link between awe of God and life satisfaction was explained by a greater sense of connection with others. In other words, theoretically, those who are in awe of God may feel more connected to others. As they feel more connected to others, they might experience more satisfaction with life. Here, we can see the potential salience of bonded connections among adults—with both God and others—which can help to enhance their level of satisfaction with all of life.

Overall, these studies elucidate that awe may be linked to both religion and spirituality in general, as well as more concrete daily spiritual experiences and practices in particular (e.g., sensing God's presence). This association between awe and spirituality might be explained, at least in part, by the notion of the small self, which is a "diminished perceived self-size"[86] and is made up of a loss of the ubiquitous human preoccupation with the self. What is more, awe of God, more narrowly, may be positively related to life satisfaction. This suggests that, at least theoretically, awe of God, not just secular awe, can be good for mental health because we might evaluate our life as positive and headed in the right direction.

Awe Summary

To summarize these findings, awe is defined as a positive emotion, which includes the experience of the vastness of the world around us and our inability

---

85. Krause and Hayward (2015a).
86. Bai et al. (2017), 187.

to fully comprehend it.[87] Awe triggers may include those that are cognitive (e.g., meditating on God's infinite power, pondering Albert Einstein's theory of relativity), physical (e.g., standing in amazement in front of the Eiffel Tower, watching the northern lights, or aurora borealis), and social (e.g., being the recipient of a virtuous act on the part of an altruistic stranger, watching Babe Ruth hit his 714th home run in professional baseball).[88] Correlation research has revealed that awe is linked to, among other psychological variables, prosocial interactions, well-being, and a small self.[89] Experimental research has illuminated that awe can actually be induced,[90] and awe can be experienced within the context of religion and spirituality.[91] When it comes to awe and mental health, the regular, dispositional experience of awe in life may, psychologically, ameliorate self-preoccupations, which are often a struggle for individuals with depressive, anxiety-related, and trauma-related disorders; improve interpersonal relationships by increasing prosocial behaviors; and offer a wider meaning and purpose in life, which might increase well-being and decrease the common symptoms of depression, anxiety, stress, and trauma.[92]

Building on this review, we now turn to the study of worship in psychology, which has a much smaller, sparse literature base when compared to the burgeoning and seemingly ever-expanding work on awe. Then, we integrate the psychology of worship and awe and offer an awe metaphor and two examples of the benefits of awe to conclude the chapter.

Worship in Psychology: Theoretical Considerations

History

In PsycINFO, which electronically houses psychology and related journal articles published over the last hundred or more years, writings on the topic of worship seemed to emerge in the early twentieth century, although there have not been as many articles, to date, when compared to awe. In the first few years of the 1900s, books on the topic of worship within the psychology (and related) literature included the psychology professor John Hylan's *Public Worship: A Study in the Psychology of Religion*[93] and the professor of medicine

---

87. Keltner and Haidt (2003).
88. Keltner and Haidt (2003).
89. Luo et al. (2021).
90. Luo et al. (2021).
91. Kearns and Tyler (2022); Van Cappellen and Saroglou (2012).
92. Monroy and Keltner (2023).
93. Hylan (1901).

Richard Cabot's *What Men Live By: Work, Play, Love, Worship*.[94] Following these two book publications, in 1916, the American physician Sanger Brown published a theoretical journal article on sex worship in the *Journal of Abnormal Psychology*, tracing the worship of sex through symbolism, religious ritual, art, mythology, and literature.[95] Then, in the late 1940s, in the *American Sociological Review*, the sociologist Orrin Klapp published a theoretical journal article on hero worship in the United States, suggesting that this unique type of worship seems to be growing as religious faith is declining.[96]

Fast-forward almost a quarter century, and Harold Ellens, a Christian psychologist and theologian, published a theoretical journal article in 1973 in the *Journal of Psychology and Theology* on the psychology of Christian worship. He argued that worship is a "celebration," with the ultimate purpose being "the achievement of emotional health and spiritual wholeness in the form of relief from destructive anxiety by means of celebration of God's grace."[97] For Ellens, Christian worship is a celebration of what God has accomplished, via his grace, in Jesus Christ—reconciling those who believe in the Son to the trinitarian God of Christianity. If grace is simply the unearned merit or favor, and corresponding salvation, that God bestows on those who "declare with [their] mouth, 'Jesus is Lord'" (Rom. 10:9), the anxiety, uncertainty, and worry that ultimately come from the fear of nonbeing[98] (i.e., ceasing to exist in embodied human form) and shame as a ubiquitous, powerful human emotion[99] can be ameliorated via celebrating who God is and what he has accomplished.

Two years after Ellens,[100] the Christian psychologist Stephen Meyer published a theoretical journal article on the relationship between neuropsychology and worship.[101] In it, he suggests that Christian worship should be both analytic and verbal (via pastors preaching God's Word, the Bible, from the pulpit on a Sunday morning) and subjective and experiential (by way of behavioral rituals on the part of congregants, like the raising of hands during the communal singing of worship music on Sunday morning), corresponding to the reality that humans have an analytical left brain and experiential right brain, respectively. Since the 1970s, very few books or theoretical or empirical journal articles seem to have emerged on the

---

94. Cabot (1914).
95. Brown (1916).
96. Klapp (1949).
97. Ellens (1973), 10.
98. Tillich (1980).
99. Kaufman (1996).
100. Ellens (1973).
101. Meyer (1975).

psychology of religious worship, whether as a psychological construct for measurement or a practice that is hypothesized to influence other psychological outcomes (e.g., mental health).

As an exception to this widespread absence, the Christian psychologist Alexis Abernethy edited a book on a multidisciplinary approach to worship, with diverse contributions from authors within theology, the arts, and psychology, among others.[102] And the Christian psychologists Brad Strawn and Warren Brown attempted to integrate psychological, neuroscientific, and spiritual perspectives on Christian worship.[103]

Nevertheless, a wide variety of empirical studies have emerged in recent years on various forms of idol worship, most notably celebrity worship. For instance, Ying-Ching Lin and Chien-Hsin Lin investigated different types of idol worship among adolescents in Taiwan, with an idol (not to be confused with biblical idols, previously mentioned in chap. 2) defined as "someone whose talents, achievements, status, or physical appearance are specially recognized and appreciated by his or her fans."[104] Results revealed that, among the participants, the most popular idols were celebrities (endorsed by about 66 percent of participants), such as actors and performers. This was followed by noncelebrities (at roughly 10 percent), like family members and friends. The reasons these individuals were valued and worshiped, according to participants, were because they were "good looking," were "attractive dressing," had an "attractive body shape," were "humorous and funny," and were "knowledgeable and clever," among other qualities.[105] As part of the study, the researchers also examined the relationship between the aforementioned traits of the idols (e.g., exterior, interior, wealth) and the extent to which they worshiped such idols (i.e., kept close track of the idol, obsessed about the idol via intense thoughts and feelings). Results revealed that the strongest (positive) relationship emerged for external traits, such as physical appearance, and idol worship.

As one more preliminary example, some authors have proposed a theory of compensation to explain the seemingly widespread idol worship that is permeating contemporary societies, with "idolizing" succinctly explained as "considering a person or person-like figure as an object for worship."[106] With this theory, idol worshipers select and worship an idol (whether an athlete, performer, YouTube influencer, or other celebrity) to compensate for a lacking

---

102. Abernethy (2008).
103. Strawn and Brown (2013).
104. Lin and Lin (2007), 575.
105. Lin and Lin (2007), 579.
106. Cheung and Yue (2012), 35.

or deficient relationship with someone else,[107] whether a deity / higher power, parent, romantic partner, or friend. Worded another way, there is a fantasy that replaces a reality, with the fantasied relationship meeting certain psychological and social needs for a perceived sense of closeness, connection, shared values, and self-worth.[108] Over time, when the worshiping individual has a "surplus" and, thus, is psychologically satisfied, they may move on to another idol to worship.[109]

To empirically investigate this theory, researchers explored the relationship between parental absence and idol worship among adolescent Hong Kong participants, with results revealing that most of the idols endorsed were celebrity entertainers.[110] Also, a positive link emerged between parental absence (for either father or mother) and idol worship, meaning that, as adolescents' father or mother was absent, they endorsed that they were more likely to worship idols, lending support to this compensation model.[111]

Of course, for Christians, only God is worthy of worship. Yet, because God designed humans to worship him via his Word (the Bible) and works, including his creation,[112] in a fallen world we will look to fill this void by worshiping lesser things, if we are not worshiping God. We now turn to more precise definitions and ingredients of worship in psychology, and then we will discuss the different types of psychology research (correlational, or the relationship between variables, and experimental, or possible causal influences that one variable has on another) on contemporary notions of worship.

Definitions

For the purposes of this chapter, the *APA Dictionary of Psychology* defines a few key terms that are important for us to consider in detail within the context of the psychological experience of worship. First, "religion" is "a system of spiritual beliefs, practices, or both, typically organized around the *worship* of an all-powerful deity (or deities) and involving behaviors such as prayer, meditation, and participation in collective rituals."[113] Notice, here, that religion involves "the worship" of a God, higher power, or deity, which means worship is central to understanding the psychological experience of religion. Moreover, "spirituality" is "a concern for God and a sensitivity to

---

107. Cheung and Yue (2012).
108. Cheung and Yue (2012).
109. Cheung and Yue (2012).
110. Cheung and Yue (2012).
111. Cheung and Yue (2012).
112. Entwistle (2015).
113. American Psychological Association (n.d.e), italics added.

religious experience, which may include the practice of a particular religion but may also exist without such practice."[114] In other words, religion *may* include spirituality, and spirituality *may* include religion. Still, spirituality *may not* include religion. Finally, "worship" is formally defined as both "*reverence* or adoration for a divine or supernatural being, a person, or a principle" and "the formal expression of religious faith in ritual, prayer, or other prescribed practices,"[115] with a synonym for "reverence" being "awe."[116]

So, religion is an organized system that often gives rise to spirituality, whereas spirituality may, but does not have to, include organized religion. Worship is embedded within religion, with a spiritual and awe-inducing experience emanating from worship, since it can be directed toward a god, deity, or higher power. Given that worship is ubiquitous, however (i.e., from a Christian perspective, humans are always worshiping someone or something, with this motivation being innate),[117] it does not have to be attached to religion. Rather, it can be a spiritual experience in pursuit of the adoration and praise of a human or idea and function outside the context of religious life.

With the above definitions in mind, in the remainder of this chapter I argue that, psychologically and spiritually, worship—including an attitude of reverence or adoration and its accompanying particular behaviors—can be directed toward *either* God *or* the self, others, or things. Put another way, we can worship either the Creator or his creation. In either case, however, we inevitably strive to worship in reverential awe, and we need to pursue vastness and mysteriousness in the process.[118]

Ingredients

In terms of the particular ingredients of the psychological (and corresponding spiritual) experience of worship,[119] it may include the following: (1) reverential awe, which is an emotional admiration and amazement directed toward someone or something; (2) adoration, which overlaps with reverence and is a deep love and respect for someone or something; (3) a contrast, meaning there is a need to compare the worshiped and worshiper, with the former perfect and holy and the latter imperfect, unworthy, or less-than on at least some level; (4) an object (whether God, the self, others, or things); (5) an emphasis on individual or group forms, suggesting that worship can

114. American Psychological Association (n.d.f).
115. American Psychological Association (n.d.g), italics added.
116. Vocabulary.com (n.d.).
117. Tozer (2009).
118. Keltner and Haidt (2003).
119. American Psychological Association (n.d.g); Britannica (n.d.).

be conducted alone, by oneself, or in a group setting that is referred to in Christianity as "corporate worship"; (6) particular behaviors, such as religious rituals, rites, sacrifices, words, songs, or prayers, which may include the worshiper bowing or kneeling to honor and praise the worshiped; (7) an application to all of life, not merely confined to a particular location (e.g., a church auditorium) on a particular day (e.g., Sunday) with specific songs (e.g., hymns) and individual guides (e.g., a worship leader on a stage); and, finally, (8) intrinsic psychological (and spiritual) motivation, with humans having an innate need and drive to worship in reverential awe, whether the object is God, the self, others, or things.

To summarize these definitions and ingredients, worship is a psychological and spiritual experience common to all of life, religious and nonreligious (i.e., secular). It is conducted either individually or collectively, with several ingredients: reverential awe; an imperfect, unworthy self and a holy, worthy object that we purposefully direct our worship toward; specific behaviors employed to carry out the act of worship; and an innate, ubiquitous drive and need to worship, whether God, the self, others, or things. Building on these definitions and ingredients, we now pivot to actual empirical research, which is somewhat sparse (especially for the religious type), on worship as a psychological construct for measurement and intervention.

Worship in Psychology: Empirical Considerations

To date, despite the abundance of diverse measures that examine the psychology of religious and spiritual functioning in general,[120] no comprehensive measures seem to have been developed that exclusively focus on religious or spiritual worship more narrowly from a psychological perspective. And this absence prevents quantitative inquiries and relegates worship to the category of an imprecise operationalized construct. It also confines it to the theoretical realm, with many psychologists using the term more generally to refer to *all* religious behaviors or church attendance (as in "church *worship* service").[121]

Still, a smaller sprinkling of individual items have been included within some measures in the psychology of religion literature, such as the Daily Spiritual Experiences Scale (DSES; "During worship, or at other times when connecting with God, I feel joy, which lifts me out of my daily concerns"),[122] Spiritual Assessment Inventory (SAI; "I am always in a worshipful mood when

---

120. Hill and Hood (1999).
121. Spilka and Ladd (2013).
122. Underwood and Teresi (2002), 32.

I go to church"),[123] and Religious Background and Behavior questionnaire (RBB; "Attended worship service").[124]

Also, as one possible exception, a recent scale, the Mindfulness During Worship Scale (MWS), has been developed that assesses a mindful approach to worship among Christian populations.[125] More precisely, the MWS includes the ingredients of concentration when worshiping God (e.g., sustained, focused attention on God), presence when worshiping God (e.g., feeling God's loving presence in the here and now), and absorption when worshiping God (e.g., being fully present and immersed in a present-moment relationship with God with total attention).[126] With a sample of UK Christian adults, the authors found empirical support for these three dimensions via factor analysis (a statistical strategy to elucidate patterns or clusters of item responses in the numerical instrument data). The researchers also revealed that mindful worship, as a psychological construct, was positively linked to general mindfulness and spirituality. Unfortunately, to date, this scale does not seem to have been used to examine its relationship with mental health variables in correlational research or measure mindful worship as a psychological intervention for mental suffering. Although religious worship has been seldom researched on its own in the psychology literature, several theoretical and empirical journal articles have elucidated a plethora of other types of worship, which we might call idol worship, including worshiping the self, others, and things.

Self Worship (Narcissism)

Within the *APA Dictionary of Psychology*, "narcissism" is succinctly defined as "excessive self-love or egocentrism,"[127] with a recent review article on the topic identifying several symptom categories, such as "grandiose narcissism" (e.g., a sense of entitlement, arrogance, and inflated self-importance; gregariousness and extraversion) and "vulnerable narcissism" (e.g., a preoccupation with the self, or egocentrism; a distrust of, and need to distance oneself from, others; neuroticism, or psychological distress and dysregulation).[128] Although "self worship" terminology is not frequently used to describe narcissism in

---

123. Hall and Edwards (2002), 354. This item, though, is employed to assess impression management, or the tendency to present oneself in an overly positive light.
124. Connors et al. (1996), 96.
125. However, because the authors combined mindfulness, a Buddhist concept, with Christian worship, additional measures are needed that begin from a biblical worldview.
126. Yousaf et al. (2022).
127. American Psychological Association (n.d.d).
128. Miller et al. (2021).

the psychology literature,[129] it is a synonym within the English language.[130] As a result, I argue in this chapter that the psychological construct of narcissism, which can in its extreme version be a diagnosable personality disorder (as in narcissistic personality disorder),[131] is a form of self worship. And this self worship often makes us miserable, both individually and collectively, as well as psychologically and spiritually.

According to recent survey data compiled from just over 270,000 participants, scores of narcissism seem to be highest in young adulthood, and men tend to score higher on measures of narcissism than women.[132] Also, narcissism appears to increase in Western societies when economies are thriving, then decrease with recessions, possibly due to the promotion of individualism when there is an abundance of monetary resources.[133] More specifically, Jean Twenge and colleagues found that, between 1982 and 2008, symptoms of narcissism increased in the United States among a sample of roughly 35,000 college students, which aligned with a period of affluence and prosperity due to US economic conditions (e.g., lower unemployment rate). Then, symptoms of narcissism decreased from 2009 to 2013, possibly due to an economic recession (e.g., higher unemployment rate).

In either case, widespread narcissism—with the narcissistic personality disorder (NPD) prevalence rate within the US population ranging from approximately 1 percent to 17 percent, depending on age and race[134]—may be at least partially explained by the rise of social media in the last several decades. Researchers have discovered that, among a sample of over 23,000 Norwegians between the ages of sixteen and eighty-eight years old, social media addiction was positively linked to scores of narcissism.[135] Research has also revealed that, among a combined sample of Finnish university students and community adults, the self worship of narcissism was positively related to depression and anxiety and negatively related to well-being.[136] These findings suggest that in contemporary societies narcissistic self worship may pose a whole host of problems related to mental health.

129. For an exception in psychology, see the psychologist Paul Vitz (1994), who argues that contemporary Westerners are living in a socially narcissistic age of self worship. In a similar vein, in returning to the chapter 2 theme of idolatry, the famous theologian Augustine of Hippo suggests that idolatry is, in the end, self worship (Cavanaugh, 2024). Thus, combined, we might say that for Christians narcissism is the idolatry of self worship.
130. Roget's Thesaurus (2003).
131. American Psychiatric Association (2022).
132. Weidmann et al. (2023).
133. Twenge et al. (2021).
134. Males (2018); Yakeley (2018).
135. Andreassen et al. (2017).
136. Henttonen et al. (2022).

Yet, researchers have also found that, among a sample of US college students, intrinsic religiousness (i.e., religion as central to life and an end in and of itself, not a means to some other end, such as mere self-fulfillment or self-promotion) was negatively related to narcissism.[137] This suggests that religion (and its corresponding emphasis on worshiping God, not the self; see Exod. 20:3–6) may help to ameliorate narcissistic self worship, at least theoretically. In other words, religion points the worshiper to God, without whom we may be prone to worship the self.[138]

What is more, since the emotion of awe (i.e., reverence) is embedded in worship, it may be helpful to examine research on awe and narcissism, or self worship. In a study among adults from the United States, United Kingdom, Canada, Germany, and Australia who reported taking psychedelics (e.g., psilocybin, peyote) in the last five years and, in the process, having an awe-inducing experience, researchers found that their self-reported awe was negatively related to symptoms of narcissism through connectedness to nature / the world.[139] In other words, a sense of connectedness mediated the negative association between awe and narcissism in this study.

With this study in mind, theoretically, an awe-induced experience of connection with nature and others may help to reduce symptoms of narcissism such as a grandiose self and self-entitlement. Of course, the previous study[140] has major limitations, given that many people (including Christians) would prefer to avoid relying on psychedelics as a tool for awe induction. At any rate, these studies suggest that the self worship of narcissism may negatively impact mental health, with religion potentially helping to protect against worshiping the self. In addition, awe may aid in providing a sense of connectedness, which can ameliorate narcissistic self worship. Beyond self worship, which has almost exclusively been researched in psychology in the form of narcissism, other forms of worship have gained greater traction, such as celebrity worship.

Other Worship (Celebrity)

Although narcissism scores may have gone up from the 1980s to 2008 and then declined after 2008, celebrity worship appears to continue to be on the rise.[141] Lynn McCutcheon and Mara Aruguete examined thirty-five studies from 2001 to 2021 that used a measure of celebrity worship. Results

---

137. Watson et al. (1984).
138. Vitz (1994).
139. van Mulukom et al. (2020).
140. van Mulukom et al. (2020).
141. McCutcheon and Aruguete (2021).

revealed that scores that rise to the level of "celebrity worshipers" have greatly increased over this designated time.

To facilitate this line of research, McCutcheon and colleagues developed the Celebrity Worship Scale (now apparently referred to after additional research as the Celebrity Attitude Scale).[142] Recruiting a sample of US community adults, the researchers administered a pool of thirty-three items to participants. After analyzing the data, they ended up with a final set of seventeen items, which included themes of obsessing about celebrities' lives, living vicariously through celebrities, being psychologically impacted by celebrities' successes and failures in life, thinking about celebrities as a way to avoid the stressors of life, finding pleasure in learning about and following celebrities, and bonding with others through talking about and following celebrities. At the conclusion of this pioneering scale-development study, the authors suggested that absorption and addiction may explain celebrity worship. With the former, absorption, celebrity worshipers might engage in "an effortless focusing of attention," leading to "a heightened sense of reality of the idolized celebrity."[143] When this happens, worshipers may develop the view that they have a unique bond, motivating them to continue to attain more information and details about the celebrity's life and, consequently, the intimacy they long for. With the latter, addiction may play a role, according to the authors, given that celebrity worshipers might attempt to use this type of worship as a way to fill the void left by an "empty self." As with other addictions, celebrity worshipers may engage in compulsive, addictive behaviors to meet their deep-seated need to fill a psychological void, emptiness, or hollowness, with increased tolerance leading to more and more extreme behaviors to continue to meet such a need.[144]

Among different populations, the study of celebrity worship has produced interesting results. For instance, among a sample of UK community adults, researchers investigated the relationship between religiosity and celebrity worship, with results revealing a negative relationship.[145] In other words, as participants reported greater religiosity (e.g., religion is an important part of all of life), they endorsed less celebrity worship.[146] However, this result was not replicated just over a decade later. In a follow-up study among US college students, McCutcheon and colleagues did not find a significant negative link between religiosity and celebrity worship, suggesting that further research

142. McCutcheon et al. (2002).
143. McCutcheon et al. (2002), 81.
144. McCutcheon et al. (2002).
145. Maltby et al. (2002).
146. Maltby et al. (2002).

is still needed to better understand whether organized religion, including Christianity's teachings on forbidding idol worship (see Exod. 20:4–5), can ameliorate celebrity worship in contemporary societies.[147]

As the celebrity worship literature has grown over the years, authors have conducted literature reviews to better understand the accumulated research on this important construct. Samantha Brooks, for instance, conducted a comprehensive review of the celebrity worship literature, identifying sixty-two studies for further investigation.[148] Themes that emerged included a negative link between age and celebrity worship, meaning it may be less of an issue with time. Also, women might be more likely to engage in celebrity worship than men. Moreover, some evidence suggests there is a positive association between narcissism and celebrity worship, along with a negative relationship between cognitive flexibility (e.g., adjusting thinking based on new information, integrating two different concepts at the same time, switching between important tasks) and celebrity worship. Finally, there are some data that suggest well-being (including life satisfaction) is negatively linked to celebrity worship. These key findings from the Brooks review illuminate that a range of psychological struggles are related to celebrity worship. In addition to these themes,[149] Randy Sansone and Lori Sansone conducted their own review of the literature, focusing mainly on celebrity worship and mental health.[150] Themes that emerged included some empirical evidence for a positive association between celebrity worship and depression, anxiety, and addiction.

Overall, this growing body of research suggests that celebrity worship may be associated with a range of psychological struggles, such as cognitive inflexibility, addiction, depression, and anxiety. This suggests that worshiping celebrities does not bring with it the mental health that may be sought among such worshipers. Building on these themes of self (narcissism) and other (celebrity) worship, let us now turn to thing (money, material possessions, and food) worship, which also brings with it a range of potential psychological struggles.

Thing Worship (Money, Material Possessions, Food)

In addition to self and other worship, the worship of things has certainly been an area of investigation in the psychology literature. According to the *APA Dictionary of Psychology*, "materialism" is defined as "a value system that

---

147. McCutcheon et al. (2013).
148. Brooks (2021).
149. Brooks (2021).
150. Sansone and Sansone (2014).

emphasizes the pursuit and acquisition of material goods and luxuries, typically perceived by the individual as a measure of personal worth and achievement, often at the expense of moral, psychological, and social considerations."[151] Although not as well researched as awe or celebrity worship, materialism and attitudes toward money and other tangible possessions (what I refer to in this chapter as "thing worship"), as well as their relationship to other areas of psychological functioning, have been researched in the psychology literature.

For example, among a sample of US college students, researchers found a positive link between materialism (e.g., possessions are an extremely important part of life and define success) and unhealthy attitudes toward money (e.g., money is the only thing in this world that is trustworthy, money defines ability level and success, personal wealth should be bragged about to others).[152] This study suggested that those who embrace materialism may end up employing money as a "self-aggrandizement" tool to inflate and advance the self.[153]

As one more example, Rik Pieters longitudinally and bidirectionally investigated the influence that loneliness (e.g., feeling isolated and left out by social groups) has on materialism (e.g., a preoccupation with buying things for pleasure and purpose in life) and materialism has on loneliness.[154] Among a sample of participants sixteen years old and older in the Netherlands, the researcher collected data on loneliness and materialism over a six-year period of time during five different time periods. Results revealed that loneliness positively influenced materialism over the six-year period and vice versa. In other words, as loneliness increased, so did materialism, and as materialism increased, so did loneliness, lending support to the theoretical notion that lonely people turn to material possessions to soothe their pain. Of course, overly pursuing material possessions may only lead to more loneliness, as conventional wisdom might suggest, given they are no substitute for a real relationship with other human beings.

More recently, Giulia Sesini and Edoardo Lozza reviewed the literature on attitudes toward money (e.g., money is highly important and offers status, money should be loved and worshiped), highlighting several key themes across over two hundred studies.[155] Specifically, a pattern emerged that suggests those who tend to view money as a source of control, status, and personal worth may be more materialistic and compulsive in their buying habits and have lower life satisfaction.

151. American Psychological Association (n.d.c).
152. Christopher et al. (2004).
153. Christopher et al. (2004).
154. Pieters (2013).
155. Sesini and Lozza (2023).

To better understand some of these findings, theoretically, Marsha Richins has suggested that materialistic adults may begin to learn in childhood to rely on tangible things in the external world (e.g., money, clothing) for a sense of self-worth, rather than intangible things in the internal world (e.g., developing an area of expertise or knowledge base, cultivating a skill set or behavioral competencies).[156] Over time, per Richins, this overreliance on tangible things may leave the individual lacking, vulnerable, and unstable, in terms of their sense of self. This may be because the strategy of accumulating things is often unreliable, and attitudes toward such things are always shifting because of changes in style, technology, and so forth, which may make it hard to keep up.[157]

In terms of materialism and mental health, research has revealed a positive relationship between preoccupations with financial success and psychological struggles.[158] For instance, among a sample of US college students, endorsing financial success as a "guiding principle" for life was positively linked to symptoms of both depression and anxiety.[159]

As another example, with a sample of US college students, believing that money will offer power and prestige was positively linked to narcissism and negatively associated with intrinsic religiosity (e.g., believing that religion should be applied to all of life).[160] This finding suggests that those who are preoccupied with money as a vehicle through which power and status can be attained may be more self-absorbed and entitled, whereas those who are less concerned with money may be more religious.[161]

Finally, employing a sample of Chinese college students, Gouzhou Wang and colleagues investigated the relationship between materialism and mental struggles, with mindfulness as a possible moderator (i.e., a variable that explains the strength of the relationship between two other variables).[162] Results-wise, this study illuminated a positive relationship between materialism (e.g., strongly desiring material possessions, such as cars and houses) and mental struggles (e.g., symptoms of depression and anxiety), with mindfulness (e.g., staying focused on one task for sustained periods of time, being nonjudgmentally aware of present-moment experiences) functioning as a moderator. In other words, as participants reported greater mindfulness-related skills,

---

156. Richins (2017).
157. Richins (2017).
158. Kasser and Ryan (1993).
159. Kasser and Ryan (1993).
160. Watson et al. (2004).
161. Watson et al. (2004).
162. Wang et al. (2017).

the strength of the relationship between materialism and mental struggles was weakened. With these results in mind, the researchers concluded that "individuals with higher level of mindfulness could be immune from the detrimental effects of materialism on their mental health."[163]

In addition to materialistic tendencies and preoccupations with money, food may be another form of idol worship. As a quick example, in a theoretical article, K. Schneider suggests that compulsive eating disorders may be a type of food worship.[164] If psychotherapy clients learn to ask the question, "How adaptive is my form of worship, how helpful and meaningful is it to my life?" they can begin to replace unhealthy forms of worship with healthy forms.[165] By asking this key question, they are also taught to manage the corresponding anxiety that inevitably comes from shifting from habitual and unhelpful forms of worship to helpful ones that enrich life and provide meaning and purpose.[166]

Nonetheless, thus far, the bulk of worship research in psychology has been quantitative and correlational, focused on worship as a construct for measurement (e.g., the self, others, and things), not an intervention to ameliorate mental struggles. What is more, no comprehensive lines of research seem to have emerged on religious worship, whether as a construct for measurement or intervention. Still, at least *some* research—albeit qualitative, not quantitative, with smaller sample sizes and, thus, an inability to generalize from smaller samples to larger populations—has been conducted on religious worship among Christians, most notably by Abernethy.

Worship and Religion/Spirituality

In a qualitative study among a small group of US Christian church worship leaders, Abernethy and colleagues attempted to identify themes of worship that may contribute to "spiritual transformation," defined as spiritual and corresponding behavioral change among Christian congregants.[167] After they conducted interviews, the themes that emerged—which the worship leaders believed may contribute to spiritual change within the context of worship—included sensing God's presence, focusing attention on God, honoring God, and using God's Word, among others.

What is more, although quantitative studies on worship as a psychological intervention seem to be generally lacking in the psychology literature,

---

163. Wang et al. (2017), 134.
164. Schneider (1990).
165. Schneider (1990), 96.
166. Schneider (1990).
167. Abernethy et al. (2015).

Abernethy and colleagues qualitatively investigated the worship experiences of a small sample of US Christian adults, asking them particular questions related to their level of transformation (i.e., a personal change in life) following a worship service.[168] Qualitative interview results revealed that almost three-fourths of the participants reported they had a transformational worship experience because, at least in part, they dually confessed sin to God and experienced God's forgiveness. This finding suggests that Christian worship may have a powerful relational element of Christians expressing perceived shortcomings, a sort of cathartic interpersonal experience, and perceiving that they received God's undeserving merit or favor, despite their wayward ways.

In yet another article, Abernethy and colleagues describe a psychological program for pastoral burnout that included different forms of Christian worship, although the manualized intervention and corresponding empirical data do not, to date, appear to have been published in the peer-reviewed psychology literature.[169] Yet, we can draw implications related to mental health from this body of worship literature, described next.

Worship and Mental Health

To date, no correlational or experimental (intervention) studies seem to have emerged on religious worship and mental health, other than the aforementioned study on mindful worship,[170] which seems to be a syncretized amalgam of Buddhist (mindfulness) and Christian (worship) practices. In this study, though, no other mental health variables were included (e.g., depression, anxiety, stress), other than mindfulness and spirituality measures, to investigate its relationship to psychological functioning.

Nevertheless, theoretically, pivoting from self, other, and thing (creation) worship to religious (Creator) worship may have a range of psychological and spiritual benefits, based in part on the previous review of the psychology literature on worship. When worshiping with the mental skills of concentration, awareness, and absorption,[171] worshipers may be able to shift their attention and awareness from self-preoccupations to God, which can help them to get unstuck from unhelpful, distracting cognitive and emotional patterns (e.g., self-criticism, worry, low mood, anxiety). Also, worshipers might be able to receive optimal soothing comfort from God to ameliorate an "empty self," which seems to be common with a range of different types of idol worship

168. Abernethy et al. (2016b).
169. Abernethy et al. (2016a).
170. Yousaf et al. (2022).
171. Yousaf et al. (2022).

(e.g., celebrity).[172] Additionally, worshipers (of celebrities) may struggle with psychological flexibility.[173] Thus, learning to notice when one is engaged in unhealthy idol worship and shift to proper, healthy forms of worship (God, not self, others, or things) is key, drawing on the mental skills of concentration on God, present-moment awareness of God, and full, total absorption in the experience of worshiping God. Finally, worshiping God, as opposed to the self, others, and things, may ameliorate loneliness,[174] given that worshiping God involves a real, personal, give-and-take, reciprocal relationship with the Creator and Sustainer of all. This is opposed to self worship (which leaves worshipers in utter isolation and reliant on themselves for soothing comfort and satiation), other worship (which may include a delusional sense of intimacy with a celebrity who does not know the worshiper exists), or thing worship (which leaves worshipers overly reliant on unreliable, tangible, fleeting, and temporary things in the outer world that will never fully satisfy their inner needs).

Worship Summary

To summarize this review of worship in psychology, other than Abernethy and colleagues' qualitative research[175] and Omar Yousaf and colleagues' scale on mindful worship,[176] no psychologists—whether Christian or non-Christian—seem to have developed a line of research on the psychology of religious worship. Yet, self (e.g., narcissism), other (e.g., celebrity), and thing (e.g., materialism, money) worship have been explored, with a pattern emerging that suggests these types of creation worship may not fully satisfy and, instead, may be related to a variety of mental health struggles. With this review in mind, we now pivot to an integrative view of the psychology of worship and awe, including the mental health implications and limitations in the current psychology literature.

Worship and Awe: An Integrative Perspective

Although it is not acknowledged as such in the psychology literature, secular awe is a form of creation worship, which is a lesser form of worship when compared to Creator worship, since Christians believe God to be the

172. See McCutcheon et al. (2002).
173. Maltby et al. (2004).
174. Richins (2017).
175. Abernethy et al. (2015, 2016b).
176. Yousaf et al. (2022).

Creator and Sustainer of all (Col. 1:16–17). If (1) "awe" is simply defined as "the experience of admiration and elevation in response to physical beauty, displays of exceptional ability, or moral goodness" and includes "vastness" and "incomprehensibility,"[177] and (2) "worship" is succinctly captured as "reverence or adoration for a divine or supernatural being, a person, or a principle,"[178] then as humans we can experience worshipful awe toward anyone or anything, and worship is the mechanism through which an experience of reverential awe is pursued, whether we realize it or not. Moreover, given the many objects of worship (whether God or the self, others, or things), we are *always* worshiping someone or something, and our mental health is always being impacted, sometimes outside of our awareness and for better or worse.

In chapter 1, I defined Christian worship as follows:

An adoring, surrendering, meaning-deriving, self-minimizing and Other-maximizing grateful response of reverential awe to the trinitarian God of the Bible. When we worship God, we honor him for who he is as infinitely good, wise, powerful, present, and holy. We adore him for his actions as Creator, Sustainer, and Redeemer, especially his ultimate act of redemption via the birth, life, death, resurrection, and ascension of Jesus Christ. Finally, we honor him for his providential care, or his perfect, loving, and guiding governance that is personally and intimately extended to all creation. Christian worship is carried out via intentional and purposeful psychological and spiritual disciplines with all our being, including our thoughts and images, emotions, and actions. By regularly acknowledging and worshiping God at the center of existence, we can celebrate all of life across the areas of family, church, work, school, community, and leisure.

I argue that worshipful awe, which is often neglected in contemporary Christian circles as an intentional, purposeful spiritual discipline extended to all of life on a moment-by-moment basis, has far-reaching implications for Christian psychological and spiritual health. Because of this, Christians should learn to shift from lesser, creation worship (which gives rise to lesser, self-derived meaning and purpose in life) to greater, Creator worship (leading to greater, God-derived meaning and purpose in life), possibly doing so via the modified *AWE* technique mentioned in chapter 1,[179] which will be covered in greater detail in chapters 4, 5, and 6.

---

177. American Psychological Association (n.d.a).
178. American Psychological Association (n.d.g).
179. Eagle and Amster (2023); Feldman et al. (2007); Lawrence (1993); see the figure in chap. 1.

Mental Health Implications

Nevertheless, for now, an enduring worshipful awe that is anchored to Christianity as a daily psychological and spiritual discipline and part of a coherent, comprehensive religious worldview[180] may help Christians to have a sense of the present-moment slowing down of time; a small, humble self (in contrast with a prideful, elevated, narcissistic self); a greater sense of connection with people, places, and the world around us;[181] and gratitude and appreciation[182] for moment-by-moment awe-inducing worshipful experiences. This dispositional, worshipful awe can be triggered by people (including God), ideas (such as a grand theory that changes history), and physical locations and structures (such as the vastness of the Milky Way),[183] with Christian worshipful awe inevitably pointing us back to our Creator, Sustainer, and Redeemer to celebrate with and through.

Theoretically, worshipful awe may result in increased well-being,[184] including meaning, purpose, and satisfaction in life;[185] greater altruistic care for others[186] and humility;[187] less rumination;[188] greater acceptance of life's uncertainties, which are inevitable;[189] and healthier religious and spiritual functioning and practices.[190] Conversely, when worship is directed to the self, others, and things, Christians may end up struggling with a whole host of psychological challenges, such as depression and anxiety[191] or loneliness.[192] Because of this, the ability to flexibly pivot from creation worship to Creator worship may be key via the mental skills of concentration, present-moment awareness, and absorption.[193]

---

180. Knabb et al. (2025).
181. Yaden et al. (2019).
182. Büssing et al. (2018).
183. Keltner and Haidt (2003).
184. Zhao et al. (2019).
185. Chirico and Gaggioli (2021); Monroy and Keltner (2023).
186. Jiao and Luo (2022).
187. Stellar et al. (2018).
188. Chirico and Gaggioli (2021).
189. Luo et al. (2021).
190. Büssing (2021); Kearns and Tyler (2022).
191. Henttonen et al. (2022).
192. Pieters (2013).
193. Yousaf et al. (2022). For Christians, of course, these ubiquitous meditative skills come from the Christian religious tradition, not Buddhism. As a result, I have intentionally chosen not to refer to them as "mindful skills." For a review of the similarities and differences between Buddhist mindfulness and Christian meditation and contemplation, including the overlapping skills within each, see Knabb (2021).

Current Limitations

Turning to shortcomings in the current awe and worship psychology literatures, one major limitation cannot be overlooked, since most theoretical and empirical works that have been published are secular and exclude God as Creator, Sustainer, and Redeemer, which has massive real-world implications for twenty-first-century Christ followers. Above all else, the psychology literature (whether theoretically or empirically focusing on awe or worship) commonly neglects to distinguish between creation and Creator worship, which is problematic for Christians who adhere to a biblical worldview, given that the Bible prohibits idol worship (Exod. 20:4–5). Indeed, when Christians wrongly worship people or things—by placing themselves, not God, at the center—humankind's telos cannot be fully realized,[194] which is to worship God and enjoy him for his own sake.[195] For optimal Christian mental and spiritual health, therefore, a regular, moment-by-moment pivot seems to be needed, since Christians believe that we were designed to worship God as the Source, not merely his creation, divorced from him.

Yet, in a way, secular psychologists may have a better understanding of worshipful awe than Christians, since secular psychologists seem to acknowledge, through ever-expanding lines of research, that creation worship can be applied to *all* of life. On the other hand, Christians sometimes tragically believe that worship (and its corresponding emotional experience of awe) should be confined to Sunday morning services and nowhere else. In other words, Christians might disappointingly have a far too narrow view of the impact of worshipful awe when compared to secular psychologists, who continue to examine its far-reaching implications. In either case, like all others throughout history, Christians are vulnerable to creation worship because we live in a fallen, broken world as fallen, broken humans. To better illustrate this point, a metaphor can help, presented next.

Worship and Awe and the "All-Knowing Adolescent" Metaphor

Like "all-knowing adolescents" who want nothing to do with their parents and believe they fully grasp all of life and have everything figured out, we can often believe we are all-knowing. We may think we are omniscient, which can rob us of the opportunity to enjoy life's mysteries in the way that comes so naturally to children. In fact, children are often effortlessly able to stand in awe of the

---

194. Knabb et al. (2025).
195. *Westminster Shorter Catechism* (n.d.).

vastness and mysteriousness[196] of life, given that they are, both physically and psychologically, small. Kids literally stare up at the world around them. They are reliant on adults for survival and limited with developing fine and gross motor skills, strength and endurance, and cognition and intelligence. Yet, gradually, as we develop both physically and psychologically and move into our teenage years, we start to believe we have everything figured out. When this happens, we move from mystery, awe, and gratitude to pseudo-certainty, boredom, and resentment. In turn, we may miss out on the childlike wonder that so naturally permeates our early-life experiences.

So, how do we fight against the all-knowing adolescent inside us that is making us miserable, cheapening moment-by-moment experiences, and preventing us from enjoying the bigness of ideas, people, and places that we inevitably encounter on the roads of life? First, we need to simply acknowledge and recognize the all-knowing adolescent inside each of us that attempts to control our inner and outer world. Second, when we notice this adolescent is attempting to dominate our experiences, we can gently shift toward embracing a younger version of ourselves, attitude-wise, the "unknowing child" who looks up at all of life with a smile and is overwhelmed (in a good way) by just how big the world can be. Ultimately, combined, we are engaging in a two-step process of noticing and shifting,[197] doing so repeatedly, given the all-knowing adolescent wants to take over on a moment-by-moment basis. However, the unknowing child can help to enliven the here and now and bring new meaning and fulfillment on the adventurous roads of life. With this metaphor in mind, let us now shift to an example of worship and awe in daily living, before concluding with a clinical example in psychotherapy.

Worship and Awe in Daily Life

I can still remember the day. I was driving my usual route to pick up my two kids from school midafternoon, some twenty to thirty minutes from my home. On this day, it was a bit rainy, with dark clouds surrounding me as I traveled down the busy street. Worrying about the tasks that still awaited me when I returned home, I was lost in the frantic busyness of my mind and struggling to stay present to the unfolding moment.

I had traveled this familiar route too many times to count, whether in the morning, midday, or evening, but in the flash of a moment I shifted my attention from my overactive, worrying mind to the bright, brilliant, vivid rainbow

---

196. Keltner and Haidt (2003).
197. Knabb (2021).

that effortlessly descended from the rain clouds above down to the landscape of houses off in the distance. Overwhelmed with the vastness and beauty of this rainbow, I was no longer preoccupied with the struggles of the day, like an earthquake that instantaneously shifts one's focus from the mundane activities of the present moment to the sheer power of a rocking earth below.

Without spending any time or energy at all, I allowed myself to ride this wave of awe, giving glory to God in the process, as I trekked toward my children's school on an otherwise uneventful Monday in December. In this passing moment, the rainbow was big and I was small, in a good way, and I stepped outside of myself, psychologically speaking, to enjoy God's creation.

To this day, I can still remember the emotional experience of being captivated by the combination of colors, arc, and sheer size of this magnificent display; my finite human mind could not fully comprehend it all, which was okay. In fact, it brought me a sense of peace in knowing that I did not need to futilely strive for control or certainty as I moved about the day. With this personal example of worshipful awe in mind, we now shift gears to explore a clinical example in psychotherapy.

Worship and Awe in Psychotherapy

Juan was a middle-aged Latino adult who came to psychotherapy due to a gambling addiction. Diagnosed with a gambling disorder—which included long-term struggles with gambling money, restlessness upon attempting to stop, a constant preoccupation with thoughts and images associated with gambling, gambling to avoid the sadness and anxiety he constantly felt, and the loss of his job due to gambling[198]—Juan was desperate for help. In fact, due to his long-term gambling, he had lost his high-paying administrative job in the medical field and his house and car, and his wife had moved out with their two young children to live with her mother about ninety minutes away. Because of these experiences, not only was Juan in distress due to the gambling disorder itself, he was also seeing the widespread consequences of such a costly addiction.

Upon working with his psychotherapist over the course of several months, Juan disclosed that he would bet large sums of money on college sports. He frequently believed he had a "sure thing" and would be able to secretly replace the money he had taken from savings, retirement, and other bank accounts he shared with his wife. Gradually, Juan and his psychotherapist began to identify Juan's struggles with money, traced back to his childhood

---

198. American Psychiatric Association (2022).

years. Growing up, Juan lived in a single-parent home, with his mom working multiple jobs around the clock to simply make ends meet. With two older siblings, Juan often felt unloved, as well as ashamed for being the poor kid in school, which led him to pursue materialistic needs to feel better about himself and be accepted by his school peers. He was constantly striving to purchase the most popular sneakers or clothes to impress his friends, and in middle school things got progressively worse. As he moved into his adolescent years, all Juan could think about was buying the newest things to get praise from those around him.

To support his spending habits, he turned to gambling, frequently playing craps or other betting games with his friends, which eventually led to high-dollar wagers. Increasingly, Juan enjoyed the money he earned, the possessions he accumulated to feel less poor, and the rush of gambling. He convinced himself he was good at it and there was no rush that compared.

Juan and his psychotherapist, in one particular session, discussed the Christian concept of worship. Since both Juan and his psychotherapist identified as Christian, they decided together to integrate the Christian faith into his treatment, exploring the role that worship played in Juan's life. More specifically, Juan's psychotherapist brought up the psychology literature on worship, including some of the research on the worship of money and materialism, which had a range of unhealthy mental health correlates. About halfway through the fifty-minute session, Juan broke down crying. He disclosed that he believed he was worshiping money and material possessions, which was making him miserable. Although he had talked about his childhood struggles in previous sessions, Juan truly began to realize his current challenges could be traced back to his childhood years and his desire for praise from his friends, given that he did not feel loved at home.

Over the next several sessions, Juan and his psychotherapist worked on developing a set of mental skills—psychological and spiritual disciplines—for shifting from worshiping money and material possessions to worshiping God, which also aligned with the twelve-step program Juan was participating in at the time (Gamblers Anonymous). Such skills included noticing the thoughts and feelings that Juan was experiencing when he was preoccupied with money worship, then flexibly shifting (via attention, awareness, and absorption)[199] to God throughout the day. Upon doing so, Juan started to realize that he was engaging in creation, not Creator, worship, which never brought him the inner satisfaction and love he longed for growing up. Although it took some time for Juan to integrate into daily life this practice of noticing when

---

199. Yousaf et al. (2022).

he was engaged in creation worship and shifting to Creator worship,[200] upon the conclusion of treatment, he did end up feeling more meaning and purpose in life and less loneliness. This led to him being less preoccupied with money, materialism, and gambling.

Conclusion

In this chapter, we have explored both awe and worship in the psychology literature, focusing on theoretical and empirical works, mental health implications, and current limitations. Although this growing literature base can help Christians to better understand the psychology of worshipful awe, with worship being the moment-by-moment vehicle through which we pursue awe, it has a major limitation. Secular psychologists do not recognize God at the center and, as a result, do not distinguish between creation and Creator awe, with the former, from a Christian perspective, being a lesser version of the latter and a potential form of idolatry.

For contemporary Christians, then, a regular shift is needed on the roads of life, pivoting from worshiping in reverential awe the people, places, and things God has created to rightfully acknowledging that God is the Source of all. Until we do so, we will continue to be miserable, both psychologically and spiritually. Now that we have explored an introduction to worship and awe, along with the theology and psychology of the topic, we will be shifting toward the chapters on application. We will begin with worship and awe with thoughts and images (chap. 4), then worship and awe with behaviors (chap. 5) and, from there, relationships (chap. 6).

200. Knabb (2021).

CHAPTER FOUR

Christian Worship and Awe with Thoughts and Images

I meditate on all your works and consider what your hands have done.
—Psalm 143:5

The worship of God and the enjoyment of God in worship and meditation are not merely instrumental goods but intrinsic goods. Being in the presence of the God who loves us intensely is the Christian's highest joy and pleasure. While it is instrumentally good in that it energizes us for service and mission, this enjoyment of God is good in itself, for it is indeed the realization of the highest purpose for which we were made.
—John Jefferson Davis, *Meditation and Communion with God*

Introduction

In the next three application chapters, I attempt to help you target three awe triggers: cognitive/conceptual through intentional thoughts and images, physical/sensory through intentional behaviors, and social/relational through intentional relationships.[1] We will pay particular attention to thoughts and images in this chapter. I begin by reviewing both biblical and psychological perspectives on worship and awe with thoughts and images, which can function as cognitive/

---

1. Eagle and Amster (2023); Keltner and Haidt (2003).

conceptual triggers for awe. Then, I combine these theological and psychological insights to present an integrative understanding of how your thoughts and images, as a Christian, can be presented to God as an act of worship. This can help you move toward reverential awe before God, greater meaning and purpose in life, and, consequently, Christian mental and spiritual health. In turn, I offer a log to keep track of your thoughts and images and several activities to help you cultivate reverential awe before God with thoughts and images. For these activities, I draw on classic Christian psychological and spiritual practices/disciplines (e.g., meditation, prayer, and contemplation within Puritan, Jesuit, and medieval Christianity) and the modified *AWE* practice[2] mentioned first in chapter 1 under the heading "An Integrative Practice." I also provide journaling exercise prompts along the way to help you reflect on your thoughts and images. I conclude the chapter by offering examples of worship and awe with thoughts and images from both Scripture and psychotherapy.

My hope is that this chapter can help you begin to recognize the importance of worshipful, thankful thoughts and images before God, pivoting from self to Other, others to Other, and things to Other. This pivot can move you toward awe of God and greater meaning, purpose, and Christian mental and spiritual health. Worshipful awe of God is a daily, moment-by-moment thankful wonder and grateful amazement at God and, through him as Creator, Sustainer, and Redeemer, his creation. With worshipful awe, human thoughts and images play a foundational role in our stance before and relationship with the triune God. Worship is an intentional, purposeful psychological and spiritual discipline,[3] extended to all of life, not just confined to Sunday morning corporate worship in a church building.

A Biblical Perspective

For centuries, the human mind has played a prominent role in Christians' ability to worship God in thankful, reverential awe with thoughts and images. In Genesis 1:27, we read that God created humankind in his image, which means Adam and Eve were "free for the worship of the Creator," according to the Lutheran theologian Dietrich Bonhoeffer.[4] In his exegesis of Genesis, Bonhoeffer goes on to point out that God placed the tree of life, which represents life and dependence on God, and the tree of the knowledge of good and evil, which represents death and the human attempt to be like God, in

---

2. Eagle and Amster (2023); Feldman et al. (2007); Lawrence (1993).
3. Calhoun (2015).
4. Bonhoeffer (1959), 39.

the center of the garden of Eden. This famous story ends with Adam and Eve eating from the tree of the knowledge of good and evil and wanting to be like God, not dependent on him.

Fast-forward to the present day, and we, as fallen human beings, continue to place ourselves, not God, at the center of the proverbial garden. We often desire to be like him, as infinite, independent, and worshiped, not finite, dependent, and worshipful. Because of this, life can be an ongoing struggle of being preoccupied with the self, others, or things, captured with our thoughts and images, which we place at the center of life. As we do so, we may as Christians struggle to live out our God-given purpose. This purpose is to worship God in awe, which we will eventually and inevitably do when we are face-to-face with God in heaven. Yet, on the roads of life, we may experience added struggle because of the fall.

Throughout the Old and New Testaments, we read about the salience of worshiping God in grateful, reverential awe, including what can happen when we prioritize ourselves, others, and things above him.[5] Defined as "a response by the worshipper of adoration, humility, submission, and obedience to God," worship in the Bible can involve doing so with thoughts and images.[6] Examples include when we read the Bible, meditate on verses in the Bible, pray to God, and contemplate God. These four practices combined have been historically referred to, in monastic Christianity, as *lectio divina*, which is Latin for "divine reading" and was briefly discussed in chapter 2.[7] From a Christian perspective, using the mind via the God-given medium of thoughts and images to worship our Creator can certainly contribute to grateful, wonder-inducing awe.[8] This distinctly biblical form of awe can simply be defined as "an emotion combining honor, fear, and respect before someone of superior office or actions," which "most appropriately applies to God."[9] What follows is a breakdown of three of the key steps within *lectio divina*—meditation, prayer, and contemplation—applied to worship and awe with thoughts and images and building on the cursory exploration of the practice in chapter 2.

Lectio Divina: *A Short Introduction*

The Christian psychological and spiritual discipline of *lectio divina* grew out of the monastic tradition, with early references to various forms of the

---

5. Forrest et al. (2021).
6. Holman (2004d), 1052.
7. Upper Room (2003i).
8. Van Cappellen et al. (2021).
9. Holman (2004a), 63.

practice around the sixth century.[10] With each step, the practitioner is interacting with Scripture to cultivate and maintain a more intimate, worshipful encounter with God. The twelfth-century monk Guigo II used the metaphor of eating food to capture each of the four steps. With reading, we are taking an initial bite out of the text of the Bible, slowly interacting with the words line by line.[11] With meditating, we are beginning to chew the text, thinking deeply about, pondering, and ruminating on the words.[12] With praying, we start to taste the text by interacting and conversing with God.[13] Finally, contemplating captures savoring the text via resting in God in loving silence.[14] Given the importance of using thoughts and images to worship God, what follows is a brief review of the second, third, and fourth steps. Then, we'll move on to a psychological understanding of awe and the various practices in the chapter to cultivate worshipful awe before God with thoughts and images.

Meditation

Among the strategies for worshiping God with thoughts and images, meditating on God's Word can be especially powerful. This is because Scripture reveals who God is (infinitely good, wise, powerful, present, and holy), what he has done (as Creator, Sustainer, and Redeemer), and his grand plan for humankind (the grand biblical narrative of creation, fall, redemption, and restoration). "The Bible concerns itself with who or what we worship and with what we meditate about—directing our minds to Scripture, creation and redemption."[15] So, "at the most basic level, meditation is our dwelling on, obsessing over, scheming about, daydreaming about or fantasizing over something we value."[16] As humans, we are always meditating—that is, ruminating—on something. We are always slowly chewing on cognitive material with our ongoing mental activity like a cow methodically chewing cud in a field, to use a famous image from monastic life.[17] Certainly, the question isn't whether we are meditating and worshiping from moment to moment. Rather, the question relates to what we are intentionally choosing to meditate on and, consequently, worship, which reveals what we love.[18]

---

10. Wilhoit and Howard (2012).
11. Guigo II (2012); Wilhoit and Howard (2012).
12. Guigo II (2012); Wilhoit and Howard (2012).
13. Guigo II (2012); Wilhoit and Howard (2012).
14. Guigo II (2012); Wilhoit and Howard (2012).
15. Wilhoit and Howard (2012), 77.
16. Wilhoit and Howard (2012), 77.
17. Wilhoit and Howard (2012).
18. Smith (2016).

There are multiple words in the Old and New Testaments to capture meditation. In the Old Testament, the Hebrew word *hagah* is employed a variety of times. It means to "meditate, to murmur, to ponder, to speak, [and] to utter."[19] It is captured in Joshua 1:8, Psalm 1:2 and 77:12, and Isaiah 33:18.[20] *Siyach* is found in a plethora of Old Testament locations and defined as "to put forth, meditate, muse, commune, speak, ponder, [and] sing."[21] It is reflected in Psalm 119:15 and 119:23.[22] In the New Testament, the Greek word *meletaō* is defined as "to take care of, revolve in the mind, imagine," as employed in 1 Timothy 4:15 ("Be diligent").[23]

As the second of the four steps of *lectio divina*, to meditate means to repeat, ponder, think deeply about, ruminate on, or imagine God's Word.[24] When we meditate, we use a mantra (e.g., a passage in Scripture) or image (e.g., the cross).[25] With biblical meditation, we are attempting to use our entire selves, including the body (via verbalizing the passage), the memory (via remembering the passage), the intellect (via comprehending the passage), and the will (via living out the passage).[26] So, Christian meditation is about using the mind via thoughts and images to worship God. We do so with our God-given body, memory, intellect, heart, and will.[27]

The early desert Christians—monks who lived in the deserts of Egypt, Syria, and other similar arid locations in the third to sixth centuries—meditated on the Psalms as a way to shift from tempting, compulsive thoughts to God.[28] One such desert monk, Evagrius, compiled a comprehensive list of verses in the Bible to "talk back" to these distracting, ongoing thoughts.[29] An example of a tempting, compulsive thought is captured in the theme of pride, which prevented them from prioritizing God's presence in daily life. So, to recite the Psalms in response to prideful, self-focused thoughts, an early desert monk might recite Psalm 44:6: "I put no trust in my bow, my sword does not bring me victory."

Fast-forward about a thousand years, and the Puritans—devout Protestant Christians in seventeenth-century England and American colonies that

---

19. *Strong's Lexicon* (n.d.b).
20. *Strong's Lexicon* (n.d.b).
21. *Strong's Lexicon* (n.d.b).
22. *Strong's Lexicon* (n.d.b).
23. *Strong's Lexicon* (n.d.a).
24. Wilhoit and Howard (2012).
25. Upper Room (2003e).
26. Robertson (2011).
27. Gray (2009); Robertson (2011).
28. Burton-Christie (1993).
29. Evagrius of Ponticus (2009).

attempted to apply an orthodox reading of the Bible to all of life—strongly advocated for biblical meditation. One Puritan succinctly defined it as "the steadfast and earnest bending of the mind on some spiritual and heavenly matter."[30] For example, in his book *Gospel Worship*, the Puritan Jeremiah Burroughs argues for the importance of meditating on God's attributes during worship: "When I am to worship God, I am to look on him as the Living God, as that God that has *life* in himself, and gives life to his creatures."[31] In addition to meditating on God as the living God, Burroughs teaches that Christians should meditate on God as the Almighty God:

> I come to seek for some great thing, and I come to seek to a great God, that has all power in heaven and earth, and infinitely more power than there is in all creatures in heaven and earth. I am praying to a God that can create peace and create help. My condition cannot be so desperate, but this infinite Almighty God is able to help me. Let me make him the object of my faith as he is so infinitely Almighty. What a full object of faith is this God that has all power in Him? Let me come to him as a strong Tower.[32]

So, Burroughs recommends meditating on God's attributes (such as his infinite goodness, wisdom, power, presence, and holiness) as a form of worship. If meditation is the foundation for Christian worship via pondering and ruminating on who God is with God's attributes found in the Bible, it is essential to employ our God-given mind to do so. We can commune with God by worshiping him with awe-inspiring thoughts and images.

The following list provides a few examples of God's attributes in the Psalms, which can be meditated on to cultivate and maintain awe of God in an act of reverential worship. The worship of who God is by way of his attributes is threaded across the Psalms, a collection of "prayers, praises, hymns, meditations, and liturgies" dating back three thousand years,[33] so these verses may be especially fitting.

- *Goodness:* "Taste and see that the LORD is good; blessed is the one who takes refuge in him" (Ps. 34:8).
- *Wisdom:* "How many are your works, Lord! In wisdom you made them all; the earth is full of your creatures" (Ps. 104:24).

---

30. Ball (2016), 25.
31. Burroughs (2018), 152.
32. Burroughs (2018), 153.
33. Ross (2011), 25.

- *Power:* "Praise the Lord, my soul. Lord my God, you are very great; you are clothed with splendor and majesty" (Ps. 104:1).
- *Presence:* "Where can I go from your Spirit? Where can I flee from your presence? If I go up to the heavens, you are there; if I make my bed in the depths, you are there" (Ps. 139:7–8).
- *Holiness:* "You are enthroned as the Holy One; you are the one Israel praises" (Ps. 22:3).

With these wonder-inspiring attributes of God in mind, in this chapter we further explore and practice biblical meditation. We pay particular attention to meditating on the Psalms, which capture God's infinite goodness, wisdom, power, presence, and holiness, to worship God in reverential awe. In addition to biblical meditation, Christian prayer is a strategy for cultivating and maintaining worshipful awe before God.

Prayer

Within the Christian tradition, prayer is a key practice for interacting with God. It is defined as "communication with God through thoughts, words, and gestures whereby we express what we believe about God and our relationship to God and to one another."[34] There are a variety of prayer practices that employ thoughts and images to worship God in awe and, thus, draw closer to and commune with him. Among several types, prayers of adoration and thanksgiving focus on praising God in reverential awe, whereas prayers of petition and intercession involve a request to God to intervene in some way.[35] As a third type, monologic prayer captures the repetition of a short word, phrase, or mantra to focus the mind, quiet and still the mind, practice God's presence, and guard both the mind and heart from tempting, compulsive thoughts.[36] Themes of such compulsive thoughts may include pride, anger, lust, envy, gluttony, and worry.[37] Finally, prayer can focus on the use of the imagination or confession of sin.[38]

To provide more detail, prayers of adoration involve thanking, praising, and worshiping God[39] in awe for who he is and what he has done. So, in solitude and silence, we might simply say, "Lord our God: we adore you. When we

---

34. Upper Room (2003h).
35. Upper Room (2003h).
36. Goodwin (1999).
37. Goodwin (1999).
38. Upper Room (2003h).
39. Foster (1992).

look at the heavens, the work of your hands, we wonder why we have been chosen to share such delights, and we join with all creation in praise to you and for what you have done."[40] To offer another example, the Puritans were especially fond of prayers of adoration. Within their famous work *The Valley of Vision*, which is a collection of Puritan prayers, the "Praise and Thanksgiving" entry includes the following:

> O my God, thou fairest, greatest, first of all objects, my heart admires, adores, loves thee, for my little vessel is as full as it can be, and I would pour out all that fullness before thee in ceaseless flow. When I think upon and converse with thee ten thousand delightful thoughts spring up, ten thousand sources of pleasure are unsealed, ten thousand refreshing joys spread over my heart, crowding into every moment of happiness.[41]

Here, we see a rich, detailed theme of thanksgiving, praise, worship, and awe of God beyond the more common prayers of petition (e.g., asking God for things) that many Christians are used to.

Yet one more example of prayer, roughly a thousand years before the Puritans, is a simpler, shorter, monologic form of prayer that was employed to engage in worshipful awe before God. This type of prayer comes to us from the early desert Christians. Short passages in Scripture (e.g., the Psalms) were repeated as monks engaged in labor (e.g., basket weaving) in order to focus the mind on God and away from tempting, compulsive thoughts.[42] Also called "arrow prayers," these concise prayers evolved into the Jesus Prayer (i.e., "Lord Jesus Christ, Son of God, have mercy on me"), which is popular in the Eastern Orthodox Church.[43] In its shortest form, the Jesus Prayer consists solely of the name Jesus and is repeated internally in a slow, soft, and simple manner. These monologic prayers, such as the Jesus Prayer, can certainly be a way to practice worshipful awe before God throughout the day.[44] This is especially true if the goal of the prayer is to cry out to Jesus for mercy, or his loving-kindness and responsiveness to our human needs, and practice God's presence by "pray[ing] continually" (see, e.g., Mark 10:47 and 1 Thess. 5:17).

To offer one final type of prayer that can be employed to worship God, within the Jesuit Christian tradition the imagination is commonly used to interact with the Gospels in a more experiential manner. Among the Jesuits,

---

40. Rice and Huffstutler (2001), 119.
41. Bennett (1975), 15.
42. Johnson (2010a); McGuckin (2010).
43. Johnson (2010a); McGuckin (2010).
44. Zaleski (2011).

a worldwide Catholic group, Ignatian spirituality is embraced. Ignatius of Loyola was a Spanish Catholic who lived in the fifteenth and sixteenth centuries. He started the Society of Jesus, or Jesuits, and wrote *Spiritual Exercises*, which is a collection of writings on spiritual strategies for meditation, prayer, and contemplation within the Christian tradition.[45] Jesuit practitioners who engage in this practice, referred to as "imaginative contemplation," attempt to embed themselves in a Gospel story by seeing themselves in the story, seeing the other characters in the story, watching the other characters of the story interact, hearing what the other characters of the story might be saying, and actually interacting themselves with the other characters of the story.[46] They do so by relying on the human skill of imagination.[47] In other words, using the five senses, we can experience the Gospels in new ways, such as imagining we are one of Jesus's disciples worshiping him in resurrected form in Matthew.[48] So, we may use our sense of sight to imagine what it might be like to see Jesus with our own eyes. Or, we might employ our sense of touch to embrace him. With our imagination and God-given senses, we can worship the Jesus of the Gospels in new, awe-inducing ways. Although we often think about meditating on God's Word and praying to God, we may not fully consider the role that the imagination and senses can play in worshiping God to induce awe of God. Imagination can be especially effective in interacting with the Gospels in creative, life-enhancing ways.

Contemplation

In addition to Christian meditation and prayer, the second and third steps, respectively, in *lectio divina*, Christian contemplation can be employed to cultivate reverential, worshipful awe before God. It is succinctly defined as "focused attention of the soul toward the Divine."[49] Christian contemplation often consists of sitting in present-moment silence and solitude and resting in the God of love by downplaying our reliance on words and images to spend time with him.[50] Over the centuries, the monastic Christian tradition has advocated for Christian contemplation as the fourth and final step of *lectio divina*, given its emphasis on resting in God with a loving awareness of him.

---

45. Ignatian Spirituality (n.d.).
46. Gallagher (2008).
47. Gallagher (2008).
48. See Warner (2010) and Matt. 28:16–20.
49. Upper Room (2003b).
50. Knabb and Bates (2020).

This is just like when we are getting to know a good friend.[51] We may initially learn about the friend by listening to them describe who they are and their life experiences, which is consistent with the reading and meditating steps of *lectio divina*. Then, we may converse with them to get to know them on a deeper level, like the praying step of *lectio divina*. Yet, at a certain point, we may recognize there are moments when we can sit with them in silence, since we know them and want to just enjoy the experience. This may be like watching a sunset at the beach together, reminiscent of the contemplating step of *lectio divina*.

The most detailed instructions on Christian contemplation may come to us from the *Cloud of Unknowing*, which is an anonymous, fourteenth-century English book. In it, the author advocates for reaching up to God in love in a "cloud of unknowing" and placing all other knowledge beneath a "cloud of forgetting" below.[52] To focus the mind on God and return to him as the point of attention when the mind inevitably drifts, the *Cloud* author suggests using a short prayer word, such as "God" or "love."[53] In the process, the practitioner is worshiping God authentically and wholly, as the *Cloud* author teaches in his second book, *The Book of Privy Counseling*: "My dear friend in God, go beyond your intellect's endless and involved investigations and worship the Lord your God with your whole being. Offer him your very self in simple wholeness, all that you are and just as you are, without concentrating on any particular aspect of your being. In this way your attention will not be scattered nor your affection entangled, for this would spoil your singleness of heart and consequently your union with God."[54]

In another Christian contemplative work, *Treatise on the Love of God*, the sixteenth- and seventeenth-century French Catholic Francis de Sales suggests that meditation involves "dwelling on a single thought with great attention," whereas contemplation consists of an "adoring, uncomplicated, and enduring attention of the soul to divine things."[55] In other words, meditation "examines the details," and contemplation "considers the larger picture."[56] So, to use a camera metaphor, Christian meditation zooms in to focus on the details of Scripture, including God's attributes and actions, whereas Christian contemplation zooms out to see the bigger picture and rest in God's love. In either case, at least some use of thoughts and images is employed to worship God in reverential awe.

51. Knabb, Vazquez, Garzon et al. (2020).
52. Johnston (2014).
53. Johnston (2014).
54. Johnston (2014), 203.
55. de Sales (2011), 43, 46.
56. de Sales (2011), 49.

Before turning to the exercises in this chapter, I'd like to explore what the psychology literature has to say about employing our thoughts to cultivate awe.

A Psychological Perspective

In their pioneering theoretical article on the psychology of awe, psychologists Dacher Keltner and Jonathan Haidt start with an acknowledgment that awe is easily recognizable in the world religions, including the apostle Paul's conversion experience (see Acts 9:3–7).[57] Within this theoretical article, which, at the time of this writing, has been cited over two thousand times according to Google Scholar, the authors define awe as the human experience of something or someone vast. This vastness, for the authors, is coupled with the need to adjust our thinking and understanding to make room for this source of amazement and wonder. And in another article that developed an awe measure, an element of gratitude was added,[58] which means that awe is grateful wonder or thankful amazement toward the bigness and vastness we experience in life.

Keltner and Haidt, along with others over the years, also have suggested that there are three major types of triggers for awe.[59] These triggers include those that are cognitive/conceptual (e.g., having some sort of epiphany, insight, or revelation about a big idea; trying to comprehend God's infinite power; meditating on a spiritual experience or God), physical/sensory (e.g., being overwhelmed by staring at the Grand Canyon, listening to worship music), and social/relational (e.g., spending time in solitude and silence with God).[60] Each of the three triggers can lead to awe, which has mental health benefits.

In support of this notion, a recent study among US college students interested in meditation found that the positive relationship between spirituality (e.g., feeling connected to the surrounding world) and well-being was explained by awe (along with the positive emotions of love, peace, and gratitude).[61] Worded another way, as college students reported a higher level of spirituality, they also endorsed a higher level of awe. And as they indicated they experienced a higher level of awe, they also reported a higher level of well-being. Research has illuminated that the practice of meditation can actually

57. Keltner and Haidt (2003).
58. Büssing et al. (2018).
59. Keltner and Haidt (2003).
60. Eagle and Amster (2023); Keltner and Haidt (2003).
61. Van Cappellen et al. (2016).

be a way to induce awe.⁶² And the number of times we meditate per day has a positive relationship with awe, meaning the more we report that we meditate, the more we report feeling awe.⁶³ More specifically, research has revealed that mantra meditations, such as loving-kindness meditations that involve repeating short, compassionate phrases about the self and others (e.g., "May I be happy," "May others be at ease"), can be helpful in improving awe.⁶⁴

In general, meditation can simply be defined as a "sustaining quiet, simple focus."⁶⁵ It involves the basic steps of moving from relaxation (e.g., being physically relaxed and calm, at peace, and content), to a simple and quiet focus (e.g., sustained attention on a specific point of focus, present-moment awareness, reduced mental agitation, fewer racing and/or scattered thoughts, and acceptance of the inner world), to a greater awareness of oneself and the world (e.g., the ability to nonjudgmentally observe inner and outer events with a perceived sense of distance and open curiosity), to a sense of transcendence (e.g., experiencing the vastness and mystery of the world and a more reverential sense of meaning and purpose that surpasses the self).⁶⁶ With these general steps, Christians can confidently draw from our own religious heritage and sacred text to meditate on God's attributes as a sort of alternative Christian mantra meditation in place of Buddhist (and Hindu) mantra meditation. In turn, we can experience worshipful awe of God.

For this chapter, awe can certainly be triggered by a cognitive, conceptual, imaginative understanding that God is the Creator, Sustainer, and Redeemer and infinitely good, wise, powerful, present, and holy. In other words, as Christians, we have a real relationship with a personal God who created the universe, humankind, and all that is worthy of awe. Thus, there is a thought and image component to awe of God; we can be amazed by him because he has revealed who he is, including his attributes and actions (past, present, and future), via his special revelation, the Bible.⁶⁷ Without his generous special revelation, we would be left to know him by solely looking to his general revelation,⁶⁸ or creation, which gives us glimpses of him, but by no means elucidates his goodness, wisdom, power, presence, and holiness. So, what follows is an integrative perspective on worship and awe with thoughts and images, paying particular attention to worshipful awe of the God of the Bible.

62. Preston and Shin (2017).
63. Büssing et al. (2018).
64. Fredrickson et al. (2008).
65. Smith (2021), 39–47.
66. Smith (2021), 39–47.
67. Wilson (2021).
68. Wilson (2021).

An Integrative Perspective

We now return to the modified *AWE* method first mentioned in chapter 1,[69] which removes Buddhist-derived mindfulness and, in its place, inserts Christian worshipfulness as a worldview-sensitive alternative. With this method, we take the three intentional steps of attending to God, worshiping God, and enhancing worship of God via being thankful for and enjoying *all* his creation. These steps are key for cultivating Christian awe. In other words, as Christians, we are learning to stand in appreciative awe toward God and, through God, his creation. We are also learning not to worship lesser things that are empty, dead ends in and of themselves because they are not rightfully acknowledged as emanating from him. Along the way, we are practicing God's presence. This intentional practice is reminiscent of Brother Lawrence's famous instructions,[70] with the skills of attention on God, present-moment, worshipful awareness of God, and awe-inducing acceptance of God as Creator, Sustainer, and Redeemer. God is sovereign over all of life and governing everyone and everything as the Benevolent King.[71]

In support of this understanding, a few years ago I developed with colleagues a Christian gratitude assessment tool to measure a distinctly Christian form of gratitude in empirical research.[72] Within the six-item scale, items included "I should thank God daily for his forgiveness," "I often feel grateful to God for his daily gifts," "I often praise God for the life he has given me," and "I often meditate on God's goodness."[73] Among an online sample of Christians, we found that Christian gratitude was positively correlated with well-being (e.g., having a positive outlook on the future, believing the problems of life are being effectively handled).[74] Therefore, building on this understanding, remaining in appreciative awe of God as the infinitely good Creator, Sustainer, and Redeemer is key for mental health. And we can do so from moment to moment in life. In other words, we can be intentional about being in wonder and amazement before the triune God, and then extend this thankfulness to his creation.

In the context of thoughts and images, for Christians, the first step is to shift our attention from ourselves, others, and things to God because we are often preoccupied with attaining awe-inducing thoughts and images that are

---

69. Eagle and Amster (2023); Feldman et al. (2007); Lawrence (1993).
70. Lawrence (1993).
71. Knabb (2021).
72. Knabb et al. (2023).
73. Knabb et al. (2023), 310.
74. Knabb et al. (2023).

not inspired by him. This is what we call in Christianity "idol worship."⁷⁵ In other words, we need to recognize we are chasing after the wrong awe triggers when we don't have an awareness of the Source, such as human- and creation-derived social (e.g., the kindness of a stranger), physical (e.g., the vastness of the Pacific Ocean), and cognitive (e.g., a paradigm-shifting idea to illuminate a new insight into life) awe triggers.⁷⁶

So, we may have unilateral human thoughts of self-importance or be preoccupied with attaining a perfect reputation before others, with corresponding fantasies and images of self-worth and receiving the seemingly due praise of those around us. We may be distracted by the need to be endlessly "liked" on social media or for our grand ideas, jokes, or memes "going viral" online. Related to others, we may engage in celebrity worship, tirelessly following Hollywood stars' or professional athletes' every move, from their professional careers and fashion choices to their tumultuous personal lives. Along the way, we may try to induce a sense of awe and amazement. Finally, we may worship things, chasing a fleeting sense of awe via worldly possessions, such as a new sports car, breathtaking work of art, mansion in a gated part of town, or fancy jewelry, to display before others and serve as a status symbol of our worth.

In each of these instances, we may be ineffectively pursuing creation awe. That is, we may chase after a sense of bigness, vastness, and amazement, coupled with the need to adjust our understanding of the world to fit this larger-than-life perspective into our current thinking.⁷⁷ From a Christian perspective, though, with these feeble attempts, we are not living out our God-given purpose when we worship lesser things. This is especially true when they are divorced from an awareness of the Creator, Sustainer, and Redeemer. Because of this, a moment-by-moment, intentional shift is needed that commences with our thoughts and images.

This shift can occur when we practice the modified *AWE* exercise introduced in the first chapter. With *A*, we are focusing our *attention* on God, not the self, others, or things, with a recognition that God's creation will not provide the greatest sense of awe when we do not recognize the Source.⁷⁸ Then, with *W*, we are breathing in God's presence as we say something like, "My God," recognizing God's presence within as an act of reverential *worship*.⁷⁹ Finally, with *E*, we are breathing out as we say something to the effect of "you are good," resting in an awareness that God is the Creator and Sustainer of

75. Beale (2008).
76. Keltner and Haidt (2003).
77. Keltner and Haidt (2003).
78. Eagle and Amster (2023); Lawrence (1993).
79. Eagle and Amster (2023); Lawrence (1993).

all, which means we can *enhance* our appreciation for his creation with a sense of gratitude and amazement directed toward *all* that he has made.[80] Along the way, with our thoughts and images, we are learning to focus on God by repeating a short saying, such as "My God, you are good." This phrase can serve to reset our thinking and help us shift from creation to Creator as we learn to worship God and, through him, all of creation, not place ourselves, others, or things at the center of creation.

Ultimately, we can use thoughts and images to focus our attention on God—whether through meditation, prayer, or contemplation—with a short phrase that is paired with a present-moment activity. This can be followed by breathing in God's presence as an act of worship as we pair our in-breath with the first part of a short phrase, such as "Sovereign Lord," to capture how amazing he is in the here and now. As the third step, we can breathe out to rest in him, aligning the out-breath with the remainder of a short phrase, like "you are the Creator and Sustainer of all." This last step captures a sense of awe because God has created such a beautiful world to enjoy. Before engaging in a variety of practices to worship God in awe, however, I would like us to better understand the types of thoughts and images that we entertain throughout the day. With these thoughts and images, we are often preoccupied with creation and divorced from an awareness of God as the Creator, Sustainer, and Redeemer. If meditation is simply pondering or ruminating on something, what we choose to ruminate on is key in each unfolding moment.

A Daily Log

In this initial exercise for chapter 4, I'd like you to log during six time periods throughout the day the types of thoughts and images that you ended up entertaining or ruminating on to cultivate a sense of amazement and awe. These may be cognitive, creation awe triggers related to the self, others, and things. To get you started, I've added a few examples for the morning. Feel free to log these in a separate notebook to give yourself ample room for writing.

Once you have completed the exercise, try to journal for a moment on a separate piece of paper. Write down the patterns, in terms of recurrent thoughts and images, that emerged. Also write down the costs of being preoccupied with (or maybe even worshiping) the self, others, or things to feel awe.

- What patterns did you notice, in terms of your thoughts and images concerning yourself? How about thoughts and images about others?

---

80. Eagle and Amster (2023); Lawrence (1993).

Time	The Self	Others	Things
Morning	I woke up and eagerly checked my social media accounts first thing this morning, thinking it'd feel amazing to get more "likes" with some of yesterday's meme postings and imagining what it'd be like to have a meme posting that "went viral."	At the breakfast table, I found myself watching sports highlights on my smart phone, believing I'd feel a sense of awe if I could get a quick glimpse of some amazing plays from the night before and imagining the perfect three-point shot in the basketball game. I didn't engage with my family around me.	As I got into my car this morning to head to work, I had the vivid image of driving a new European sports car, not the ten-year-old American minivan that I own and am accustomed to, which would seemingly lead to a feeling of amazement when heading in to work.
Midmorning			
Noon			
Afternoon			
Evening			
Bedtime			

What about thoughts and images about things? Are these results surprising? Why or why not?
- What is the spiritual impact, in terms of your relationship with God, in being preoccupied with (or maybe even worshiping) yourself, others, or things?
- What is the psychological impact, in terms of your mental health, in being preoccupied with (or maybe even worshiping) yourself, others, or things?

Now that you have had the opportunity to identify some of the thoughts and images that may be distracting you from worshipful awe of God, I'd like us to begin to practice several exercises to help you, as a Christian, shift from the self, others, and things to awe of God on the roads of life as you place one foot in front of the other from moment to moment.

EXERCISE: Puritan Meditation

Among the Puritans, devout Protestant Christians in seventeenth-century England who attempted to apply an orthodox reading of the Bible to all of life, biblical meditation was paramount. For example, in *Gospel Worship*, the Puritan Jeremiah Burroughs advocates for meditating on God's attributes, including his infinite goodness, wisdom, power, and holiness, to enter a state of worship. So, in this ten-minute exercise, I'd like us to practice Puritan meditation to cultivate worshipful awe of God with thoughts, drawing on the Psalms, which consists of the following steps:

1. Find a quiet location, free from distractions, and select a short portion of Scripture to attend to. Select a verse within the Psalms that emphasizes God's infinite goodness, wisdom, power, presence, or holiness.
2. Say a brief prayer to God. Ask him to be with you in the midst of this meditative practice and accept this time spent with him as an act of worship. Begin to meditate on his attributes with the chosen verse as a form of worship to God.
3. Slowly and gently repeat the designated passage in Scripture with all your attention as an act of worshipful reverence to God.
4. Move from your "head" to your "heart." Consider the feeling of awe and amazement that comes from meditating on God's infinite goodness, wisdom, power, presence, or holiness.
5. Continue to feel this awe of God as you recite the verse from the Psalms.

6. Whenever you notice your attention has shifted to yourself, another person, or something else, just gently bring it back to the selected passage in the Psalms and corresponding feeling of awe before God.
7. Say a short prayer to God. Thank him for his infinite goodness, wisdom, power, presence, and holiness, as revealed in Scripture. Express gratitude to God for the ability to worship him with reverential awe as Creator, Sustainer, and Redeemer.[81]

Key passages in the Psalms to meditate on may include the following:

- Goodness: "Good and upright is the LORD" (Ps. 25:8).
- Wisdom: "[God's] understanding has no limit" (Ps. 147:5).
- Power: "Great is our Lord and mighty in power" (Ps. 147:5).
- Presence: "Where can I go from your Spirit?" (Ps. 139:7).
- Holiness: "You are enthroned as the Holy One" (Ps. 22:3).

Upon completing the exercise, please reflect on the experience with the following questions:

- What was it like to meditate on God's attributes? How well were you able to focus your attention on God via the selected Bible verse?
- What feelings came up as you engaged in the practice? How well were you able to cultivate awe before God?
- What distractions, if any, got in the way of worshipful awe before God? Thoughts about the self? Others? Things?
- How can you integrate this practice into daily life so you can draw on God's Word to worship him in reverential awe?

EXERCISE: Puritan Prayer of Adoration

In addition to Puritan meditation, a wide variety of Puritan prayers can be employed to cultivate worshipful awe of God. We can pray them with our thoughts and images, especially those that express adoration and thanks to God. In *Piercing Heaven: Prayers of the Puritans*, one prayer by the Puritan Matthew Henry, titled "The Heavens Declare Your Glory," is especially powerful. For this exercise, simply read through the following prayer as an act of worship before God, doing so in reverential awe. As you read the words,

---

81. Ball (2016); Beeke and Jones (2012); Hall (2007); Knabb (2021), 192–93; Watson (2014).

try to go at a slow pace so they resonate and represent your sincere thoughts to God. Overall, the purpose of this exercise is to slowly praise God in the here and now, focusing your attention on him, worshiping him in reverential awe, and thanking him for his amazing creation.

> The heavens declare your glory, O God, and the firmament shows your handiwork. And by the things that are made, we clearly see and understand your eternal power and divine nature. . . . Who is a God like you, glorious in holiness, fearful in praises, doing wonders? Who in the heavens can be compared to you? O Lord of Hosts, who is a strong Lord like you? . . . And there are no works like your works. For you are great, and do wondrous things. . . . As heaven is high above the earth, so are your thoughts above our thoughts, and your ways above our ways. . . . You are God, and you do not change. . . . The everlasting God, the Lord, the Creator of the ends of the earth, who does not faint or grow weary—there is no searching your understanding. Amen.[82]

Now that you have slowly read through the prayer, try to reflect on the experience by answering the questions below:

- What was it like to use these centuries-old words, written by Matthew Henry, to pray to God? How well were you able to focus your attention on God as you slowly read through the prayer?
- What feelings came up as you prayed to God? How well were you able to cultivate awe before God?
- What distractions, if any, got in the way of prayerful, worshipful awe before God? Thoughts about the self? Others? Things?
- How can you integrate this type of prayer practice into daily life so you can worship him in reverential awe with your thoughts?

EXERCISE: Ignatian Prayer

Spiritual Exercises was written by Ignatius of Loyola in the 1500s and consists of a plethora of practices, such as meditation, prayer, and contemplation, to cultivate a deeper relationship with God.[83] Among the exercises, the "Prayer of the Senses" helps practitioners to use the five senses (sight, sound, taste, touch, and smell) to experience the Gospels in new ways, embedding themselves in

---

82. Elmer (2019), 236–37.
83. Endean (1990); Hansen (2012); Ivens (1998).

the various stories of Jesus and his followers.[84] In this exercise, I would like you to use your God-given senses and corresponding imagination to worship God in reverential awe. Locate yourself in the story of Jesus's resurrection. The purpose is to stand in awe before him as the resurrected Lord. Worship him in amazement as you imagine falling before his feet to praise him as the risen Messiah.

To begin, set aside ten minutes and find a quiet location that is free from distractions. Sit up straight in a supportive chair. Close your eyes to use your imagination to worship God in reverential awe. When you are ready, slowly move through these steps:

1. Start by saying a short prayer to God, asking that he accept this practice as an act of worship toward him as the Creator, Sustainer, and Redeemer of your life. Ask that he reveal himself to you in this very moment.
2. Next, slowly read through the biblical text of Luke 24:36–44:

   While they were still talking about this, Jesus himself stood among them and said to them, "Peace be with you."

   They were startled and frightened, thinking they saw a ghost. He said to them, "Why are you troubled, and why do doubts rise in your minds? Look at my hands and my feet. It is I myself! Touch me and see; a ghost does not have flesh and bones, as you see I have."

   When he had said this, he showed them his hands and feet. And while they still did not believe it because of joy and amazement, he asked them, "Do you have anything here to eat?" They gave him a piece of broiled fish, and he took it and ate it in their presence.

   He said to them, "This is what I told you while I was still with you: Everything must be fulfilled that is written about me in the Law of Moses, the Prophets and the Psalms."

3. Once you have read this passage, use your God-given senses to imagine you are with the disciples as they experience and interact with the risen Jesus.
   a. What do you *see* as you observe his hands and feet and look him in the eyes? Try to use your sense of sight to stand in amazement and wonder as you observe what is unfolding before your eyes.
   b. What does it feel like, in terms of *touch*, to embrace Jesus as a friend, rabbi, and the Son of God in bodily, resurrected form? Try to use your

---

84. Endean (1990); Hansen (2012); Ivens (1998).

sense of touch to fully experience, with amazement and wonder, the reality that Jesus has risen from the grave.

   c. What *smells* do you experience as you embed yourself in this story within first-century Palestine? What might the surrounding trees and vegetation smell like? What might the dust of the ground smell like? Try to use your sense of smell to, with amazement and wonder, take in the surrounding aromas as you interact with the risen Lord.
   d. What *sounds* do you experience, including Jesus's voice? What is it like to directly hear from him as the resurrected Messiah, especially when he confidently declares, "Peace be with you," in this very moment? Try to use your sense of sound to, with amazement and wonder, listen to the noises that emerge as you powerfully interact with and worship the Son of God.
   e. What *tastes* do you experience as you eat broiled fish with Jesus, the risen Lord? Try to slow down to, using your sense of taste, savor this meal with him, recognizing you are communing with the God of the universe.
4. Now that you have used your senses to interact with the risen Jesus in worshipful awe, imagine you have alone time with him and can walk up to him, look him in the eyes, and ask him a question. In reverential awe, what might the question be and how might he respond? For example, you might ask, "How is this possible? How could you have come back to life?" In turn, you might imagine Jesus replying, "I am the Creator, Sustainer, and Redeemer. I died for your sins and rose again so that you, too, can have eternal life and be with me forever. I did this because of the love I have for you."
5. As the final step, imagine worshiping Jesus in reverential awe as a response to his answer. Thank him with amazement and wonder for what he just did. He died for your sins and rose again to conquer death. Praise him, worship him, and adore him, knowing that only the Son of God could do such awe-inducing things.
6. When you are done with the above steps, say one more brief prayer to God. Ask him to continue to help you stand in reverential awe before him throughout the day. Recognize, with your God-given imagination and senses, that he is the Creator, Sustainer, and Redeemer of your life.

Upon completion of these steps, try to journal for a few minutes on a separate piece of paper to reflect on the experience.

- What was it like to use your God-given imagination and senses to worship the risen Lord? How well were you able to focus your attention on and worship Jesus within the practice?
- What feelings came up as you embedded yourself in the story and conversed with the Son of God? How well were you able to cultivate awe before him?
- What distractions, if any, got in the way of worshipful awe before Jesus? Thoughts about the self? Others? Things?
- How can you integrate this type of prayer practice into daily life so you can worship Jesus in reverential awe with your imagination?

EXERCISE: Medieval Contemplation

Within the *Cloud of Unknowing*, an anonymous medieval English work from the fourteenth century that presents detailed instructions on Christian contemplation, the author advocates for imagining reaching out to God in love in a "cloud of unknowing" above.[85] He also advocates for placing everything else—such as thoughts, emotions, images, and memories—beneath a "cloud of forgetting" below. Using the image of clouds, the author teaches that contemplating God involves downplaying the use of all thoughts and images other than the God of love. In other words, our knowledge of God gets us only so far in our imperfect attempt to directly experience God, which, via contemplation, is an act of love. In this process, we are embracing the mystery and awe of God. We are not trying to somehow contain him in our own categories of the mind. So, there's a vastness we are embracing as we reach for God in love, not with human knowledge, during such moments. God is knowable, since he has given us his divine revelation, the Bible, and taken on human form as the Son of God. And God is unknowable, given that he is so much greater than we could ever fathom with our fallen, limited, finite human mind. Ultimately, although we cannot fully know God with our human mind, we can love him during moments of contemplation. This is the aim of the *Cloud* author's instructions.

In order to love God in worshipful awe and amazement, the *Cloud* author suggests using a very short word, such as "God" or "love," to focus the human attention on him, since the human mind is prone to wander.[86] As we imagine reaching out to God in love in this mysterious cloud of unknowing, we are placing all else, including human knowledge, beneath a cloud of

---

85. This discussion of the *Cloud of Unknowing* is based on Cooper's (2017) interpretive text.
86. Johnston (1973).

forgetting. In essence, this practice is a simple way to rest in God, with love (not knowledge) leading the way. As we rest in God, we are using the imagery of clouds: one cloud of love, awe, and unknowing is above, and one cloud of forgetting is below and helps us gently place beneath it earthly distractions that pull us away from God. Overall, we reach for heaven with the powerful image of a cloud that represents our faithful, loving, awe-inducing worship of God. And we set aside earthly distractions by moving them underneath a second cloud, one that helps us keep our worship on God, not the things of the world.

For this exercise,[87] try to set aside ten minutes, find a quiet location, and sit up straight in a supportive chair with your eyes closed. When you are ready, follow the below steps in a slow and deliberate manner:

1. Say a short prayer to God. Thank him for who he is as Creator, Sustainer, and Redeemer and his beautiful creation.
2. Imagine that there is a "cloud of unknowing" above and "cloud of forgetting" below. Imagine reaching toward God in love within the cloud of unknowing, doing so experientially.
3. To experientially reach for God in an act of love, not merely think about him, begin to say the word "love" internally as a symbol of your worshipful desire to spend this time with him as Creator, Sustainer, and Redeemer.
4. In a gentle, unhurried manner, set all other thoughts and images—including those about yourself, others, or things—beneath a cloud of forgetting.
5. Repeatedly, in an unhurried, slow, soft, and simple manner, recite the word "love" within. This word imperfectly, yet authentically, captures your worshipful, thankful desire to reach for God in the cloud of unknowing.
6. Whenever another thought or image emerges, which will inevitably happen, gently place it beneath the cloud of forgetting.
7. Continue this practice for ten minutes, then conclude by praying to God. Thank him for giving you his perfect love as Creator, Sustainer, and Redeemer.

After completing this exercise, try to reflect on the experience by journaling with a separate piece of paper in response to the following questions:

---

87. Johnston (1973); Knabb (2021); Knabb and Bates (2020).

- What was it like to use your God-given imagination to reach for God in love within a cloud of unknowing? How well were you able to focus your attention on and worship God within the practice?
- What feelings came up as you reached for God in love within the cloud of unknowing? How well were you able to cultivate a grateful awe before him?
- What distractions, if any, got in the way of reaching for God? Thoughts about the self? Others? Things?
- How can you integrate this type of contemplative practice into daily life so you can worship God in thankful wonder with your imagination?

EXERCISE: *Lectio Divina*

For this next exercise,[88] I'd like us to combine reading, meditating, praying, and contemplating to worship God in reverential, thankful awe. You will be slowly moving through the four steps of *lectio divina*, doing so by interacting with a verse in the Psalms that offers thanks to God.

To start, find a quiet location that is free from distractions, and sit up straight in a supportive chair. Now, when you are ready, follow the steps below, doing so slowly, gently, and reverentially before God:

1. Slowly *read* Psalm 9:1–2 line by line and with intentionality and gratitude before God: "I will give thanks to you, LORD, with all my heart; I will tell of all your wonderful deeds. I will be glad and rejoice in you; I will sing the praises of your name, O Most High." Imagine reading these verses like you are taking the first bite out of a delicious meal.
2. *Meditate* on a selected portion of the first verse, "I will give thanks to you, LORD, with all my heart." Slowly, gently, and simply repeat these words internally. Imagine you are beginning to chew the bite of a delicious meal.
3. *Pray* to God. Thank him for his many "wonderful deeds" in your life. Imagine tasting God's goodness as you continue to chew God's Word.
4. *Contemplate* God. Take an even shorter portion of the passage, "thanks," to simply rest in God in loving, grateful silence. Sit in awe before your Creator, Sustainer, and Redeemer. Again and again, in a slow, soft, and simple manner, repeat "thanks" to God. Imagine that you are savoring this bite of food right here and now.

---

88. Guigo II (2012); Wilhoit and Howard (2012).

Now that you have concluded this short exercise, try to journal for a moment with separate paper by reflecting on the following questions:

- What was it like to move through the four steps of *lectio divina* to give thanks to God in reverential awe? How well were you able to focus your attention on and worship God within the practice?
- What feelings came up as you thanked God? How well were you able to cultivate a grateful awe before him?
- What distractions, if any, got in the way of thanking God for his "wonderful deeds?" Thoughts about the self? Others? Things?
- How can you integrate this type of practice—the four steps of *lectio divina*—into daily life so you can continue to intentionally worship God in grateful amazement?

EXERCISE: Classic Hymn

For this exercise, I would like us to draw from the classic nineteenth-century Christian hymn, "This Is My Father's World," by Maltbie Babcock (1901). This hymn fittingly captures the amazement and gratitude we should have when walking with God as our Creator, Sustainer, and Redeemer on the roads of life. Feel free to either meditate on the verses or sing them to yourself if you know the song or want to follow along with a version online.

To meditate on the hymn, as in the previous exercises, find a quiet location that is free from distractions. When you are ready, follow along with the verses. Do so by intentionally saying them within (or singing them) line by line:

> This is my Father's world,
> And to my listening ears
> All nature sings, and round me rings
> The music of the spheres.
> This is my Father's world:
> I rest me in the thought
> Of rocks and trees, of skies and seas;
> His hand the wonders wrought.
>
> This is my Father's world,
> The birds their carols raise,
> The morning light, the lily white,
> Declare their maker's praise.
> This is my Father's world,

He shines in all that's fair;
In the rustling grass I hear Him pass;
He speaks to me everywhere.

This is my Father's world.
O let me ne'er forget
That though the wrong seems oft so strong,
God is the Ruler yet.
This is my Father's world:
why should my heart be sad?
The Lord is King; let the heavens ring!
God reigns; let the earth be glad![89]

Once you are done, try to journal for a few minutes with separate paper. Reflect on the following question:

- What was it like to move through the hymn, acknowledging "this is [your] Father's world?" How well were you able to focus your attention on and worship God in reverential awe within the practice?
- What feelings came up as you acknowledged "this is [your] Father's world?" How well were you able to cultivate a thankful awe before him?
- What distractions, if any, got in the way of acknowledging "this is [your] Father's world?" Thoughts about the self? Others? Things?
- How can you integrate this meditative practice or song—whatever medium you choose—into daily life so you can continue to intentionally worship God with thankful wonder?

EXERCISE: Practicing *AWE*

In this last exercise[90] for the chapter, I would like you to use the modified *AWE* exercise first mentioned in chapter 1. You will be going on a walk in nature, building on the previous hymn's central theme that "this is [your] Father's world." For this ten-minute practice, find a safe path (e.g., sidewalk, trail). Spend the time slowly moving through the three *AWE* steps. (For those whose mobility is limited, consider sitting on your porch or at a location outdoors. You may wish to say "This is my Father's world" internally as you work your way through prayer beads or a prayer rope.)

---

89. Lyrics are from hymnary.org and are in the public domain.
90. Eagle and Amster (2023); Lawrence (1993); Sturm et al. (2022).

1. *Attend.* As you start to walk, place one foot in front of the other. Focus your attention on God by beginning to slowly, gently, and internally say, "This is my Father's world." Whenever another thought or image distracts you, especially those related to the self, others, or things, just gently bring yourself back to the phrase, "This is my Father's world."
2. *Worship.* Continuing to walk, breathe in God's presence as you internally say, in a simpler, more condensed manner, "Father." As you do so, you are breathing in an awareness, second by second and step by step, that the world in which you walk belongs to your Father as Creator and Sustainer. You are also aware that he has generously shared it with you as you walk with him.
3. *Enhance.* Continuing to walk even farther, breathe out as you say, "Thank you." Rest in the reality that God is with you right here and now and has created the world that you inhabit as you walk with him, step by step and breath by breath. As you breathe out, extend this awareness of God to his creation. Express your gladness with another "Thank you" to him for creating your ears to listen; the rocks, trees, skies, and seas to admire; and the birds, light, and grass to enjoy, as "This Is My Father's World" reveals.

Upon completing your time outside, try to journal for a few minutes on a separate paper. Reflect on the following questions:

- What was it like to walk with God, in reverential awe, inspired by "This Is My Father's World?"
- What feelings came up as you walked with God within his world? How well were you able to cultivate gratitude to him as you walked and talked with him?
- What distractions, if any, got in the way of appreciating your Father's world? Thoughts about the self? Others? Things?
- How can you integrate this practice of attending, worshiping, and enhancing (*AWE*) into daily life so you can continue to intentionally worship God with appreciation and amazement?

Before concluding the chapter, I'd like to offer both a biblical and a life example of worshipful, grateful awe before God to capture the salience of using our God-given thoughts and images to experience God's creation with thankfulness and wonder.

A Biblical Example

Within the pages of the Old Testament, we read about the importance of biblical meditation to take delight in God. According to Psalm 1,

> Blessed is the one
>   who does not walk in step with the wicked
> or stand in the way that sinners take
>   or sit in the company of mockers,
> but whose delight is in the law of the Lord,
>   and who meditates on his law day and night.
> That person is like a tree planted by streams of water,
>   which yields its fruit in season
> and whose leaf does not wither—
>   whatever they do prospers. (vv. 1–3)

In this instructional wisdom psalm,[91] which commences this famous book of worship,[92] we read that someone is "blessed" (the Hebrew word *esher*, meaning "happy") when they "delight" (the Hebrew word *hephets*, which can be defined as attempting to attain something that is highly desirable).[93] They are also "blessed" when they "meditate" (the Hebrew word *hagah*, which captures reflecting, pondering, or muttering with the mind and heart) on God's teachings and promises.[94] This form of biblical meditation is "verbalized rumination."[95] With it, we speak softly and allow the words to penetrate the heart.[96]

The person who travels down the correct path, wherein they meditate on the Bible, will be happy (in contrast with the wicked). Along the way, they are delighting in God's teachings and promises and praising and worshiping him.[97] Writing on the link between the Psalms, meditation, and worship, one author offers the following: "As Christians immerse themselves in God's revealed Word and meditate on it, they learn what is pleasing to him and develop a biblical vocabulary and grammar for worship. Biblical meditation is not an emptying of the mind in an attempt to enter some sort of transcendental spiritual state, but is rather a concerted focusing on the Lord and his Word for

---

91. deClaisse-Walford et al. (2014).
92. Longman (2014).
93. *Strong's Lexicon* (n.d.b).
94. *Strong's Lexicon* (n.d.b).
95. deClaisse-Walford et al. (2014), 61.
96. Moore (2021).
97. Goldingay (2006).

the purposes of appreciating and understanding."[98] Overall, for the twenty-first-century Christian, meditating on God's teachings and promises is key for happiness, according to the very first two verses of the very first chapter of Psalms. To do so, as Christians, we need to be intentional about using our God-given thoughts and images to worship God in reverential awe. We need to walk with him each step of the way as we enjoy him as Creator, Sustainer, and Redeemer. We need to also appreciate, with wonder and amazement, his beautiful creation.

A Psychotherapy Example

Wendy, a twenty-one-year-old Latina female, presented to psychotherapy due to trauma-related symptoms. These symptoms included intrusive memories from past abuse and impaired functioning, since she struggled to keep a job and maintain close friendships. In the first session, Wendy reported that life was always difficult. Growing up living with her grandparents, she never really felt like she had a home, or a caregiver to trust for that matter. She told her psychotherapist that, especially in her adolescent years, she could remember crying alone in her room, with no one to console her. In these moments, she would often have vivid memories of prior abuse at the hands of her father, who was now in prison. In response to these difficult memories, she started to ask a wide variety of "Why" and "What if" questions to try to make sense of the distressing events. This led to constant sadness and shame. "Why did he abuse me?" she would ask herself repeatedly, along with "What if it happens again?" Although she wanted so desperately to get answers to these questions, they never seemed to come, especially since she was all alone in her efforts to sort them out.

As she grew older, the intrusive, unwanted, distressing trauma-related memories continued, so much so that she would commonly get lost in her mind. She would struggle to be present to whatever was in front of her, whether interacting with a teacher in high school or college or with a friend sharing a story over coffee. In fact, she would regularly feel like she was on automatic pilot, not connected to each unfolding moment. Because of this, not only did she have the intrusive memories, but she also reported she had a hard time simply getting through each day as she moved into her young adult years.

Yet, after her initial psychotherapy session, a powerful experience occurred one evening in a church group she was invited to by a friend. The pastor was talking about the salience of meditating on God's Word and gave some specific instructions for how to do so. Prior to this night, she never really thought

---

98. Moore (2021), 223.

about the thought patterns that occupied her mind. And she regularly felt like she was all alone to walk through life.

As the pastor shared, she began to consider that God, rather than her own self-preoccupations, could be the focus of her life. She also considered that worshiping God, rather than ruminating on her isolation and history of trauma, might bring her the greatest happiness. With this novel perspective in mind, she made the intentional decision right in the middle of the group in the auditorium to worship God with her thoughts.

As the words of Psalm 119 were prominently displayed on the big screen within the packed auditorium, she immediately focused in on verse 37: "Turn my eyes away from worthless things; preserve my life according to your word." At that very moment, Wendy was in awe of God. She thanked him for preserving her life over the years, even though she had suffered so much. She recognized the importance of focusing her mind on him (including who he is and his promises and plan for her), rather than getting lost in rumination, worry, and doubt. She could, with her thoughts and images, turn her attention to him to worship him. In the immediacy of the moment, this brought her overwhelming gratitude and delight.

The next week, in her second psychotherapy session, she shared this powerful experience as tears rolled down her face. Sensing the importance of this event, her psychotherapist worked with her to build on this encounter. Her therapist taught her a more formal, classic Christian spiritual practice, *lectio divina*, to pivot from "worthless things" to God throughout the day in order to utilize cognitive triggers to experience worshipful awe of God. Gradually, Wendy was able to integrate *lectio divina* into daily life to cultivate thankful wonder more regularly toward God as Father, Son, and Holy Spirit and Creator, Sustainer, and Redeemer. She drew upon a range of powerful verses from the Psalms to do so.

Wendy would continue to struggle with intrusive memories of past trauma and corresponding, and often unproductive, "Why" and "What if" questions. Yet, she worked with her psychotherapist to develop an intentional strategy for worshiping God in reverential awe to "turn [her] eyes away from worthless things." Rather than trying to be like God, somehow omniscient like him, she could gently shift her attention toward who God is, as found in Scripture, and his promises to her.

Conclusion

In this chapter, we focused on worshipful awe with thoughts and images. We recognized that they can serve as awe triggers to cultivate and maintain a thankful wonder before God. As a worldview-sensitive alternative to Buddhist-derived meditations, Christian meditative practice involves focusing on God's Word, with Christians directing their thankful wonder to him. As key ingredients, worshiping God involves both gratitude and amazement, combined to form Christian awe before the Creator, Sustainer, and Redeemer, who is infinitely good, wise, powerful, present, and holy. Because of this, in each unfolding moment, as Christ followers, we can shift our attention from ourselves, others, and things to God. Upon doing so, we can worship him with thankfulness and wonder and, through him, admire and appreciate his entire creation. My hope is that the various exercises in this chapter have helped you move closer toward effectively using your God-given thoughts and images to worship the Source and get into the habit of using the modified *AWE* exercise throughout the day. In the next chapter, we will be expanding this approach to include physical/sensory triggers by employing deliberate behaviors to cultivate and maintain worshipful, appreciative awe before God.

CHAPTER FIVE

Christian Worship and Awe with Behaviors

In the beginning God created the heavens and the earth.
—Genesis 1:1

You can worship God at your desk, on an elevated train, or driving in traffic. You can worship God washing dishes or ironing clothes. You can worship God in school, on the basketball court. You can worship God in whatever is legitimate and right and good.
—A. W. Tozer, *Tozer Speaks*, vol. 1

Introduction

In chapter 5, we review physical/sensory awe triggers, cultivated via intentional and purposeful actions in the real world (e.g., listening to music, hiking, sightseeing monuments) by using our God-given senses of sight, sound, taste, touch, and smell. A review of worship and awe with behaviors is presented separately within Christianity and psychology. Then, an integrative understanding of how Christians can worship God in thankful, reverential awe with behaviors is offered. From this perspective, worshipful awe with behaviors in our environment can be pursued using our God-given senses. Indeed, Christian worship is a psychological and spiritual discipline to be behaviorally practiced on a moment-by-moment basis and extended to every domain of life (e.g., work, family, community, church). It is not just confined to corporate worship on Sunday mornings while we passively sit in the pews of a local church building. With worship as a spiritual discipline, every second of life can be enhanced. We can recognize that God is the Author of all that is immense, beautiful, and inexplicable.

Throughout the chapter, concepts are defined, exercises are presented (including the modified *AWE* exercise applied to physical/sensory awe triggers),[1] and biblical and clinical examples are offered. Journaling exercises are also embedded to help you, as a twenty-first-century Christian, process and reflect on each exercise. You'll be able to do so with an acknowledgment that God is "holding all things together" at the center of existence (Col. 1:17). We begin this chapter with a biblical perspective, paying particular attention to Christian worshipful awe with intentional behaviors in God's wonderful creation. In God's world, we must rightfully and regularly recognize him in the middle of all that exists.

A Biblical Perspective

We start with a biblical view of the very world that God created for us to move about in, live in, and enjoy. We recognize that "worship" is simply defined as a relationship "between the created and the Creator, which finds expression in both specific events and lifestyle commitments."[2] It is really about "focusing on and responding to God" in all of life.[3] As Christians, we believe that God created us to worship him,[4] and we will eventually worship God in heaven (see Rev. 4 and 5). When it comes to God's creation, we can stand in reverential awe of all that he has made for us, whether we are admiring a physical structure (both natural and human-made), listening to music, or gazing upon a work of art. In the process, we can "focus on and respond to God." As we respond to him, worship functions as an intentional, purposeful spiritual discipline to acknowledge God as Creator, Sustainer, and Redeemer in every domain, moment, and season of this short life he has blessed us with.

Since awe is about acknowledging the vastness and mysteriousness[5] of God's creation and inevitably embedded in worship, and since worship is a spiritual discipline that can be cultivated, maintained, and applied to our appreciation for God's works (i.e., God created everything in this world, either

---

1. Eagle and Amster (2023); Feldman et al. (2007); Lawrence (1993).
2. Pierce (2008), 18.
3. Whitney (2014), 102.
4. Calhoun (2015).
5. Keltner and Haidt (2003).

directly or indirectly), we will be focusing in this chapter on worshipful awe with particular behaviors in response to physical/sensory awe triggers in God's vast, magnificent creation. God has created this world for us to enjoy from moment to moment on this side of heaven. In essence, God created us with five unique senses (sight, sound, taste, touch, smell) to enliven and enrich, with a sense of awe-induced wonder, our interactions in the physical world, which we unpack together in this chapter.

General Revelation and Common Grace

As a quick review, returning to a key theme from chapter 2, God reveals himself to us in his creation (see, e.g., Rom. 1:18–21), referred to in Christian language as "general revelation." This means that all humanity can know something, albeit in a limited way, about who God is by observing, studying, and appreciating the natural world (e.g., objects like rocks, structures such as mountains, living beings like humans or animals, elements like water or fire, or phenomena like rainbows) that he created.[6] We can worship him, in reverential awe, by exploring, with an open and inquisitive curiosity, all that he has fashioned and formed for us to enjoy and marvel at with a profound sense of mystery.

Another relevant Christian concept mentioned earlier is "common grace," defined as "gifts God distributes to humans through created means" such as "blessings found in the natural world and innate capacities of the human mind."[7] So, God reveals his loving, benevolent grace, an undeserved merit or favor generously directed to humankind, in even secular communities via achievements, advancements, and thriving. God's common grace may be extended to beautiful architecture, scientific knowledge, or art. Because of this, we can worship God, in reverential awe, by appreciating *all* the blessings he has generously offered, even to secular communities via human talents, skills, and other God-given abilities (see, e.g., James 1:17).

Combined, general revelation and common grace elucidate that Christians can worship God in reverential, adoring, thankful awe. We can appreciate both his natural creation and those (even secular individuals and communities) who have used their God-given talents and skills (whether they realize the Source or not) to create, build, expand, and advance humanity across the arts, sciences, and other disciplines to make this fallen world a better place. There is *always* someone or something to admire with wonder and amazement in

---

6. Sproul (1997); Wilson (2021).
7. Treier (2017), "Grace," para. 4.

God's vast, mysterious world just as long as we acknowledge the Source of all—the triune God as Father, Son, and Holy Spirit.

God at the Center of Creation

In essence, the Christian behavioral act of worshiping God involves the moment-by-moment acknowledgment that he and he alone is at the center of all of creation (Col. 1:17). This intentional and purposeful acknowledgment of God at the center of his, not our own (as if we were all-powerful and all-knowing like him), creation involves particular behaviors as we move about the God-given physical world and utilize our God-given senses. These behaviors are illuminated for us in the Old Testament of the Bible—written thousands of years ago, yet still highly relevant today for psychological and spiritual insights into the human condition. Such behaviors are also captured in the centuries-old spiritual practices/disciplines Christians have developed for daily life that are still used in twenty-first-century Christian communities of worship.

GOD AND THE OLD TESTAMENT

Within the Old Testament, God is commonly acknowledged as sovereign, presiding over all creation on his magnificent, powerful throne (see Ps. 22:3).[8] Therefore, a Christian view of worshipful awe will inevitably recognize this reality, anchored to a firm, unwavering biblical foundation. Rather than worshipful awe emanating from the self, others, or things at the center—in some sort of humanistic, purely materialistic manner, as is often the case with the study of worship and awe in the secular scientific discipline of psychology—we must, as twenty-first-century Christ followers, maintain a moment-by-moment awareness of God as King on his throne.[9] To do so, as has been mentioned in chapters 1 and 2, we can look to God's special revelation, the Bible, to illuminate his plan for worship, beginning with the Old Testament.

Within the first several chapters of Genesis, we learn about a God who is both set apart as holy and personal/relational.[10] This God "created the heavens and earth," as well as Adam and Eve, and then went on to provide for them by creating trees "good for food" (see Gen. 1 and 2, esp. 2:19). So, Genesis 1 and 2 establish that God is both the Creator and Sustainer.

---

8. Pierce (2008).
9. Pierce (2008).
10. Pierce (2008).

After the fall of humankind in Genesis 3, a new type of relationship develops, wherein God pursues a wayward, fallen, estranged humankind, over and over again, with the human requirement to worship God as Creator and Sustainer as a theme. In fact, postfall, we first learn about worship in the story of Cain and Abel in Genesis 4, wherein only one of the brothers (Abel) offers God something worthy ("fat portions from some of the firstborn of his flock," Gen. 4:4).

Further along in the Old Testament, we find out that God is holy (see, e.g., Exod. 15:11; 1 Sam. 2:2), which means he is worthy of our worship. Time after time, God is referred to as holy in the Old Testament, meaning that he is separate, set apart from humans, perfect, and pure (Isa. 6:1–5).[11] The Old Testament also reveals the importance of (1) unique places and behaviors of worship, such as remembering who God is and what God has done via creating altars, tabernacles, and temples for prayer and animal sacrifice (e.g., killing and burning animals before God to atone for human sin) at particular locations and times;[12] (2) living a life of "service and distinctiveness,"[13] that is, obeying God and remaining separate from the world, not acting like gentile (i.e., non-Jewish) nations (see, e.g., 1 Sam. 15);[14] and (3) praying to God, which means, among other components, formally thanking God, adoring God, repenting of sin, and acknowledging God's character and promises (see, e.g., 1 Kings 8:15–61).[15]

This Old Testament worship can help us, as contemporary Christians, to better understand both God's holiness as a set apart, transcendent deity deserving of our formal, adoring worship and the specific patterns of behavioral action called for throughout history. Such behaviors include acknowledging God in a range of locations at particular times; living a life that is distinct from those who do not believe in, follow, and prioritize him at the center of all; and communicating with God to thank him, revere him, sing to him, and ask him for forgiveness.[16]

God and the Spiritual Disciplines

In addition to understanding the who (the triune God as Father, Son, and Holy Spirit), how (the particular behaviors required by God in the Old Testament to worship him), when (the specific times when God has called humans

---

11. Holman (2004b); Pierce (2008).
12. See Josh. 8:30–35; see also Lee (2021); Pierce (2008).
13. Pierce (2008), 174.
14. See Lee (2021); Pierce (2008).
15. See Lee (2021); Pierce (2008).
16. Pierce (2008).

to worship him), where (the plethora of locations, via altars, tabernacles, and temples, where worship takes place), and why (because God is holy, set apart, transcendent, and the Creator and Sustainer of all) of worship found in God's special revelation to humankind, the Bible, we can learn from Christian spiritual writers throughout the centuries. These writers have attempted to identify and operationalize distinct spiritual practices/disciplines for Christian worship, extended to every domain and season of life in God's wonderful, stunning world.

Throughout the ages, Christians have engaged psychological and spiritual practices/disciplines to worshipfully commune with God and become more like his Son, Jesus Christ (e.g., meditating, praying, contemplating, singing). Sadly, one distinctive spiritual discipline, worship, is sometimes overlooked by the contemporary Christian church. This may be because it is more narrowly, and erroneously, viewed as merely singing songs on a Sunday morning in corporate church settings.

Yet, for the contemporary Christian professor, pastor, and spiritual writer Donald Whitney, "Worship is the God-centered focus and response of the soul; it is being preoccupied with God. So no matter what you are saying or singing or doing at any moment, you are worshiping God only when He is the center of your attention."[17] Whitney goes on to poignantly state,

> Worship is a Spiritual Discipline insofar as it is both an end and a means. The worship of God is an end in itself because to worship, as we've defined it, is to focus on and respond to God. No higher goal or greater spiritual pleasure exists than focusing on and responding to God. But worship is also a means in the sense that it is a means to godliness. The more we truly worship God, the more—through and by means of worship—we become like Him. The worship of God makes believers more godly because people become like their focus.[18]

If spiritual disciplines help us to be more like Christ (via behaviorally displaying the fruit of the Holy Spirit mentioned in Gal. 5:22–23, like love, joy, peace, patience, and kindness)[19] from the inside to the outside, worshiping God helps us to recognize that God is at the center. He is worthy of our adoration and praise. And as we worship him, we are slowly and deliberately becoming like the person we are venerating.

---

17. Whitney (2014), 105.
18. Whitney (2014), 113.
19. Wright (2017).

For this chapter, this inside-to-outside worship can be extended to all of God's creation, including interacting with nature, listening to music, and appreciating architecture or art. And, building on the insights gained from the elucidation of Old Testament worship (e.g., the frequent display of unique and diverse locations, times, behaviors, and prayer practices), we can recognize that the daily worship of God consists of an array of particular locations and times within his creation (not just on Sunday morning in a church building) with intentional behaviors that set us apart from the world (e.g., attempting to live a righteous life because God is holy and the Holy Spirit dwells within).[20] We can also have ongoing, moment-by-moment, prayerful, and worshipful communication with God, acknowledging who he is as holy and set apart and his promises to us as wayward and fallen human beings in need of a Redeemer.[21]

Historically, Christians have used very specific, well-defined spiritual disciplines to commune with and worship God, many of which we will combine in this chapter with insights from the worship and awe literature in psychology. For example, *visio divina* is a form of prayer that involves deepening our relationship with God within his vast, beautiful creation, covered further along in this chapter in more detail.[22] As another spiritual discipline of worship, labyrinth prayer consists of simultaneously physically walking within a labyrinth and mentally praying, doing so in order to symbolically "journey toward God" at the center of the labyrinth, also expanded on as a practice in this chapter.[23] To offer yet one more example, we will be practicing combining Christian meditation and walking based on a pilot study I conducted and published with colleagues on this unique blend of outdoor mental and physical activity to ameliorate daily stress.[24] Also, practicing the presence of God,[25] first mentioned in chapter 1 and which we will explore in the second half of this chapter, can be applied to any worshipful activity within God's creation. In each of these historic Christian spiritual practices/disciplines, the focus is on worshiping God within his creation and giving him the honor and praise as the Creator.

In essence, worshipful awe for Christians involves acknowledging on a moment-by-moment basis *all* of God's vast, incomprehensible, mysterious, beautiful creation.[26] Within the context of this chapter, worshipful awe is,

20. Pierce (2008).
21. Pierce (2008).
22. Calhoun (2015).
23. Calhoun (2015).
24. Knabb, Pate, Sullivan et al. (2020).
25. Lawrence (1993).
26. Keltner and Haidt (2003).

simply put, seeing beauty in God's creation and rightfully attributing it to the Creator. We can do so by appreciating (among other aspects of God's creation) nature, architecture, music, art, and food. Yet, a fundamental difference exists between Christian and secular versions of worship and awe. For Christians, we must intentionally pivot from creation to Creator worship—that is, self to Other, others to Other, and things to Other—in secular society. This is because secular communities often do a good job of, to use an art metaphor, acknowledging the rich, diverse, beautiful colors of paint (God's creation) on the canvas of life, but not celebrating the artist doing all the painting (God as Creator).

To summarize a biblical perspective on worship and awe with behaviors and physical/sensory awe triggers, worship is about a relationship between God, the Creator, and humans, the created, acknowledging that God is holy, transcendent, perfect, and, thus, set apart.[27] God's general revelation, which illuminates at least something about who he is as Creator and Sustainer within his beautiful creation, and common grace, which elucidates the advancements, talents, and skills God has blessed even secular communities with, provide humans with an opportunity to celebrate and worship God, in reverential awe. We are worshiping God's vast, wonderful, awesome creation on a moment-by-moment basis, whether via nature, architecture, music, art, or some other magnificent sensory experience in his big, grand world.[28] To do so, Scripture, especially the Old Testament of the Bible, offers at least some insight into what this might look like, behavior-wise. We can look to the altars, tabernacle, and temple in particular physical locations employed to celebrate God, designated behaviors that illuminate that God's chosen people are set apart from the world, and prayer practices that rightly acknowledge who God is as holy and his promises to those who put their faith in him.[29] Drawing inspiration from the Old Testament, we can see all of life as an act of worship fueled by the spiritual emotion of awe[30] in the here and now. Let us now turn to psychology to better understand worship and awe with behaviors within the context of physical/sensory awe triggers.

A Psychological Perspective

As a review, "awe" can be succinctly defined as "the feeling of being in the presence of something vast that transcends your current understanding of the

---

27. Pierce (2008).
28. Keltner and Haidt (2003); Sproul (1997); Wilson (2021).
29. Pierce (2008).
30. Keltner and Haidt (2003).

world."[31] It includes the combined experiences of vastness, mysteriousness, and gratitude.[32] And there are three main awe trigger categories: (1) thoughts and images (covered in chap. 4; e.g., meditating on God's attributes, pondering a grand theory, trying to understand how big the universe is); (2) behaviors and the physical world (covered in this chapter; e.g., watching a natural phenomenon, staring at a large natural or human-made landmark, listening to live music at a music festival, admiring a famous painting in a museum); and (3) social encounters (discussed in chap. 6; e.g., fellowshiping with God, watching an elite athlete perform, observing someone carry out a virtuous act directed toward a stranger).[33]

Although psychologists (both theorists and researchers) do not tend to use the term "worship" to describe the vehicle through which awe is cultivated and maintained, it may be a good fit. This is because the *APA Dictionary of Psychology* defines "worship" as, once more, "*reverence* or adoration for a divine or supernatural being, a person, or a principle,"[34] and "reverence" is a synonym for "awe." As humans, we are always worshiping someone or something, since we have an innate, God-given need to experience awe, both psychologically and spiritually, on a regular basis. So, when we are using our God-given senses (sight, sound, smell, touch, taste) to interact with the vastness and mysteriousness of the physical world,[35] whether we are listening to music, enjoying a work of art, or admiring a natural or human-made landmark, we are engaging in the behavioral act of psychological and spiritual worship.

Physical/Sensory Awe Triggers with Behaviors[36]

To offer more detail, the psychological and spiritual emotion of awe can arise because of a variety of worshipful experiences in nature. Such experiences may include observing natural phenomena (e.g., a bright rainbow after a storm, a sunset over the Pacific Ocean); staring at a natural landmark (e.g., water cascading down the Niagara Falls, the unique colors and contours of the famous rocks of Joshua Tree, the vastness of Half Dome in Yosemite National Park); or watching animals in nature (e.g., a lion hunting a gazelle in the heat of the Sahara desert, a polar bear catching a fish in the icy cold of Alaska). Awe may be triggered by human-made experiences, too, such as

---

31. Keltner (2023), 7.
32. Büssing et al. (2018); Keltner and Haidt (2003).
33. Büssing et al. (2018); Keltner and Haidt (2003).
34. American Psychological Association (n.d.g), italics added.
35. Keltner and Haidt (2003).
36. This section is based on Eagle and Amster (2023) and Keltner and Haidt (2003).

enjoying architecture (e.g., the Taj Mahal in India, the Empire State Building in New York City), listening to music (e.g., an orchestra's contemporary rendition of Mozart's Requiem Mass in D Minor), or eating food (e.g., filet mignon or crème brûlée at a gourmet restaurant). Finally, awe can be triggered behaviorally via engaging in everyday, not just standout, physical/sensory experiences. These experiences may include walking around a neighborhood and noticing the intricacies of the local architecture, trees, or animals, enjoying a simple breakfast meal at a local diner, or appreciating live music at a "mom and pop" coffee shop. For Christians, when we are not acknowledging our Source of awe, we are worshiping God's creation, not him as Creator, which can quickly turn into idolatry (in biblical terms).

Theory

Theoretically, experiencing physical/sensory-induced awe by way of behaviorally moving about and interacting within our immediate environment may help us to integrate new information for survival.[37] This is because we often rely on previously established schemas (i.e., human mental models, cognitive structures, or abstract outlooks to understand, predict, or solve problems in our environment), heuristics (i.e., human mental shortcuts for decision making or problem solving), or other relatively fixed mental lenses through which to view and understand our surroundings.[38] This reliance can prevent us from taking in the new information necessary to problem solve, plan, and make decisions.[39] This experience, accommodation, combined with vastness (i.e., a physical structure or sensory experience is perceived to be too big or immense to fully take in)[40] in nature and the rest of the outer world can enhance and enrich life.

For authors Jake Eagle (a professional counselor) and Michael Amster (a physician), these types of awe-inducing behavioral experiences in the physical world with the five senses (i.e., seeing, tasting, touching, hearing, smelling) are facilitated by at least three basic steps,[41] mentioned previously in chapter 1. These steps include (1) *attention*, meaning we concentrate in a sustained manner on the object in our awareness that is amazing, vast, mesmerizing, and beautiful; (2) *wait*, capturing the ability to slow down to experience the

---

37. Shiota et al. (2014); Taylor and Workman (2022).
38. Shiota et al. (2014); Taylor and Workman (2022).
39. Shiota et al. (2014); Taylor and Workman (2022).
40. Keltner and Haidt (2003).
41. Eagle and Amster (2023). Although the two authors reported results from laboratory research, aside from what is mentioned in their book, I could not locate the research in any published peer-reviewed journal articles.

object, via the senses, in the immediacy of the here and now, doing so by taking a slow, deep, natural breath as we inhale the magnificence of the moment; and (3) *exhale and expand*, suggesting that we need to slowly breathe out to further allow the awe-inducing sensory experience and interaction with the designated object to be encountered as we pay particular attention to the data gathered from our senses. This simple acronym, *AWE*, can be a useful tool for taking awe "on the road," given that it is easy to remember and can help us to savor the beauty, vastness, and mysteriousness of the world with a sense of gratitude.[42]

In support of this theoretical understanding of the role that a mindfulness-based *AWE* acronym can play in facilitating awe in our everyday environments, researchers recently investigated the role that mindfulness plays in explaining the link between awe and life satisfaction among a sample of adolescents in China, with results supporting this relationship.[43] In other words, as awe increases, so do mindful skills (e.g., focused attention, present-moment awareness, nonjudgmental acceptance of unpleasant inner experiences). And as these mindful skills increase, so does life satisfaction (e.g., believing life is currently going well and optimal). So, mindfulness may explain the awe and life satisfaction link, functioning as the mechanism of action to explain how people with greater dispositional awe end up with greater life satisfaction. They may have a present-moment, compassionate awareness and acceptance of the various thoughts, feelings, sensations, memories, and images—whether pleasant or unpleasant—that are encountered daily.

Applied to nature, it may be that awe—including the ingredients of the small self, connectedness, a sense of vastness, and the ability to shed prior schemas and other entrenched perspectives[44]—can help to practice mindfulness in the natural world. When we are hiking up a mountain, for instance, mindfulness might aid us in being more grounded in the present moment. We may be able to focus, with sustained attention, on the vegetation, animals, rocks, and other surroundings with an open curiosity. It may also help us to be more absorbed in the experience. We may be fully engaged, rather than distracted by an overactive, critical mind. This approach to the natural world may, in turn, help us to feel more satisfied with life (e.g., believing life is going well). This may be because we are more present, with an open curiosity, to the world around us, not distracted by rumination, worry, and self-judgments in our often-noisy head.

42. Keltner and Haidt (2023).
43. Dong and Geng (2023).
44. Monroy and Keltner (2023).

Research

To lend empirical support to the notion that nature induces awe, among a sample of US college students, researchers assigned participants to sit in either nature (i.e., in a botanical garden) or a human-built location (i.e., in a stadium or parking lot) for fifteen minutes and then measured their experience of awe.[45] Results revealed that the nature group reported a greater increase, pre- to postintervention, in awe than the (human-made) stadium group. The nature group also indicated they experienced a greater amount of absorption, which is "a state of feeling captivated and engrossed in the features of the environment."[46]

This experience of awe in nature, possibly due to absorption, may enhance well-being, as evidenced by recent research. In a study of Chinese university students, researchers randomly assigned participants to either a positive awe group (i.e., a video of the earth from an extremely high altitude), negative awe group (i.e., a video of storms), or a neutral group (i.e., a video of someone providing step-by-step directions for cleaning a floor).[47] Results revealed that students in the positive awe condition, but not the negative awe or neutral conditions, reported increases in both life satisfaction and well-being. This study illuminates that positive experiences with nature might increase well-being.

Interventions

Physical/sensory awe intervention studies—emphasizing behavioral action in the real world—may include, but are not limited to, sitting in a local environment for periods of time to observe the surroundings,[48] watching videos of nature,[49] listening to music,[50] going on "awe walks" (which involve walking at a slow to moderate pace with no cell phone or other electronic device and simply noticing the wonder and mystery of the environment),[51] and engaging with virtual reality (VR) technology to create simulated experiences of awe in nature.[52]

As an empirical example, researchers examined possible changes in well-being and stress-related symptoms among a combined sample of military veterans and at-risk youth after an awe-inducing whitewater rafting trip, with

---

45. Ballew and Omoto (2018).
46. Ballew and Omoto (2018), 29.
47. Liu et al. (2023).
48. Ballew and Omoto (2018).
49. Liu et al. (2023).
50. Pilgrim et al. (2017).
51. Sturm et al. (2022).
52. Chirico et al. (2018).

results revealing an increase in well-being and decrease in post-traumatic stress disorder symptoms.[53]

These studies seem to show that one vehicle through which awe can be pursued is behavioral action in the real world with physical/sensory triggers. Such behavioral action may include interacting in nature (e.g., observing a natural landmark, staring at a human-made landmark, engaging in whitewater rafting), listening to music live and in person or via headphones, or taking in the beauty of art at a museum.

Still, for Christians, these types of awe triggers may end up moving us toward idol worship if disconnected from their Source, with "idolatry" succinctly defined as adoring someone or something in place of God. For Christ followers, this type of forbidden worship will never truly satisfy, psychologically or spiritually, unless we pivot from creation to Creator worship with reverential, thankful awe of God as the active ingredient.

An Integrative Perspective

To make this needed pivot, a modified *AWE* exercise[54] for worship and awe with physical/sensory triggers is key. This modified *AWE* practice is the Christian spiritual discipline of worship, applied to all of life. It is a fitting, worldview-sensitive alternative to Buddhist mindfulness. Rather than *attention, wait,* and *exhale and expand,*[55] Christians are taking the three intentional, modified steps of *attending* to God, *worshiping* God, and *enhancing* worshipful awe by recognizing God is the Creator and Sustainer. With the "enhancing" step, Christians are also offering God an ever-expanding gratitude and adoration for who he is, what he has done, and what he will do as the grand narrative of the Bible comes to full fruition with a new heaven and earth (Rev. 21).

Overall, worshipful awe with physical/sensory triggers involves worship as an intentional, purposeful psychological and spiritual Christian discipline to behaviorally shift from creation to Creator worship and rightfully acknowledge God at the center of all of creation. Along the way, we are acknowledging that *all* the immense, mysterious beauty in this world comes from God and God alone, whether directly or indirectly. In this chapter, therefore, I offer several behaviorally anchored Christian practices/disciplines within the context of worship and awe with physical/sensory triggers in God's beautiful, breathtaking world. I also offer examples in the Bible and psychotherapy.

---

53. Anderson et al. (2018).
54. Eagle and Amster (2023); Feldman et al. (2007); Lawrence (1993).
55. Eagle and Amster (2023).

Upon doing so, my hope is that you will dually deepen your relationship with God and improve your mental and spiritual health. This is because you are living out your God-given telos, which provides meaning and purpose on the proverbial roads of life. Let us now begin with a daily log to better understand your current experiences of physical/sensory triggers in the real world as you behaviorally move about God's vast, beautiful garden called Earth.

A Daily Log

Rather than worshiping God in reverential awe as Creator, Sustainer, and Redeemer, we can often get caught up in pursuing lesser, creation awe. In the context of physical/sensory triggers via intentional behaviors, we may strive to visit a natural landscape, admire architecture, listen to music, or stand speechless in front of a brilliant piece of art. When we do so, we may forget to give honor, praise, and glory to the Creator. If this happens, we are certainly pursuing our innate need for worshipful awe, but we are doing so without the one who instilled or embedded it. As a result, it can be helpful to begin to recognize when we are engaged in lesser, creation worship and need to pivot to greater Creator worship, especially since our desire for awe will remain because it is God-given. Yet, our acknowledgment of God as the Source may be lacking, given that we are fallen, broken human beings who commonly wander from him due to our ubiquitous, enduring struggles with sin and idolatry.

With this perspective in mind, in this first exercise for chapter 5 (like chap. 4), I'd like you to log during six time periods throughout a chosen day the types of physical/sensory, creation, "thing" triggers (and corresponding behaviors) that you ended up pursuing to induce the emotion of awe. Use this chart as a model. To get you started, I've added an example for the morning.

Once you have completed the exercise, try to journal for a moment with separate paper. Write down the patterns, in terms of behaviors, that emerged, along with the costs of being preoccupied with (or maybe even worshiping) the physical/sensory things of the world in an attempt to feel awe.

- What patterns did you notice, in terms of your behaviors toward these things? Are these results surprising? Why or why not?
- What is the spiritual impact, in terms of your relationship with God, in being preoccupied with (or maybe even worshiping) things?
- What is the psychological impact, in terms of your mental health, in being preoccupied with (or maybe even worshiping) things?

Time	Things
Morning	Instead of attending Sunday worship service this morning, I drove alone to the local beach about an hour away, since I felt anxious about the week ahead and was worrying about my strained relationship with my boss. The night before, I read online that a storm was passing through, which meant there would be a massive swell—with waves up to fifteen feet high—impacting the coastline. To feel awe, not anxiety, I sat on the beach by myself for roughly two hours, staring at the huge waves crashing against the shoreline. Upon driving home, though, I realized I was avoiding God. At no point during my beach trip did I acknowledge him as the Creator and Sustainer of all. Instead, I was simply worshiping his creation, divorced from him. As I sat in traffic on the way home, I prayed to God, thanking him for creating this beautiful world and giving me my sense of sight to watch such magnificent waves on an otherwise uneventful Sunday afternoon.
Midmorning	
Noon	
Afternoon	
Evening	
Bedtime	

Now that you have had the opportunity to identify some of the behaviors that may be distracting you from worshipful awe of God, I'd like us to begin to practice several exercises to help you, as a Christian, shift from awe of created things to awe of the Creator God as you explore God's beautiful, vast, mysterious world with him.

EXERCISE: Mirror Metaphor

Several years ago, the Christian professor and writer Donald Whitney pointed out that the word "worship" comes from a Saxon word, *worthship*, meaning that worship is about acknowledging God's infinite worth.[56] The more we fellowship with the triune God—Father, Son, and Holy Spirit—the more we recognize that God is holy and set apart. We also recognize we are privileged to be able to worship him in right relationship because of Christians' union with Christ. When we worship God, we are to function as a sort of mirror, reflecting God's awesomeness back to him in reverential gratitude.[57]

For this exercise, you'll be using your God-given sense of sound paired with mental imagery to cultivate worshipful awe before God. To do so, I'd like you to select one of your favorite worship songs, whether classic or contemporary. You'll pair listening to the song with a mental image of yourself functioning as a mirror and, as a result, simply reflecting God's awesomeness back to him during the five or so minutes you are listening to music and worshiping. (If you have hearing or vision loss that prevents you from participating in this exercise, please feel free to skip it and move on to the next one.)

With this simple exercise,[58] find a quiet location, free from distractions, and sit up straight in a supportive chair with your eyes closed. Be ready to play the song through headphones or speakers, whichever you prefer. When you are all set, follow the instructions below.

1. First, say a short prayer to God. Ask him to help you function as a mirror that reflects his awesomeness back to him during this designated time of worship.
2. Second, play the selected worship song. Attend to it by focusing all your attention on the words of worship directed to God. If you know the words, consider singing along out loud, directing them to God as Creator, Sustainer, and Redeemer. As you do so, imagine that you are a mirror, reflecting who God is back to him as you sing to him in the here and now.

---

56. Whitney (2014).
57. Whitney (2014).
58. Eagle and Amster (2023); Whitney (2014).

3. Continuing to listen to the song, begin to worship God in reverential awe, recognizing he is vast and impossible to fully comprehend with your finite human mind. He is the perfect, infinitely good Creator and we are imperfect, flawed creatures. As you worship him, continue to imagine you are a mirror that reflects God's unending benevolence back to him.
4. Persisting in your worship, begin to focus your breathing. Slowly inhale God's vastness and infinite goodness, wisdom, power, and presence as you reflect these perfect attributes of God back to him. Then, slowly exhale to enhance your worship experience.
5. As you exhale, thank God for benevolently creating you to be in relationship with him and giving you this very moment with him. In the process, continue to hold the image of a mirror in your mind, reflecting who God is back to him as you worship him with amazement and wonder.
6. As you reach the final few seconds of the worship song, continue to slowly exhale. Rest in the vastness and mystery of God, who is both knowable, via Scripture, and unknowable, because he is ineffable and beyond human comprehension. Reflect God's immense mystery back to him as you thank him and adore him.
7. When the song ends, sit in silence for a moment or two. Bask in the reverential awe you feel toward God as your personal Creator, Sustainer, and Redeemer, thanking and praising him for who he is.

Upon completing the exercise, try to journal for a few minutes on separate paper, reflecting on the following questions:

- What was it like to worship God in reverential awe by singing a song to him and functioning as a mirror by reflecting back to him who he is?
- What feelings and other sensory experiences came up as you worshiped him? How well were you able to express gratitude to him as you worshiped him via singing a song and functioned as a mirror to reflect his greatness back to him?
- What inner distractions, if any, got in the way as you sang to God? Thoughts? Feelings? Sensations? Memories? Images? Preoccupations with the self, others, or things? Environmental distractions such as a car passing by on the street or family members talking in another room?
- How can you integrate this spiritual discipline of worship by way of attending, worshiping, and enhancing (*AWE*) into daily life so you can continue to intentionally worship God with appreciation and amazement?

EXERCISE: *Visio Divina*

According to the Christian spiritual director and author Adele Calhoun, the famous Christian spiritual discipline of *lectio divina*, or "devotional reading," is about praying God's Word.[59] Conversely, *visio divina*, or "holy seeing," is about "praying with our sense of sight" by slowly interacting with and savoring a powerful biblical image that reflects a Christian truth of some kind.[60] Examples of this type of "praying with the eyes" include the Christian use of particular Christian visual imagery, like the cross, stained glass portraits in churches, or statues of biblical figures.[61] *Visio divina* utilizes our God-given sense of sight and the spiritual discipline of worship to spend time with God in reverential awe and gratitude.

For this exercise,[62] you will be using your sense of sight and an image of Christ on the cross to worship the triune God as Father, Son, and Holy Spirit. Try to find an image, whether it is one you already possess (e.g., a framed picture or painting) or a downloadable image on the internet, that captures the essence of Jesus's crucifixion. Once you have an image selected, set aside ten minutes to follow along with the below directions.

1. Find a quiet location that is free from distractions. Sit up straight in a supportive chair. Rest your chosen image of Jesus on the cross either in your lap or on display close by.
2. Say a short prayer to God. Ask him to be with you as you worship him by gazing upon, through your God-given sense of sight, Jesus as the Son of God on the cross.
3. Allow your eyes to gently gaze at the details of the image. Scan every inch of the depiction by zooming in (to use a camera metaphor). Attend to the details as you worship God in reverential awe. Recognize what he accomplished on the cross for you. God the Father sent God the Son to die for you to generously and lovingly reconcile you to him. As you do so, slowly, gently, and naturally breathe in and out.
4. Allow your eyes to gently gaze at the image as a whole. Zoom out (to use a camera metaphor once more). Continue to breathe in and out slowly, gently, and naturally. As you zoom out to see a "bigger picture" perspective, continue to worship God as Father, Son, and Holy Spirit. Recognize how amazing the atonement is. God the Father sent God the

---

59. Calhoun (2015), 336.
60. Calhoun (2015), 79.
61. Calhoun (2015), 79.
62. Calhoun (2015); Eagle and Amster (2023); Upper Room (n.d.).

Son to die for you, and the Holy Spirit now dwells within you in the here and now. Consider how the atonement is ultimately incomprehensible. Yet, on a basic level, you can trust in the reality that you have been reconciled to God through your union with Christ.
5. Enhance your visual worship by thanking God for the plan laid out before you. Jesus suffered and died on a lonely wooden cross, motivated by his infinite love, so you can have eternal life and be reconciled to God. You are now friends, not enemies, with God. As a result, you can confidently walk with him on the proverbial roads of life as a trustworthy traveling companion.
6. Say a brief prayer to God. Adore him and thank him for Jesus's finished, yet still mysterious, work on the cross to die for your sins, reconcile you to God, and save you from eternal separation from him. Ask God to continue to show you this amazing, awe-inducing image throughout the day as a reminder of his infinite love and goodness.

Once you have finished the exercise, try to journal for a few minutes on separate paper. Reflect on the following questions:

- What was it like to worship God in reverential, thankful awe by gazing at Jesus on the cross?
- What feelings and other sensory experiences came up as you worshiped him? How well were you able to cultivate gratitude to him as you worshiped him, via *visio divina*?
- What inner distractions, if any, got in the way as you gazed upon Jesus on the cross? Thoughts? Feelings? Sensations? Memories? Images? Preoccupations with the self, others, or things? Environmental distractions?
- How can you integrate this spiritual practice of attending, worshiping, and enhancing (*AWE*) into daily life so you can continue to intentionally worship God with appreciation and amazement?

EXERCISE: Travel a Labyrinth

Within historic Christianity, pilgrimages, or "spiritual journeys to sacred places,"[63] were an important part of the burgeoning faith. Within the Old and New Testaments, one of the most famous examples consisted of Jews traveling to the temple. This journey still takes place today via Christians and

---

63. Welch (2014), ix.

Jews making the trek to the Temple Mount. Yet, many people throughout history could not, and still cannot to present day, make these types of journeys for various reasons (e.g., family commitments, financial limitations).[64] This barrier to travel has resulted in labyrinths being embedded in cathedrals for Christians to symbolically make such a spiritual journey, doing so by simply traveling to their local cathedral.[65] Pilgrimages, whether actual or symbolic, have historically allowed Christians to travel away from the busyness and distractions of life and toward God, who dwells at the very center, then back to their local community to live their life for him.[66]

Simply defined as a "single pathway, turning and curving upon itself in a complex pattern around a central point," Christian labyrinths may have first been constructed in the fourth century to function as a symbolic spiritual discipline.[67] Practitioners slowly journey to the middle, which represents God dwelling at the center of existence.[68] Upon deliberately walking through the labyrinth, travelers are slowly, intentionally, and quietly praying, meditating, and worshiping God.[69] They are surrendering to him as they, step by step and turn by turn, draw closer to him and further away from societal distractions.[70] As a quick example, labyrinth travelers may wish to slowly walk toward the center as they meditate on Psalm 84:5: "Blessed are those whose strength is in you, whose hearts are set on pilgrimage."

Within the context of worship and awe, walking labyrinths offer Christians the opportunity to symbolically—yet also behaviorally and relying on the God-given senses—interact with God. And they are worshiping him in the process. Since this spiritual practice is behavioral and offers physical/sensory triggers, it can allow us to better elucidate the role that worshipfulness plays within each step we take on the proverbial roads of life.

For this exercise, try to find a labyrinth in your local community, often found indoors or outdoors at a variety of churches and other community-oriented settings. For example, World-Wide Labyrinth Locator[71] offers a directory and search tool to find labyrinths across a wide variety of countries. Then, once you have located a labyrinth that is close enough for local travel, follow the below instructions to engage in the spiritual discipline of worshipful

---

64. Welch (2014).
65. Welch (2014).
66. Calhoun (2015).
67. Upper Room (2003d); Welch (2014), 1.
68. Upper Room (2003d); Welch (2014).
69. Calhoun (2015).
70. Calhoun (2015).
71. See https://labyrinthlocator.org.

labyrinth prayer.[72] If you do not have access to a local labyrinth, there are a wide variety of finger labyrinths online. These labyrinths are printed on paper and can be easily traced with the finger as an alternative to walking a labyrinth at a local church.

1. Say a short prayer to God. Ask him to be with you as you symbolically journey to him at the center of existence in worshipful, thankful awe.
2. Begin to intentionally walk toward God. Attend to him as you slowly, gently, and internally recite Psalm 84:5: "Blessed are those whose strength is in you, whose hearts are set on pilgrimage."
3. Continue to slowly walk toward God. Attend to him by pairing the physical/sensory experience of walking and cognitive experience of meditating. As you do so, notice what you (a) see with your God-given sense of sight, (b) hear with your God-given sense of sound, (c) feel with your God-given sense of touch, and (d) smell with your God-given sense of smell.
4. As you journey to God at the center and ponder Psalm 84:5, adore God, in worshipful awe, as the Creator and Sustainer of all. He is infinitely powerful and holds the entire world in the palm of his proverbial hand.
5. Enhance your worship of God by thanking him for his perfect presence. Recognize he is always at the center of existence, which means that your spiritual journey begins and ends with him as the Source.
6. As you reach the center, say another prayer to God in reverential, thankful awe. Acknowledge him as infinitely good, wise, powerful, present, and holy and the Creator, Sustainer, and Redeemer of your life. Upon doing so, sit or stand in silence with him. Recognize his vastness and mysteriousness in the here and now.

Once you have concluded the exercise, attempt to journal for a few minutes on a separate paper. Reflect on the following questions:

- What was it like to worship God in reverential, thankful awe by prayerfully and behaviorally walking a labyrinth with all of its corresponding physical/sensory triggers?
- What feelings and other sensory experiences came up as you worshiped him along the symbolic journey? How well were you able to cultivate gratitude to him as you worshiped him via the labyrinth prayer?

---

72. Calhoun (2015); Eagle and Amster (2023); Keltner and Haidt (2003).

- What inner distractions, if any, got in the way as you walked the labyrinth and meditated on Psalm 84:5? Thoughts? Feelings? Sensations? Memories? Images? Preoccupations with the self, others, or things? Environmental distractions?
- How can you integrate this practice of pairing a symbolic spiritual pilgrimage and attending, worshiping, and enhancing (*AWE*) into daily life so you can continue to intentionally worship God with appreciation and amazement?

EXERCISE: Meditative Walking

Throughout Christian history, Christians have meditated on God's Word, which is the second step within the four-step process of *lectio divina* (mentioned in detail in chap. 4). Simply defined as "a method of prayer where reasoning predominates the pondering of God's activity and presence in human history and activity,"[73] meditation is a way to ruminate in a positive manner. We are mentally chewing on God's attributes, actions, and promises revealed in Scripture. The seventeenth-century Puritan John Ball captured meditation with the following: It is "the steadfast and earnest bending of the mind on some spiritual and heavenly matter."[74] Combined with the daily activity of walking, Christian meditation may help to reduce daily stress among Christian populations.[75]

To "walk with God" and ponder his attributes and actions may be one of the ultimate spiritual disciplines, given that we are pairing the use of our God-given mind with physical activity. We are doing so as we employ our God-given senses (e.g., our sense of sight by watching God's creation, like the birds, trees, and surrounding mountains or hills; our sense of sound by listening to the birds chirping in the trees or dogs barking in the background; our sense of touch by feeling our feet make contact with God's stable earth below us or the cool breeze make contact with our face as we slowly walk through our neighborhood) to enjoy God's magnificent, vast, mysterious world.

In this next exercise,[76] you will be walking around your local neighborhood. You will pair the physical/sensory, behavioral act of walking with the mental act of meditating on God's special revelation, the Bible. Upon doing so, you will be worshiping God in reverential awe and gratitude by immersing

---

73. Upper Room (2003e), 190.
74. Ball (2016), 25.
75. Knabb, Pate, Sullivan et al. (2020).
76. Eagle and Amster (2023); Keltner and Haidt (2003); Knabb (2021); Knabb et al. (2023).

yourself in his grand, mystifying world. He created this world for you to steward and enjoy as you fellowship with him. Ultimately, you are learning to walk with him to your eventual destination and home—being face-to-face with the triune God as Father, Son, and Holy Spirit in heaven.

Before beginning, find a convenient twenty-minute time to walk around your neighborhood, such as in the morning when the sun is rising or evening when the sun is setting. Write down or print out the following verse, which you will be meditating on as you walk: "The whole earth is filled with awe at your wonders; where morning dawns, where evening fades, you call forth songs of joy" (Ps. 65:8). With this short practice, you will be gazing on God's beautiful creation during your allotted time with him as you pair the behavioral act of walking and the mental act of meditating. When you are ready, follow along with the instructions below. Although this exercise will consist of walking at a slow to moderate pace, ensure that you have clearance from your physician or healthcare provider if you have any health-related challenges before engaging in physically demanding activities. If you are unable to walk due to limited mobility, feel free to move on to the next exercise in this chapter.

1. Say a short prayer to God. Ask him to be with you and reveal his majesty to you as Creator and Sustainer of all.
2. Begin to walk. Use your God-given senses to attend to your surroundings. Use these senses to see (e.g., the blades of grass on a neighbor's lawn; bright, colorful flowers in a nearby field; a squirrel running across the street), hear (e.g., a bird chirping in a tree, a dog barking in a backyard), and feel (e.g., the wind gently brushing against your cheek, your feet making contact with the loose gravel or pavement) your God-given neighborhood.
3. Begin to introduce the passage for meditation: "The whole earth is filled with awe at your wonders; where morning dawns, where evening fades, you call forth songs of joy" (Ps. 65:8). Try to say the verse slowly, gently, and internally as you walk and steadily chew on God's Word.
4. Worship God by feeling a sense of reverential, thankful awe for all he has created for you to enjoy. Feel a sense of joy in knowing that God has blessed you with a neighborhood to walk in and surrounding world to sensorily consume with wonder and mystery. Continue to ruminate on Psalm 65:8.
5. Enhance your worshipful awe by thanking God for being your very own Creator and Sustainer. In this moment in the here and now, God is giving you life and a breathtaking world to walk and talk with him in.

Thank him for how vast and mysterious he is, knowing he is infinitely powerful and in full control. He is big and you are small, which you can be grateful for. This relationship is like a child being held in a parent's arms, knowing everything will be okay.

6. As you conclude your walk, ask God to reveal his vastness and mysteriousness to you as you continue to walk through life in the minutes, hours, days, and weeks ahead.

Upon concluding this worshipful spiritual discipline and exercise, try to journal for a few minutes on a separate paper with the following questions:

- What was it like to walk with God in reverential, thankful awe by prayerfully and behaviorally trekking through your neighborhood, reliant on physical/sensory triggers?
- What feelings and other sensory experiences came up as you walked with God? How well were you able to cultivate gratitude toward him as you worshiped him, via the neighborhood walk?
- What inner distractions, if any, got in the way as you walked with him and meditated on Psalm 65:8? Thoughts? Feelings? Sensations? Memories? Images? Preoccupations with the self, others, or things? Environmental distractions?
- How can you integrate this practice of pairing walking and meditating with attending, worshiping, and enhancing (AWE) into daily life so you can continue to intentionally worship God with appreciation and amazement?

EXERCISE: Practicing the Presence of God

Returning to our discussion of Brother Lawrence in chapter 1, one of his most important contributions was in teaching Christians to recognize God's presence in all of life. Sensing God's presence may take place during either exciting moments or seemingly mundane activities like washing laundry, taking out the trash, or engaging in a variety of other household chores. For this humble French monk, practicing God's presence simply involves "[taking] delight in and [becoming] accustomed to his divine company."[77]

To practice God's presence, we can effortlessly pair the physical/sensory, behavioral activity with a remembrance of God in the present moment. We

---

77. Lawrence (1993), 38.

can engage in the activity "slowly," "carefully," "deliberately," "gently," and "lovingly."[78] When dually carrying out the task and keeping our mind on God, we can say a short phrase within, recommended by Brother Lawrence, such as "My God, I am completely yours."[79] We can do this to prevent our mind from wandering away from our Creator and unilaterally toward his creation, tragically divorced from him as the Source.

Gradually, we may benefit from this psychological and spiritual discipline of worship in several ways, including the following: "The soul becomes so intimate with God that it spends practically all its life in continual acts of love, adoration, contrition, trust, thanksgiving, oblation, petition, and all the most excellent virtues."[80] Perpetually practicing God's presence with adoration and thanksgiving may be awe inducing, since God is vast and mysterious and gives us no shortage of opportunities to appreciate his wondrous world. These opportunities may include staring at a fly that has landed on our shoe or hiking down to the bottom of the Grand Canyon. We will be practicing God's presence while going on a hike in nature, reliant on physical/sensory awe triggers as we worship God in reverential, grateful awe.

Prior to starting this exercise,[81] find a block of time to hike up a local hill or mountain in nature. Also, like the previous practice, although this exercise will consist of walking at a slow to moderate pace, ensure that you consult your physician or healthcare provider if you have any health-related challenges that may get in the way of such an activity. Feel free to modify the exercise in consideration of whatever natural setting is immediately available, such as a local park. Once you are ready, follow along with the instructions below.

1. Say a short prayer to God. Ask him to be with you and reveal his majesty to you as the Creator and Sustainer of all.
2. Begin to hike. Use your God-given senses to attend to your surroundings. Try to really see (e.g., the rocks that surround you), hear (e.g., the blades of grass rustling in the distance), and feel (e.g., the wind gently brushing against your cheek, your feet contacting the dirt path you are walking on) the mountain or hill you are hiking up.
3. As you hike, attend to the task of walking in God's presence. Do so "slowly," "carefully," "deliberately," "gently," and "lovingly." Recognize that God is at the center of the experience as your Creator and Sustainer.

---

78. Lawrence (1993), 38.
79. Lawrence (1993), 43.
80. Lawrence (1993), 45.
81. Eagle and Amster (2023); Keltner and Haidt (2003); Lawrence (1993).

4. Begin to worship God by introducing Brother Lawrence's recommended phrase, "My God, I am completely yours." Recognize that God is big, and vast, and mysterious, and incomprehensible, and independent, and worthy of your adoration and praise. You are small (in a good way), and finite, and dependent. In this very moment, you can surrender to him because he is in control of each unfolding moment.

5. As you continue to hike with God within his amazing world, enhance your worship by thanking him. Transcend your self-preoccupations by focusing on who he is as Creator and Sustainer of all, not your own limitations or perceived shortcomings.

6. As you conclude your hike with God, say another short prayer. Ask him to reveal his majesty to you in each unfolding moment of the day, whether walking from your home to the mailbox or traveling to the grocery store to pick up a carton of milk. Ask that God, as the Source and center of all, would make himself plainly known in all you do in his big, vast, amazing world and allow you to use your God-given senses to recognize his omnipresence.

Now that you have concluded your worshipful awe hike with God, attempt to journal for a few minutes on a separate paper with the following questions:

- What was it like to hike with God in reverential, thankful awe by prayerfully and behaviorally traveling up a mountain or hill with him, reliant on physical/sensory triggers?
- What feelings and other sensory experiences came up as you hiked with him? How well were you able to cultivate gratitude to him as you worshiped him by way of the mountain hike?
- What inner distractions, if any, got in the way as you hiked with God and repeated Brother Lawrence's recommended phrase to keep your focus on him? Thoughts? Feelings? Sensations? Memories? Images? Preoccupations with the self, others, or things? Environmental distractions?
- How can you integrate practicing God's presence via attending, worshiping, and enhancing (*AWE*) into daily life so you can continue to intentionally worship God with appreciation and amazement?

EXERCISE: Puritan Prayer of Praise

Among the Puritans formal prayers were commonplace. Such prayers astutely articulated their love for God. In *The Valley of Vision*, a variety of Puritan authors offer up prayers to God on topics ranging from confession to adoration and everything in between.[82] As a more recent example, *Piercing Heaven* explicates an abundance of Puritan prayers, capturing the highs and lows of the Christian life and Christians' communion with God.[83] These kataphatic prayers paint a rich tapestry of awe-inducing worship and praise toward God's vast and mysterious ways as Creator and Sustainer. They vividly depict a personal God who is simultaneously known and unknown.

For this next exercise,[84] we will be pairing the recitation of a portion of the prayer "Counting God's Glory," by Puritan Matthew Henry, with washing some dishes. You will want to have the text (found after step 3 in the instructions that follow) readily available before you begin.[85]

My hope is that you will be able to practice God's presence and celebrate God's gift to you, life, in even the most commonplace of daily activities. Try to set aside ten minutes. Find a time that is quiet in your kitchen so you can spend time with God as you humbly and intentionally wash dishes with him. When you are ready, follow along with the instructions below.

1. Say a short prayer to God. Ask that he would be with you and reveal his vastness and mysteriousness to you in the here and now as you humbly wash—with soap, water, a sponge, a sink, dishes, and a kitchen as God's gift to you—the dirty dishes in your kitchen.

2. Begin to run the warm water as you start the activity. Use your God-given senses to (a) see the contours of the dish itself, soap making contact with the dish, and water running down the dish; (b) feel the temperature of the water, texture of the dish and sponge, and consistency of the soap; (c) hear the sound of the water making contact with the dish and sponge scrubbing the dish; and (d) smell the soap that is allowing you to clean the dish. As you do so, recognize that God, as Creator and Sustainer, has generously blessed you with these senses to interact with his creation. Attend to both the dishes and God's presence as you wash them with him.

---

82. Bennett (1975).
83. Elmer (2019).
84. Eagle and Amster (2023); Elmer (2019); Keltner and Haidt (2003).
85. Elmer (2019), 230.

3. Slowly and reverentially, with awe-inducing gratitude, worship God while reciting Matthew Henry's "Counting God's Glory" as you continue to wash the dishes:

> Holy, holy, holy. Lord God Almighty, who is, and was, and is to come. O you, whose name alone is Jehovah, and who is the Most High over all the earth. O God, you are our God, early will we seek you. Our God, we will praise you; our fathers' God, we will exalt you. . . . You are very great. You are clothed with honor and majesty. You cover yourself with light as with a garment. You are light, and in you is no darkness at all. You are love, and they that dwell in love dwell in God, and God in them.[86]

4. Enhance your worship of God by thanking him for giving you your senses and a personal relationship with him to, of all things, enjoy washing the dishes with awe and wonder. In this very moment, God, as Creator and Sustainer of all, has blessed you with the senses of sight, sound, touch, and smell to fully experience his creation.
5. As you conclude, ask God to help you continue to see him as vast and mysterious throughout the day in his beautiful, wonderful creation, doing so with physical/sensory awe triggers.

Upon concluding this simple activity of praying to God as you wash the dishes, try to journal for a few minutes on a separate paper with the following questions to reflect on the exercise:

- What was it like to wash the dishes with God, doing so in reverential, thankful awe, by praying to him and acknowledging his greatness and majesty as you were reliant on physical/sensory triggers?
- What feelings and other sensory experiences came up as you washed the dishes with him? How well were you able to cultivate gratitude to him as you worshiped him via washing the dishes?
- What inner distractions, if any, got in the way as you washed the dishes with God and prayed a portion of Matthew Henry's prayer? Thoughts? Feelings? Sensations? Memories? Images? Preoccupations with the self, others, or things? Environmental distractions?
- How can you integrate practicing God's presence via attending, worshiping, and enhancing (*AWE*) into daily life so you can continue to intentionally worship God with appreciation and amazement?

---

86. Elmer (2019), 230.

EXERCISE: Listening to a Hymn with God

Hymns have famously been defined by Augustine as "singing to the praise of God."[87] A wide variety of English hymns are still sung in Protestant worship services in the twenty-first century. These range from John Newton's "Amazing Grace" to Robert Robison's "Come Thou Fount of Every Blessing" to Isaac Watts's "When I Survey the Wondrous Cross" to Fanny Crosby's "Blessed Assurance." With these examples, among a plethora of others, the heart of Christianity is illuminated and anchored to the Bible. Capturing Christians' imperfect and imprecise thoughts, feelings, and images about the trinitarian God as Father, Son, and Holy Spirit, they serve as a reminder of the salience of worshipful awe before the Source of all.

One hymn, "When I Survey the Wondrous Cross," seems to stand out when considering the context for this chapter—physical/sensory awe triggers with purposeful, intentional behaviors. It stands out because it is thoroughly trinitarian and gets to the heart of Christian worship—namely, what Jesus accomplished on the cross.

Although theologians have debated for millennia the various theories of the atonement,[88] in its basic form, Scripture reveals that Jesus's crucifixion on a Roman cross (and subsequent resurrection and ascension to heaven) was a sacrificial death meant to pay the price for human sin for those who believe in him (John 3:16). Through this atoning act, Christians are reconciled to God (Rom. 5:6–11; 10:9–10; 1 Cor. 15). And because Jesus conquered death, Christians, too, will overcome death and have eternal life (1 Cor. 15).

Yet, tragically, we may be anesthetized to the wonders of the cross. The cross is often viewed as a popular cultural symbol (not a reconciling reality), reflected in fancy jewelry, bumper stickers, and organizational logos. Because of this, an English hymn, anchored to Scripture and drawing on the very heart of Christians of old, may help us to experience reverential awe for the amazing, mysterious cross.

For this exercise,[89] I would like us to mentally time-travel back to the 1700s vis-à-vis Isaac Watts's famous hymn about a wonderful, awe-inspiring cross. To prepare for this five-minute exercise, please locate an online audio recording of the song. Then, find a quiet environment, free from distractions, and sit up straight in a supportive chair. Once you are ready, follow along with the steps below.

---

87. Watson (1999), 2.
88. See, e.g., Beilby and Eddy (2006).
89. Eagle and Amster (2023); Watts (1707).

1. Say a short prayer to God. Ask him to be with you during this time and reveal himself to you in the form of Jesus's reconciling, life-giving act on the cross.
2. Begin to listen to the song with your God-given sense of sound. Attend to the lyrics below and imagine Jesus on the cross, dying for you to reconcile you to God:

> When I survey the wondrous cross
> on which the Prince of glory died,
> my richest gain I count but loss,
> and pour contempt on all my pride.
>
> Forbid it, Lord, that I should boast
> save in the death of Christ, my God!
> All the vain things that charm me most,
> I sacrifice them through his blood.
>
> See, from his head, his hands, his feet,
> sorrow and love flow mingled down.
> Did e'er such love and sorrow meet,
> or thorns compose so rich a crown?
>
> Were the whole realm of nature mine,
> that were a present far too small.
> Love so amazing, so divine,
> demands my soul, my life, my all.[90]

3. As you sing the song to God, worship him in reverential awe. Recognize how amazing and wondrous it is that God the Father would send his Son to die for you so that you could be reconciled to him and forgiven for your sins and could have eternal life with him.
4. Enhance your worshipful awe by thanking God for Jesus's atoning work on the cross. Recognize that he took your place. His gracious, merciful act has allowed you to now be a friend, not an enemy, of God. You can confidently walk with him along the proverbial roads of life to enjoy his creation without fear of eternal punishment or estrangement.
5. To conclude, say another short prayer to God. Ask him to remind you of the wondrous, mysterious cross from moment to moment as you walk with him and talk with him throughout your awe-inducing day.

---

90. Lyrics are from hymnary.org and are in the public domain.

Now that you have finished singing to God about the wondrous cross, attempt to journal for a few minutes on a separate paper with the questions below:

- What was it like to sing to God about the wondrous cross in reverential, thankful awe, reliant on physical/sensory triggers?
- What feelings and other sensory experiences came up as you sang to God? How well were you able to cultivate gratitude to him as you worshiped him via singing about the wondrous cross?
- What inner distractions, if any, got in the way as you sang to God about the wondrous cross? Thoughts? Feelings? Sensations? Memories? Images? Preoccupations with the self, others, or things? Environmental distractions?
- How can you integrate singing to God about his wonderful reconciling act—the atonement—via attending, worshiping, and enhancing (*AWE*) into daily life so you can continue to intentionally worship God with appreciation and amazement?

EXERCISE: Participate in Communion[91]

Among Christian communities, Communion (that is, the Lord's Supper or Eucharist) has been practiced ever since Jesus taught his disciples at the Last Supper how to eat bread and drink wine to remember Jesus and what he would accomplish on the cross (Matt. 26; 1 Cor. 11:24–26). Through his crucifixion, he offered eternal life and salvation to those who believe in him (John 3:16; Rom. 10:9–10). For Christians, Jesus's sacrificial act, and the subsequent ritual of Communion that helps us remember its significance, is a "divine mystery."[92] We can never truly grasp exactly how it reconciled wayward sinners to a holy God. Yet, this "divine mystery" can be plainly stated: "Christ has died; Christ is risen; Christ will come again."[93]

For this very last exercise of the chapter,[94] I would like us to take Communion within the context of the spiritual discipline of worship to dually remember what Jesus accomplished on the cross and fellowship with him. We

---

91. This exercise may be a better fit for Christians who are part of Christian denominations or church traditions that do not require clergy to consecrate the elements (bread and wine). Still, even Christians who only formally participate in Communion at church services may find this exercise helpful during such occasions.
92. Calhoun (2015), 57.
93. Calhoun (2015), 57.
94. Calhoun (2015); Eagle and Amster (2023).

will use the physical/sensory triggers of the five senses to cultivate reverential, thankful awe toward him. To prepare for Communion, attain a piece of bread and grape juice (in place of actual wine). Find a quiet location that is free from distractions. Sit up straight in a supportive chair. Then, when you are ready, slowly follow along with the steps below.

1. Say a short prayer to God. Acknowledge Jesus's act of reconciliation on the cross. Ask God to be with you during this time as you remember Jesus and fellowship with him in reverential, adoring, grateful awe.
2. Slowly and reverentially read 1 Corinthians 11:23–26:

   The Lord Jesus, on the night he was betrayed, took bread, and when he had given thanks, he broke it and said, "This is my body, which is for you; do this in remembrance of me." In the same way, after supper he took the cup, saying, "This cup is the new covenant in my blood; do this, whenever you drink it, in remembrance of me." For whenever you eat this bread and drink this cup, you proclaim the Lord's death until he comes.

3. Use your God-given sense of sight to attend to and examine the bread. Recognize that it symbolizes Jesus's body, broken for you so that you could be forgiven for your sins and reconciled to God. Then, after examining the bread, take a bite and slowly chew a piece, which, again, represents Jesus's body. As you do so, consider the mystery and awesomeness of the atonement. Through crucifixion and death, Jesus died for you so that you could be in right relationship with him for eternity.
4. Use your God-given sense of sight to attend to and examine the grape juice, which represents wine. The wine symbolizes Jesus's blood, spilled for you so you could be, once more, forgiven by and reconciled to the trinitarian God. Upon taking a closer look, drink the cup, which, yet again, symbolizes Jesus's blood for you. Continue to ponder the vastness and mysteriousness of God, including this act of reconciliation. Although you cannot fully know how the atonement works, it is, nevertheless, the greatest act in human history for Christians. You can participate in this history via simply believing in Jesus (Rom. 10:9–11).
5. Worship Jesus by continuing to bask in the mystery of the atonement. Recognize with wonder and amazement that, upon eating the bread that represents Jesus's broken body and drinking the grape juice that symbolizes Jesus's shed blood, you "proclaim the Lord's death until he comes" (1 Cor. 11:26). Although this mystery is impossible to fully comprehend, plainly put it means that Jesus is coming again. And because

of the atonement, you are made right with him and are now considered a friend, not an enemy, of God as Creator, Sustainer, and Redeemer.

6. Enhance your worship by thanking Jesus for what he accomplished with a simple "Thank you, Jesus." Adore, in reverential, grateful awe, what he accomplished via the incarnation. Jesus took on human form so that you could be restored to him.
7. Say a short prayer to God once more. Ask Jesus to remind you of his ultimate act of reconciling love (John 3:16). This act was accomplished on a lonely wooden cross some two thousand years ago.

Upon completing Communion as a spiritual discipline of worshipful awe toward Jesus's accomplishment on the cross, try to reflect on the experience via journaling on a separate paper for a few minutes:

- What was it like to take Communion in reverential, thankful awe, reliant on physical/sensory triggers?
- What feelings and other sensory experiences came up as you remembered what Jesus accomplished on the cross? How well were you able to cultivate gratitude to him as you worshiped him via Communion?
- What inner distractions, if any, got in the way as you took Communion? Thoughts? Feelings? Sensations? Memories? Images? Preoccupations with the self, others, or things? Environmental distractions?
- How can you integrate remembering what Jesus accomplished on the cross via attending, worshiping, and enhancing (*AWE*) into daily life so you can continue to intentionally worship God with appreciation and amazement?

A Biblical Example

As mentioned at the beginning of the chapter, God's general revelation to humankind includes the reality that he reveals at least something of himself in his creation. With such a grand and mysterious[95] natural world, there are an almost infinite number of opportunities to better understand God's greatness, mysteriousness, and Otherness as the Creator and Sustainer of all. The Psalms, for instance, frequently capture God's awesomeness by mentioning his creation. By admiring his wonderful creation, Psalm 147 elucidates that God is worthy of our praise:

95. Keltner and Haidt (2003).

Praise the LORD.

How good it is to sing praises to our God,
    how pleasant and fitting to praise him!

The LORD builds up Jerusalem;
    he gathers the exiles of Israel.
He heals the brokenhearted
    and binds up their wounds.
He determines the number of the stars
    and calls them each by name.
Great is our Lord and mighty in power;
    his understanding has no limit.
The LORD sustains the humble
    but casts the wicked to the ground.

Sing to the LORD with grateful praise;
    make music to our God on the harp.

He covers the sky with clouds;
    he supplies the earth with rain
        and makes grass grow on the hills.
He provides food for the cattle
    and for the young ravens when they call.

His pleasure is not in the strength of the horse,
    nor his delight in the legs of the warrior;
the LORD delights in those who fear him,
    who put their hope in his unfailing love.

Extol the LORD, Jerusalem;
    praise your God, Zion.

He strengthens the bars of your gates
    and blesses your people within you.
He grants peace to your borders
    and satisfies you with the finest of wheat.

He sends his command to the earth;
    his word runs swiftly.
He spreads the snow like wool
    and scatters the frost like ashes.
He hurls down his hail like pebbles.
    Who can withstand his icy blast?
He sends his word and melts them;
    he stirs up his breezes, and the waters flow.

> He has revealed his word to Jacob,
> > his laws and decrees to Israel.
> He has done this for no other nation;
> > they do not know his laws.
>
> Praise the LORD.[96]

Notice the vastness and incomprehensibility of God, as revealed by the psalmist, illuminated by the italicized words. God names all the stars, too many to count. He creates the clouds in the sky, provides the rain, and causes the grass to grow. He providentially offers food to the animals of the land. And he distributes snow and hail and sends breezes and flowing water. Our God is a God who creates, sustains, and provides. He does so because he is infinitely powerful, good, loving, and present. He desires to take care of his wonderful, mysterious creation. As this biblical example reveals, the God of the Bible is a God who did not create only to turn away in an impersonal, apathetic manner. Instead, God is a God who is both separate, transcendent, and unknowable and personal, immanent, and knowable. Because of this, let us bask in this awe-inducing, paradoxical reality.

A Psychotherapy Example

For Charlotte, a white, married mother of two young children, life always felt dangerous. Growing up in an abusive home, she experienced trauma at the hands of a stepfather who would regularly yell, throw things, hit things, and occasionally strike both her and her mother. Her birth father had died when she was only eight years old, and after this life got extremely difficult. Her mother, grieving the loss of her husband, had to find a job to support the family—two jobs, in fact. This meant her mother was struggling with significant loss and away from the house for long periods of time. Yet, when she met Charlotte's stepfather about a year after Charlotte's father's passing, life seemed like it would be stable and predictable again.

Upon moving into their new home, though, Charlotte noticed that her stepfather would frequently lose his temper, doing so several times per day. As a result, the house was a scary and unpredictable place to live, with Charlotte struggling to feel safe. She stayed in her room most days, only finding relief in leaving for school during the week and spending time with her friends away from home on the weekend.

---

96. Italics added.

In her teenage years, Charlotte began to develop trauma-related symptoms such as intrusive, vivid memories of her stepfather's abusive episodes, which increasingly involved him verbally abusing her (e.g., telling her she was "worthless" and "stupid" due to getting average grades) and slapping (and sometimes punching) her when she did not remember to clean her room or finish her assigned chores. She also struggled with avoidance, hypervigilance, and rumination and worry. With the avoidance-related symptoms, she would hide in her room, to come out only when she knew her stepfather wasn't home. She would also avoid anyone or anything that reminded her of him (e.g., tall, male authority figures with loud, deep voices like her stepfather). Regarding the hypervigilance, she was easily startled. She constantly looked over her shoulder in anticipation of another violent act on the part of her stepfather. Finally, Charlotte increasingly struggled with negative thoughts about the world. These thoughts involved a theme of danger. She perseverated on content such as "I'm going to be hurt," "I'm not safe," and "I'm going to be hit again."

Around this time, Charlotte could remember attending church with her mother on Sunday mornings. She prayed to God that he would "heal" her stepfather and take away the violence and aggression at home. For Charlotte, though, the abuse and her unpredictable home life continued, right up until she moved out to get married.

When she got married to a peer from her high school church youth group, once again, she thought things would change. She longed for a house (and world) that was safe, predictable, and certain. Although her husband was a committed Christian who was in fact safe and loving, her trauma-related symptoms persisted from her past. She would be preoccupied with them, unable to fully attend to her husband or children. Most nights Charlotte would struggle to sleep in the same bed with him, fearing he would get violent like her stepfather.

During these years, like her church experience in adolescence, Charlotte frequently prayed to God. She asked him to take away her fear and constant "on edge" feeling. Many nights, she would lament to God, "Please, God, just take the fear away! I just want to be normal!"

Over time, these symptoms—intrusive memories, avoidance, hypervigilance, and negative, danger-related thoughts about the world—impaired her functioning in both family life and church life. Because of these continuous struggles, her husband encouraged her to see a psychotherapist, which she agreed to do.

In psychotherapy, she was diagnosed with post-traumatic stress disorder (PTSD) based on the above symptoms, among others. After her psychotherapist educated her on the symptoms of PTSD, Charlotte worked with her psychotherapist on a range of basic coping skills so she could better manage her trauma-related symptoms and move toward greater intimacy and closeness with her husband.

After a period focused on the development of a set of skills to effectively respond to her symptoms (e.g., relaxation techniques, breathing exercises), Charlotte's psychotherapist introduced her to the concept of awe. This was because Charlotte mentioned she longed to feel closer to God and trust in him as her ultimate Source of security and safety.

In particular, the psychotherapist discussed the two awe ingredients of vastness and mysteriousness.[97] He noted that awe-inducing experiences may help people to shift from rumination, worry, and preoccupations with the self to someone or something bigger than the self.[98] The psychotherapist also suggested that awe might offer meaning and purpose in life, with awe-inducing moments potentially altering previously established, rigid schemas of the world.[99] Finally, the psychotherapist mentioned that awe-inducing experiences in nature may help with trauma-related symptoms, as revealed by recent research on the topic.[100]

Over the course of the next two sessions, Charlotte explored with her psychotherapist her desire to deepen her relationship with God to feel a greater sense of safety and comfort from him, something she was not able to experience in childhood. Therefore, her psychotherapist recommended that Charlotte spend some time with God in nature by going on a local hike. This hike was to help her experience the grandness and mysteriousness of God and pivot from inner preoccupations to him. Charlotte's psychotherapist also suggested that spending time with God in nature may help her begin to change her schema of danger, since she regularly drew from this deeply embedded notion that the world was a dangerous place, based on her childhood experiences. With this understanding of awe in mind and based on Charlotte's desire to pivot from the self and others to God, she committed to going on nature walks a few times per week in a local canyon that was popular among hikers.

On one outing, Charlotte hiked up a steep hill. She arrived at the top to see a bright blue sky. In this moment, she felt God's bigness and mysteriousness, which brought her tremendous peace and comfort. She knew that he was in control and, because of this, she did not have to be. During this

---

97. Keltner and Haidt (2003).
98. Bai et al. (2017).
99. Monroy and Keltner (2023).
100. Anderson et al. (2018).

encounter with God, she was able to, for a moment, let go of the belief that the world was unsafe. She simply rested in the reality that God was at the center of existence. Rather than being preoccupied with her symptoms or a dangerous world, it was simply her and God. She could adore and thank him for giving her this moment in nature. As she started to head back to her house, she began to entertain the notion that God was with her all along, even in her childhood years. He created her and was sustaining her, despite her rough upbringing. Instead of seeing the world as an entirely unsafe place, she could pivot from her own unilateral efforts of controlling through avoidance to experiencing the greatness of God. Shifting from preoccupations about herself and others to the ultimate Other may be the most effective path forward, she realized.

Upon returning to psychotherapy, Charlotte processed with her psychotherapist this understanding that, paradoxically, focusing less on herself, not more, may be the solution to her thoughts of danger and feelings of fear. Although they may always continue to emerge, she could, with God's help, pivot in worshipful awe toward him.

Conclusion

In this chapter, we have covered quite a bit of territory. We have explored Christian and psychological perspectives on physical/sensory awe triggers with purposeful, intentional behaviors. By using our God-given senses to explore God's creation, we may be able to ameliorate our self-preoccupations. These self-preoccupations can end up leaving us miserable, with added suffering. Instead, we can worship God in reverential awe, something we were designed to do. Whether we are seeing God's fingerprint in the natural world or enjoying, via common grace, the architecture, music, and art that talented secular communities produce, we can spend each moment of the day giving thanks to God. We can recognize he is at the center of it all. To do so, the modified *AWE* acronym[101] can be a trustworthy traveling companion. It can help us to prioritize God, not the self, others, or things. This shift in perspective—each moment of life in God's immense, beautiful creation gives us the opportunity to worship and thank him for his many blessings—can also help us to change our current schemas and other perspectives that may be keeping us stuck, whether psychologically or spiritually. Now that we have explored cognitive and physical/sensory

---

101. Eagle and Amster (2023); Feldman et al. (2007); Lawrence (1993).

triggers, let us turn to social triggers. This last chapter can help us to better understand how we, as Christians, can worship God in reverential awe through the medium of our relationships with God and others. We can learn to recognize that all of life offers an opportunity to locate God in the middle of existence.

CHAPTER SIX

Christian Worship and Awe with Relationships

> Awe integrates us into the systems of life—communities, collectives, the natural environment, and forms of culture, such as music, art, religion, and our mind's efforts to make sense of all its webs of ideas. The epiphany of awe is that its experience connects our individual selves with the vast forces of life. In awe we understand we are part of many things that are much larger than the self.
>
> —Dacher Keltner, *Awe*

> It is the Will of God which from nothingness drew out the universe with all its grandeur and all that lives in it, the earth with all that is on it and beneath it, all creatures visible and invisible, living and inanimate, reasonable and without reason, from the highest to the lowest.
>
> —Jean Baptiste Saint-Jure, *Trustful Surrender to Divine Providence*

Introduction

In chapter 6, our final chapter, we review social awe triggers cultivated via intentional, purposeful relationships with God and others. A review of worship and awe with relationships is presented within both Christianity and psychology. Then, these perspectives are combined to form an integrative understanding of how Christians can worship God in thankful, reverential awe by pursuing and developing deeper connections with God and others.

Throughout the chapter, concepts are defined, exercises are presented (including the modified *AWE* exercise),[1] and examples are offered within biblical and clinical contexts. Along the way, journaling exercises are embedded to help you, as a Christian, process and reflect on the practices. Worth mentioning, this chapter is different from (although somewhat overlapping with) chapter 4 on cognitive triggers in that Christians worship and serve a *real* God via a *real* relationship. Thus, in addition to more abstract, cognitive, theological notions of God, experiential triggers in an interpersonal/relational/social context are important in the Christian life. Nevertheless, we start this chapter with a biblical view. We focus on Christian worshipful awe with relationships, with God at the center of every one of our interpersonal encounters throughout the day, whether with him or others.

A Biblical Perspective

Worship and Awe with God

THE IMAGO DEI

According to Genesis 1:26–27, God declared, "Let us make mankind in our image, in our likeness . . ." To be made in God's image, the *imago Dei*, captures the "unique nature, status, and worth of all human beings as created by God."[2] For Christians, the loving generosity (combined with infinite power) of God to create—especially humans, with inherent dignity and worth in his eyes—is nothing short of awe inducing.

Christian authors have debated for generations the ultimate meaning of "the image of God" in Genesis. More common meanings include substantive (e.g., humans were created with the God-given ability to reason and make moral decisions, unlike the animal kingdom), relational (e.g., humans were created to be in relationship with God and others), and functional (e.g., humans were created to rule the earth, with the power to do so given to them by God).[3] Among such meanings, the relational view can help us to better understand our innate need for awe-inducing worship.[4]

From this perspective, God designed us to be in a real, personal, intimate, enduring relationship with him to lovingly worship him in reverential awe with all our being—heart, soul, and mind (Matt. 22:37). We were not designed

---

1. Eagle and Amster (2023); Feldman et al. (2007); Lawrence (1993).
2. Holman (2004c), 345.
3. Middleton (2005).
4. For contemporary arguments in favor of the relational view of the *imago Dei*, see, e.g., Grenz (2001) and Miller (2011).

to simply settle for a removed, aloof, impersonal, abstract understanding of and tenuous bond with him. When we venture closer to understanding who God is as Creator, Sustainer, and Redeemer (Heb. 1:3, 10; Titus 2:14), this biblical reality should inevitably function as a social trigger for the "moral, spiritual, and aesthetic emotion" of awe.[5] And this reality should flow from a daily celebration of who he is and what he has done, is doing, and will do.

Consistent with this understanding, according to the Christian professor of divinity Allen Ross, "True worship is the celebration of being in covenant fellowship with the sovereign and holy triune God, by means of reverent adoration and spontaneous praise of God's nature and works."[6] With this definition, we see that worship is an adoring, reverential celebration—based on a binding relationship between God and those who believe in him—of who God is, character-wise, and what he has done, works-wise.

Organically flowing from this relational experience of worship is the God-given psychological, spiritual, and moral emotion of awe. This is because we are small, God is big, and we need to constantly adjust our understanding of this unequal contrast to make room for the reality that he is the Creator and Sustainer of all and at the center of all of existence. If the *imago Dei* means (at least in part) that we were created by God to worship him in a covenantal relationship,[7] and the vehicle through which awe of God is cultivated is worship, worshipful awe of God is key for Christian mental and spiritual health.

Amalgamating these concepts together (e.g., a Genesis account of the *imago Dei* and worshipful awe before God), Ross further explains, "The first two chapters of the Bible provide an unparalleled revelation of the LORD, who is the majestic and sovereign God of creation. This revelation is not only foundational to the faith but is also essential for worship: The LORD God alone must be worshipped because he is sovereign over all things—he was before all things, and by him all things exist" (Col. 1:17).[8] Here, we have the ingredients of awe, including God's vastness via his sovereignty, as well as his mysterious, beautiful majesty. These ingredients point us to the Christian need to worship him at the center as the Source of existence.

GOD'S PROVIDENCE

Since God is the sovereign Creator and Sustainer, what we are really talking about here is the immense, powerful mystery of God's "*purposeful*

---

5. Keltner and Haidt (2003), 297.
6. Ross (2006), 67.
7. Osborne (2021).
8. Ross (2006), 78.

sovereignty" and "counterintuitive *wonders*."[9] This is referred to in Christian language as "providence," or "God's activity throughout history in providing for the needs of human beings, especially those who believe in him."[10] God is more than just infinitely powerful, given that he intimately, personally, and wonderfully cares for his creation. In other words, "God visits, touches, communicates, controls, and intervenes, coming before and between people and their needs."[11] Because of this, to be in an adoring, thankful, worshipful relationship with the Source of existence means we acknowledge and trust that we will be provided for, time and time again, on this side of heaven and beyond. And this God-centered relational reality is naturally awe inducing when we deeply and meaningfully ponder it and attempt to see it everywhere. This is because God's good governance—based on his caring, guiding relationship with his creation—extends to every domain and sphere of life, whether nature, humanity, politics, or the arts and sciences.[12]

God's unique combination of infinite goodness, wisdom, and power, or his purposeful care, means we worship a benevolent, wonderful God. This is the God who displays his care for and control of his creation. He operates out of the center of existence, whether guiding the smallest atomic particles or the rotation of the earth. Since this is the case, worshipful awe, consisting of God's vastness and incomprehensibility and our human need to adjust our finite minds to make room for this reality,[13] can be extended to *all* of life. And God's proverbial hand guides every one of our awe-inducing encounters on the roads of life.

Worded differently, meditating on God's providence and experiencing his guiding hand as a benevolent King in full control of reality as his kingdom is a social trigger for worshipful awe. God's providence is an awe trigger because he is so benevolently vast that he chooses to tend to all of his creation. His providential ways surpass our finite understanding.

Christians' first psychological and spiritual response to God's providence should be to worship him in reverential, grateful awe and wonder,[14] since he chose to make all that exists, and he continues to care for it in a personal, loving manner. This ability to worshipfully celebrate God's providence can certainly help us deepen our relationship with him so that each step we take in life is in unison with the triune God. There may be no greater example of this

9. Piper (2020), 17–18, italics added.
10. Elwell and Comfort (2001), 1092.
11. Elwell and Comfort (2001), 1092.
12. Piper (2020).
13. Keltner and Haidt (2003).
14. Cottrell (1984).

benevolent intimacy than the Father-Son relationship found in the Gospels, which reveals Jesus's model of the primacy of worship and awe in daily life.

Jesus's Model[15]

To better understand how to worship God with a cherished, reverential awe, we can look to Jesus as our exemplar. Jesus took on human form, lived a perfect life, and modeled how to worship God on a daily basis. For Jesus, all of life was about adoring God. He was a first-century Jew who worshiped his Father in a variety of locations (e.g., the temple, synagogues), prayed to his Father, celebrated Jewish worship festivals (e.g., annual feasts), yielded to the will of his Father, and served others.[16] Even in the face of Satan's temptations in the desert, Jesus blatantly rejected Satan's promise of the world if Jesus would simply worship Satan (see Matt. 4:8–10). Instead, "Jesus worshipped God only and all power in heaven and on earth was given him."[17]

So, thus far in this chapter, we have explored the notion that humans were created in God's image to be in relationship with God and others. We have also discussed the idea that God has continued to care for humans via his providence—or sovereign, benevolent, personal governance and guidance over all of creation—since the creation of the world. Moreover, this chapter has elucidated that Jesus regularly modeled worship via his intimate relationship with the Father and, through this dyad, the life he led. In each of these examples, we can see the salience of relationship, which has profound implications for twenty-first-century Christ followers within the context of social awe triggers and worship as the vehicle through which they are pursued.

The Grand Narrative of the Bible

We can see the need for worshipful awe in right relationship with God threaded across the entirety of the Bible in the form of the metastory of Scripture.[18] God created humans in his image to be in relationship with him. Although we turned away from him because we wanted to worship ourselves at the center of existence, God the Father sent his Son to die on a cross as the ultimate act of reconciliation. And Christians will eventually be face-to-face with God in heaven, wherein they will inevitably worship him in reverential

---

15. This section is influenced by the writings of McConnell (2021); Morris (1992); Ross (2006); and Whaley (2009).
16. Cherry (2019); McConnell (2021).
17. Morris (1992), 78.
18. This summary is based on Wolters (2005) and Wright (2013).

awe. Most importantly, there will be no more suffering when we meet God face-to-face.

Throughout this biblical narrative that spans from Genesis to Revelation, we see the power of relationships that are exemplified by God's ongoing pursuit of and providential care for his creation. God calls us, in response, to worship him with an adoring, thankful awe, not to worship the lesser self, others, or things, which gives rise to forbidden idol worship.

Since God created humans to be relational, this includes being in relationship with others, which can also trigger awe. For Christians, being in awe of others reveals God's common grace. This common type of grace means that God blesses even secular communities, and those within them, with talents and skills. These talents and skills give rise to the experience of observing, witnessing, and cheering on amazing abilities and, consequently, seeing others as big and the individual self as small (in a good way). If Christians recognize the Source as the trinitarian God, the giftings of other people can be celebrated and regularly point the celebrator back to the Celebrated.

A Relational Perspective on Worship and Awe with Others

Within a relational context, since God created humans to be relating beings, it only makes sense that we would be in awe of others' leadership, talents, skills, and virtues. As revealed in previous chapters, God's common grace means that he generously offers such talents and skills to humans, even those who do not believe in him.[19] Christians can admire, in awe and amazement, incredible, unparalleled human displays (e.g., the giftings of singers, comedians, athletes, artists, poets, and world leaders).

Yet, when we begin to worship others' accomplishments with an intense, all-consuming adoration and praise that should be reserved exclusively for God, we engage in idol worship. This idol worship is outlawed in the Bible.[20] Therefore, we need to acknowledge the Source—God and his grace, which is extended to all humans and communities in various shapes and forms—when admiring the qualities of others.

In either case, the spiritual (and moral and aesthetic) emotion of awe[21] is a God-given relational signal that dually tells us that there is more to life than ourselves and that our Creator and Sustainer has benevolently injected beauty into his creation. If emotions functionally help us better understand our relationships and motivate us to take behavioral action in our immediate

---

19. Treier (2017).
20. Beale (2008).
21. Keltner and Haidt (2003).

environment,[22] awe as an emotion certainly includes these components. Awe reminds us that we are small, God (and, by extension, the talents and skills he blesses others with) is big, and this immense God is at the center of existence. This accurate self-and-Other contrast results in our moment-by-moment need to adjust our finite, imperfect thinking to accommodate this interpersonal (and physical, psychological, and spiritual) reality.

In other words, the emotional signal of awe offers us, in the present moment, an ensuing relational contrast and cognitive decision. Will we view ourselves as small, God as big, and our finite human mind as fallen and in need of adjustment to make room for this reality? Or will we futilely try to place ourselves, and our human mind, at the center of existence, reminiscent of Adam and Eve's tragic mistake in Genesis 3?

To summarize a Christian perspective on worship and awe within the context of social and relational triggers, we were created in the image of God to be in right relationship with him. This right relationship involves a covenantal bond that endures with a big God and small self.[23] Our enduring bond with God involves the emotion of awe as a relational signal.[24] Worship is the vehicle through which we can cultivate and maintain awe of God (and, through him, how we relate to all of his creation).[25] This vehicle of worship helps us to see God's vastness and our need to accommodate[26] our finite, fallen understanding (that erroneously and frequently places us, not him, at the center) to acknowledge the reality that God is the Creator and Sustainer of all. He resides at the center of his creation on his powerful, omnipresent throne. Through authentic, heartfelt worship, which naturally gives rise to awe, we can develop a deeper, more worshipful intimacy with him. Worded differently, our relationship with God triggers awe. And this God-induced awe motivates us to deepen our relationship with him, with each influencing the other in a bidirectional manner. This reality has profound mental and spiritual health implications, given that we have a trustworthy traveling companion who providentially cares for us, guides our path, and provides meaning and purpose for our individual lives. And our lives are meaningfully placed against the backdrop of the grand story of the Bible—creation, fall, redemption, and restoration.[27]

---

22. Linehan (2015).
23. Ross (2006).
24. Linehan (2015).
25. Ross (2006).
26. Keltner and Haidt (2003).
27. Wolters (2005).

Christians' belief in God's providence—his benevolent, governing care extended to all of his vast, beautiful, mystifying creation—captures a major difference between Christian and secular versions of worshipful awe. Whereas Christians look to a (paradoxically) vast, incomprehensible, unknowable God who is also infinitely good, powerful, knowable, and personally guiding his creation (see, e.g., Exod. 15:6; 34:6), many non-Christians seem to have no such sovereign, benevolent, personal deity to turn to for awe. Instead, lesser, creation worship may be relied on as the vehicle through which awe is cultivated in a purely natural world. This lesser worshipful awe, from a Christian viewpoint, will never truly satiate the human soul, whether psychologically or spiritually. The worldview of materialism, often embraced within the scientific discipline of psychology,[28] offers no deity or higher power as the source of all that is awe-triggering. Worded differently, there is no awe of God, only awe of his creation divorced from him. And this era of disenchantment, to borrow again from the Christian philosopher Charles Taylor mentioned in chapter 1,[29] is making us miserable, both psychologically and spiritually.

To better understand what this relational, worshipful, God-centered awe looks like, we can turn to, more narrowly, the Son, Jesus Christ, and his daily life documented in the New Testament.[30] We can also look to, more generally, the grand narrative of the Bible to get a better sense of God's overall plan. Because God is big and we are small, awe is a God-given relational emotion that signals a contrast between our smallness and his bigness. Awe also signals our cognitive, mental need to adjust on a moment-by-moment basis to the reality that he is at the center of all (Col. 1:17). In other words, vastness and the need to accommodate (due to our inability to fully understand him)[31] are foundational to what it means to be a relationally driven worshiper of God. Worship is, thus, the vehicle through which we can cultivate an adoring, grateful awe before God that is applied to *all* our interpersonal life. Before exploring the exercises in this chapter, let us attempt to better understand social awe triggers in psychology.

A Psychological Perspective

Theory

From a psychological viewpoint, awe, including the key components of vastness and mystery and the need (and subsequent attempt) to mentally

---

28. Slife et al. (2017).
29. Taylor (2007).
30. McConnell (2021).
31. Keltner and Haidt (2003).

alter beliefs to make room for the new experience, can be triggered by relationships with God and others.[32] This pursuit of socially triggered awe may occur through the medium of worship, which is often unacknowledged. This is especially true if worship is considered "reverence or adoration for a divine or supernatural being [or person]."[33] In other words, we may end up worshiping others, not God, based on their beauty, talents, skills, virtues, and leadership abilities, with limited insight into this psychological and spiritual reality. Since the actual word "worship" in many contemporary circles is used in a pejorative manner (e.g., when an adolescent accuses a peer of worshiping a dating partner because the new couple is spending too much time together), we may not have good insight into our regular use of this awe-inducing mechanism.

For Christians, this is central, given awe is a God-given relational signal. It tells us we are small, he is big, and we need to adjust our finite, limited understanding of our place and purpose in the world to make room for the reality that God is at the center of all of creation. Because God is infinitely good, wise, powerful, present, and holy, we can celebrate this with gratitude. When this happens, our sense of self may be reduced, referred to as the "small self." This can help us to pivot from the self-preoccupations (e.g., rumination, worry) that commonly give rise to mental symptoms and disorders (e.g., depressive, anxiety related, trauma related) to focusing on someone else's talents, skills, virtues, and so forth.[34] For Christians, these talents can be traced back to God and God's common grace.

Regarding social awe triggers,[35] there are at least two major categories, including awe of God and awe of others, which are pursued through the medium of worship.[36] First, the experience of God can be a social trigger for awe, referred to as "supernatural causality," meaning our "perception that God or some other supernatural entity is manifesting itself . . . [which] can be glorious if the entity is perceived as benevolent."[37] Some individuals, whether religious or nonreligious, may believe that waiting for God to appear in visual or audible form is needed to experience awe of him. However, God's providence—when we look at God's activity in the world more closely—is evident in all of creation.[38] Awareness of this reality can give rise to a sort of providence-triggered social awe of him.

32. Keltner and Haidt (2003).
33. American Psychological Association (n.d.g).
34. Bai et al. (2017).
35. Keltner and Haidt (2003); Shiota et al. (2014).
36. Wolterstorff (2021).
37. Keltner and Haidt (2003), 306.
38. See Matt. 6:25–34, wherein Jesus points to God's daily care of the birds and flowers.

Second, the experience or observation of others can be a social trigger for awe. Such experiences may include being led by an inspirational, powerful, influential leader.[39] Or, we may observe an extraordinary human talent or skill (e.g., an athlete completing a game-winning play, a magician performing a death-defying magic trick, a musician singing a popular song to a sold-out stadium of fans).[40] As another example, we may watch someone display human virtue (e.g., a selfless, compassionate act, such as donating extensive time or money toward another).[41] Finally, we may observe human beauty (e.g., physical attractiveness, whether sexual or nonsexual).[42]

Research

In terms of research on awe of God as a social trigger, among a sample of US adults, researchers found that awe of God (e.g., seeing God as the creator of life's beauty, struggling to understand God's mysterious universe, being amazed by God's power and wisdom) was positively related to life satisfaction (e.g., not wanting to change life, believing one is currently living their "best years").[43] This relationship was mediated by a sense of connection with other people (e.g., recognizing the need for other people, acknowledging a "common bond" with other people). This finding suggests that, theoretically, awe of God may increase a sense of interpersonal relatedness, which, in turn, might improve a general sense of satisfaction with life.

As another example, with a sample of US adults, a study illuminated that awe of God was positively linked to life satisfaction and negatively related to symptoms of depression.[44] This awe–life satisfaction connection was explained, or mediated, by meaning in life. This finding suggests that, theoretically, awe may help people to experience greater satisfaction with life by offering meaning in life.

Regarding research on awe of others, among a sample of online adults, researchers assigned participants to one of three groups.[45] These groups consisted of an awe group that was asked to think about and write on awe toward a person, an awe group that was asked to think about and write on awe in nature, and a neutral group that was asked to think about and write on a happy time, not awe. Each participant was also given an awe measure. Results

---

39. Keltner and Haidt (2003); Shiota et al. (2014).
40. Keltner and Haidt (2003); Shiota et al. (2014).
41. Keltner and Haidt (2003); Shiota et al. (2014).
42. Keltner and Haidt (2003); Shiota et al. (2014).
43. Krause and Hayward (2015a).
44. Upenieks and Krause (2024).
45. Graziosi and Yaden (2021).

revealed that those in the relational awe group reported more awe than the neutral group. Follow-up questions were asked among the nature and relationship awe groups to better understand the awe triggers they experienced. About one-third of the relationship group disclosed that they were in awe of another person because of the virtue or character the other person displayed.

To offer one more example, researchers recruited college students from Chinese and US universities, asking them to document potential daily awe experiences over the course of two weeks.[46] Results revealed that almost one-third of the Chinese sample and about one-half of the US sample disclosed themes of relational awe during the designated time. This finding suggests this unique type of awe may be common in daily life. What is more, researchers recorded participants' experience of the small self (that is, a "diminished perceived self-size") when they documented feeling either awe or joy for the day.[47] Findings illuminated that they felt a more reduced sense of self when they reported feeling awe, more so than joy. This suggests that awe may lead to a reduced self-size (e.g., being less preoccupied with the self, experiencing a transcendent sense of self).

To summarize this psychological discussion on social awe triggers, we may experience vastness, mystery, and the need to accommodate previously held beliefs and assumptions in our interactions with both God and others.[48] This may be especially true when we believe we have had a direct experience of God or observed effective, out of the ordinary leadership, talents, skills, or virtues among those around us. When we do so, awe may be enhanced and prolonged, which can help to cultivate less self-preoccupation (via the small self) and a sense of connectedness. In turn, we can pivot from self-preoccupations toward others. This shift may promote mental and spiritual health by allowing us to see that there is more to life than our limited understanding and that the bigness of the world can offer meaning and purpose.[49] Still, for Christians, God is to be acknowledged as the Source (see, e.g., Col. 1:17). This means that an integrative perspective on the topic will inevitably be God-centered at all times.

An Integrative Perspective

In terms of an integrative perspective, Christian worship begins and ends with God, who is the Creator and Sustainer of all. He is the ultimate Source

---

46. Bai et al. (2017), 187.
47. Bai et al. (2017), 187.
48. Keltner and Haidt (2003).
49. Monroy and Keltner (2023).

of the sense of vastness and need for accommodation[50] that characterizes the psychological, spiritual, and moral emotion of awe. God is invariably at the center of the immense beauty and mystery of *all* of life. As a result, he should be regularly and fittingly acknowledged as such, with all honor and praise due to him. For Christians, to be in an authentic, personal relationship with the living God will inevitably lead to an array of social/relational/interpersonal awe triggers. To be close to God means we will experience how grand and mysterious he is. Consequently, we will not be able to fully understand him and his providential ways. There is a mystery to God's providence that we can, as followers of Jesus Christ, yield to and trust in to enrich and enhance daily life.[51] This is because God is infinitely good, wise, powerful, and present. Combined, this means he wants what is best for us, chooses what is best from all available options, and has the power to carry out what is best.[52] He does so while remaining personally present in our life.[53]

For instance, many Christians believe in "divine simplicity." This is the theological notion that God is "absolute" and "without parts."[54] For such Christians, there is still a struggle to fully understand, with our finite human minds, how God's many attributes (e.g., God is infinitely good, wise, powerful, present, and holy) are actually identical and the same, since "there is nothing in God that is not God."[55] This immense mystery and incomprehensibility can give rise to awe of God. Yet, when we end up pursuing awe by adoring and revering the self, others, or things, which involves lesser, creation worship, this might give rise to added misery. This misery may be experienced because these finite, imperfect sources will never truly satiate our psychological and spiritual need for a more enduring, sustaining, dispositional worshipful awe.[56]

In the context of social triggers, humans were created in the image of God, to be in relationship with him and others,[57] and God's common grace extends to even secular communities.[58] This means that Christians should be, first and foremost, in awe of God, who is perfect. Only then can we be in awe of others, whom God has gifted with beauty, talents, skills, accomplishments, and virtues. With this understanding in mind—social awe triggers, pursued through the medium of worship, should inevitably point us back to God—let

50. Keltner and Haidt (2003).
51. Flavel (2011).
52. Flavel (2011).
53. Flavel (2011).
54. Dolezal (2011).
55. Dolezal (2011), 2.
56. Beale (2008).
57. Miller (2011).
58. Kuyper (2010).

us now turn to the exercises for the chapter to cultivate worshipful awe of God via God-given relational/social triggers.

Daily Log

Instead of being socially triggered by Creator awe, including a widespread recognition of God's attributes, actions, promises, and providential care, we may be vulnerable to pursuing lesser, creation awe in our relationships with others. When it comes to social triggers, we might end up worshiping, whether we realize it or not, a strong, influential leader. We may also worship someone on social media or in our personal lives who has unique talents, skills, and abilities. Or, as another example, we may worship a fellow human being who displays, on either a one-time basis or frequently, virtues or moral character that stands out. Unfortunately, when we inevitably experience the relational emotion of awe, we can end up forgetting to thank the Source, the triune God, who is the Creator and Sustainer of all. Because of this ubiquitous human vulnerability to worship, in reverential awe, our fellow humans, it can be beneficial to identify when we are pursuing lesser, creation (i.e., person) awe and need to shift to greater, Creator awe.

In this first exercise for chapter 6 (consistent with chaps. 4 and 5), try to log during six chosen time periods on a selected day the types of social/relational, creation, "person" triggers (and corresponding behaviors) that you ended up pursuing to induce the emotion of awe. I've included a sample chart with an example for the morning.

Once you have completed the exercise, try to journal for a brief period on a separate paper. Jot down the patterns, in terms of behaviors, that emerged. Also record the costs of being preoccupied with (or maybe even worshiping) the gifted, talented, attractive people of the world in an attempt to feel awe.

- What patterns did you notice, in terms of your behaviors toward these individuals? Are these results surprising? Why or why not?
- What is the spiritual impact, in terms of your relationship with God, in being preoccupied with (or maybe even worshiping) other people?
- What is the psychological impact, in terms of your mental health (e.g., thoughts, feelings, behaviors), in being preoccupied with (or maybe even worshiping) other people?

Now that you have had the opportunity to identify some of the behaviors that may be distracting you from worshipful awe of God, I'd like us to begin

Time	Others
Morning	I chose to watch a TED Talk influencer describe how to live "the good life." As I watched, I couldn't help but feel awe toward this dynamic, articulate speaker. The speaker had a commanding presence on stage and captured, in easy-to-understand language, the needed steps to find happiness. Over the course of the twenty-minute episode, I found myself captivated by their intellectual gifts (including the ability to articulate complex material in a straightforward way), their physical attractiveness and sense of fashion, and their relational skills (including their well-timed use of humor). However, upon finishing the talk, which I eagerly watched on my iPhone, I realized that I had spent no time with God, the Creator and Sustainer of all. I also had not thanked God for giving this gifted speaker the skill set to deliver such a moving message. Instead, I attributed the awe-inducing talents to the influencer alone. Turning off my phone, I prayed to God. I thanked him for pursuing a relationship. I also thanked him for reminding me, through the Holy Spirit, that he is always present and extending grace to even TED Talk influencers, whether I intentionally seek him out or not.
Midmorning	
Noon	
Afternoon	
Evening	
Bedtime	

to practice several exercises. These exercises are designed to help you, as a Christian, shift from awe of created others to awe of the Creator God as you further explore your relationship with him (and, through him, the talents, skills, and abilities of others). Among the first two exercises, I'd like us to meditate on both God's creation and God's providence, illuminated in the sixteenth-century Belgic Confession.

EXERCISE: Meditating on God's Creation

The Belgic Confession was written in the 1500s as a Protestant doctrine to capture biblical beliefs about God, the Bible, humanity, sin, and, ultimately, Jesus Christ.[59] Jesus is the one whom Christians believe in and follow to be reconciled to God and attain eternal life.[60] In the twenty-first century, Protestants continue to look to the confession's concise, biblically supported summaries and explanations for a range of theological topics, which all point the reader to Jesus Christ.[61]

For this exercise,[62] I would like us to draw inspiration from the first two steps of *lectio divina*, reading and meditating—or, to use a food metaphor, biting and chewing. We will be reading and meditating on "Article 12: The Creation of All Things" within the Belgic Confession. Upon doing so, my hope is for us to engage in Creator worship to socially trigger awe before God. Therefore, find a quiet location, free from distractions. Then, when you are ready, follow these directions.

1. Say a short prayer to God. Ask him to be with you during this time and reveal himself to you, including his vastness and mystery.
2. Slowly, gently, and internally read "Article 12: The Creation of All Things" within the Belgic Confession as you attend to God. This portion of the text has been slightly modified to be personally directed to you in contemporary English.

> I believe that the Father, by the Word, that is, by his Son, has created of nothing, the heavens, the earth, and all creatures, as it seemed good to him, giving to every creature, including me, its being, shape, form, and several offices to serve its Creator. That he does also still uphold and govern every creature, including me, by his eternal providence,

---

59. Protestant Reformed Churches in America (n.d.).
60. Protestant Reformed Churches in America (n.d.).
61. See, e.g., Horton (2011). See also Fairbairn and Reeves (2019).
62. Eagle and Amster (2023); Guigo II (2012); Keltner and Haidt (2003); Protestant Reformed Churches in America (n.d.).

and infinite power, for the service of humankind, to the end that humankind may serve our God.[63]

3. Identify a smaller, modified portion of the text: "God upholds and governs every creature." Slowly, gently, and internally repeat it to conjure up relational, worshipful awe for who God is as Creator and Sustainer.
4. Whenever another thought, feeling, sensation, memory, or image inevitably arises within, simply acknowledge it (e.g., "There's 'criticism'"). Then, ever so gently, return to the phrase, "God upholds and governs every creature," as you worship God in reverential awe.
5. Expand your worship experience by thanking God for "upholding and governing every creature." Rest, with gratitude and praise, in the reality that God's proverbial hand guides all his creation. Thank him for being a benevolent King who cares for his creation with a deep love that only a parent can provide.
6. As the practice ends, pray once more to God. Ask him to remind you of his powerful hand in creation throughout the day.

Upon concluding the exercise, try to process your experience by journaling on a separate paper with the questions below.

- What was it like to move through "Article 12," acknowledging God as the Creator? How well were you able to focus your attention on and worship God in reverential awe within the meditative practice?
- What feelings came up as you acknowledged God as the Creator? How well were you able to cultivate a thankful awe before him?
- What distractions, if any, got in the way of acknowledging God as the Creator? Thoughts about the self? Others? Things?
- How can you integrate this meditative practice into daily life so you can continue to intentionally worship God with thankful wonder?

EXERCISE: Meditating on God's Providence

For this next exercise,[64] I would like us to draw inspiration, once again, from the first two steps of *lectio divina*, reading and meditating—or, to use a food metaphor, biting and chewing. As in the last exercise, we will be reading and

---

63. Protestant Reformed Churches in America (n.d.).
64. Eagle and Amster (2023); Guigo II (2012); Keltner and Haidt (2003); Protestant Reformed Churches in America (n.d.).

meditating on one of the articles from the Belgic Confession, this time "Article 13: The Doctrine of God's Providence." When completing this meditative practice, we will be continuing to pursue Creator worship to socially trigger awe before God. Therefore, once more, find a quiet location, free from distractions. Then, when you are ready, slowly follow along with the directions below.

1. Say a short prayer to God. Ask him to be with you during this time and reveal himself to you, including his vastness and mysterious providential care.
2. Slowly, gently, and internally read "Article 13: The Doctrine of God's Providence" within the Belgic Confession as you attend to God. This selected text has been slightly modified so it is personally directed to you in contemporary English.

> I believe that the same God, after he had created all things, did not forsake them, or give them up to fortune or chance, but that he rules and governs them according to his holy will, so that nothing happens in this world without his appointment: nevertheless, God neither is the author of, nor can be charged with, the sins which are committed. For his power and goodness are so great and incomprehensible, that he orders and executes his work in the most excellent and just manner, even then, when devils and wicked people act unjustly. And, as to what he does surpassing human understanding, I will not curiously inquire into, farther than my capacity will admit of; but with the greatest humility and reverence adore the righteous judgments of God, which are hid from me, contenting myself that I am a disciple of Christ, to learn only those things which he has revealed to me in his Word, without transgressing these limits. This doctrine affords me unspeakable consolation, since I am taught that nothing can befall me by chance, but by the direction of my most gracious and heavenly Father; who watches over me with a paternal care, keeping all creatures so under his power, that not a hair of my head (for they are all numbered), nor a sparrow, can fall to the ground, without the will of my Father, in whom I do entirely trust; being persuaded, that he so restrains the devil and all my enemies, that without his will and permission, they cannot hurt me.[65]

3. Take a smaller, modified portion of the text: "My most gracious and heavenly Father watches over me with a paternal care." Slowly, gently, and internally repeat it to conjure up relational, worshipful awe for who God is as the Creator, Sustainer, and Provider.

65. Protestant Reformed Churches in America (n.d.).

4. Whenever another thought, feeling, sensation, memory, or image inevitably arises within, simply acknowledge it (e.g., "There's 'worry'"). Then, ever so gently, return to the phrase, "My most gracious and heavenly Father watches over me with a paternal care," as you worship God in reverential awe.
5. Expand your worship experience by thanking God for his providence. Rest, with gratitude and praise, in the reality that God's governing hand guides all of his creation. Thank him for being a benevolent King who cares for his creation with a deep, guiding love that only a wise parent can provide.
6. As the practice ends, pray once more to God. Ask him to remind you of his providence, extended to all of creation, throughout the day.

After finishing the exercise, try to further explore your psychological and spiritual experience by journaling on a separate paper with the questions below.

- What was it like to move through "Article 13," acknowledging God's providence? How well were you able to focus your attention on and worship God in reverential awe within the meditative practice?
- What feelings came up as you acknowledged God's providence? How well were you able to cultivate a thankful awe before him?
- What distractions, if any, got in the way of acknowledging God's providence? Thoughts about the self? Others? Things?
- How can you integrate this meditative practice into daily life so you can continue to intentionally worship God with thankful wonder and see his providence in all of creation?

Building on these two exercises, I would like us to now focus on God's many blessings and Jesus's love through two additional psychological and spiritual practices/disciplines.[66] These next practices will be reliant on Puritan meditation.

EXERCISE: Meditating on God's Gifts

Returning to the topic of Puritan meditation, presented as an exercise in chapter 4, I would like us to focus on God's many blessings to cultivate worshipful awe before him. We will be drawing on the Puritan Thomas Watson's

---

66. See Watson (2012) for these two meditative topics, among many others.

work, *A Treatise Concerning Meditation*, and his concise definition, steps, and topics for Christian meditative practice.[67]

According to Watson, meditation is "[1] the soul's retiring of itself, that [2] by a serious and solemn thinking upon God, [3] the heart may be raised up to heavenly affections."[68] With these three ingredients, embedded in his concise definition, Christians are engaging in several tasks. First, we are spending time with God in solitude, silence, and intimacy, free from the distractions of the world, to cultivate a deeper communion with God as Creator, Sustainer, and Redeemer.[69] Second, we are focusing on, attending to, and thinking deeply about God, a sort of "staying of the thoughts upon the object" that is God.[70] Finally, we are conjuring up a positive emotional experience, what the Puritans called "raising of the heart to holy affections."[71]

Topic-wise, Watson advocated for meditating on a range of content areas, such as God's attributes (e.g., infinite wisdom, Ps. 147:5), promises (e.g., God will never leave his people, Deut. 31:8), Jesus's love (Eph. 3:18–19), and daily blessings (Num. 6:24–26).

In the context of worship and the God-given relational emotion of awe and anchored to Watson's insights, in the next exercise I'd like us to focus on spending time with God in solitude. We will be thinking deeply about his blessings and cultivating an adoring awe of him, since he generously provides on a moment-by-moment basis.

In a similar vein, for the contemporary pastor and author John Piper, who has drawn heavily from the Puritans in his twenty-first-century writings, the worship of God inevitably leads to an emotional experience of delight and gives rise to the affections: "Without the engagement of the heart, we do not really worship. The engagement of the heart in worship is the coming alive of the feelings and emotions and affections of the heart."[72]

Turning back to Watson, God's blessings and gifts may include, among others, protecting you, remaining patient with you amid your daily struggles with sin, and offering you grace, or undeserved favor or merit.[73]

---

67. Watson (2014).
68. Watson (2014), 1.
69. Watson (2014).
70. Watson (2014), 1–2.
71. Watson (2014), 1–2. It should be noted that, for the Puritans, affections were not *just* feelings or emotions, since they more broadly elucidated a person's drives, consisting of the heart and will. Still, there is some overlap between the term *affections*, widely used in their writings from centuries ago, and a contemporary understanding of feelings or emotions. In other words, they did have "emotional overtones," such as "love, hope, hate, fear, and so on" (Packer, 2010), 195. See also Van Engen (2015).
72. Piper (2011), 87.
73. Watson (2014).

So, in this ten-minute exercise,[74] I'd like us to practice Watson's three-step meditative exercise within the context of God's many blessings, favors, gifts, graces, and mercies. These are poured out abundantly in daily life. These key steps include spending time with God alone in silence, focusing the mind on God, and cultivating the feeling of awe before him in response to his many blessings in daily life.

To start, find a quiet location, free from distractions. Sit up straight in a supportive chair. Then, when you are ready, follow along with the steps below.

1. Say a short prayer to God, in solitude, silence, and intimacy before him. Ask that he reveal himself to you as a personal God who offers his many blessings on a daily basis.
2. Slowly read James 1:17 to draw biblical inspiration from God's Word: "Every good and perfect gift is from above, coming down from the Father of the heavenly lights, who does not change like shifting shadows."
3. Attend to God. Focus on a shorter portion of James 1:17: "Every good and perfect gift is from above." Say these words slowly, gently, internally, and reverentially. Recognize that God offers an abundance of perfect gifts to you on a moment-by-moment basis.
4. Worship God by feeling the awe that naturally emanates from being in relationship with your personal, unchanging Creator, Sustainer, and Redeemer. Deeply experience the spiritual emotion of awe, which is a God-given signal that tells you he is big and you are small. Awe also tells you that you need to let go of your finite, limited perspective to make room for this vast, incomprehensible, mystifying reality.
5. Enhance your worshipful awe of God by thanking him for every one of his "good and perfect gifts." These gifts are on display in each moment of life, from giving you life itself, to giving you daily food, water, clothing, and shelter, to pursuing a relationship with you. Allow the emotion of awe to "come alive" deep within you to feel the vastness and mystery of God right here and now.
6. Conclude the exercise by asking God to reveal his many blessings and gifts to you throughout the rest of the day and beyond as you stand in worshipful awe before him as your benevolent King, who providentially provides repeatedly.

---

74. Eagle and Amster (2023); Piper (2011); Watson (2014).

Christian Worship and Awe with Relationships 187

After concluding the exercise, try to reflect on the experience by journaling on a separate paper with the following questions:

- What was it like to meditate on God's gifts and blessings? How well were you able to focus your attention on God via the selected Bible verse?
- What feelings came up as you engaged in the practice? How well were you able to cultivate awe before God?
- What distractions, if any, got in the way of worshipful awe before God? Thoughts about the self? Others? Things?
- How can you integrate this practice into daily life so you can draw on God's Word to worship him in reverential awe?

EXERCISE: Meditating on Jesus's Love

As the second of two exercises that draw on Watson's three-step meditative process,[75] I'd like us to now focus on Jesus's love as a social trigger for worshipful awe before God. According to Watson, Jesus's love is "transcendent" (i.e., it rises above mere human love), "sovereign" (i.e., it is all-powerful), "invincible" (i.e., it endures forever), and "immutable" (i.e., it does not change).[76] Because of this, as Christ followers, we should worship him in reverential, thankful awe on a moment-by-moment basis. We should also recognize that his love far surpasses any human love we could ever hope or wish for in a fallen, self-absorbed world.

So, with this ten-minute exercise,[77] I'd like us to return to Watson's three-step meditative exercise, this time within the context of Jesus's perfect love. We will be (a) spending time with the God of love alone in silence, (b) focusing the mind on the God of love, and (c) cultivating the feeling of awe before him in response to Jesus's transcendent, sovereign, invincible, and immutable love, readily available to his followers, who have a personal relationship with him.

To start, once more, find a quiet location, free from distractions. Sit up straight in a supportive chair. Then, when you are ready, follow along with the steps below.

1. Say a short prayer to Jesus, in solitude, silence, and intimacy before him. Ask that he reveal himself to you as the Son of God who offers his perfect love daily.

75. Watson (2014), 9–10.
76. Watson (2014).
77. Eagle and Amster (2023); Piper (2011); Watson (2014).

2. Slowly read John 15:9 to draw biblical inspiration from Jesus's direct words, capturing his love for you: "As the Father has loved me, so have I loved you. Now remain in my love."
3. Attend to Jesus, focusing in on a shorter portion of John 15:9: "Remain in my love." Say these words slowly, gently, internally, and reverentially. Recognize that Jesus offers you his transcendent, sovereign, invincible, and immutable love on a moment-by-moment basis.
4. Worship Jesus by feeling the awe that naturally emanates from being in relationship with him as your personal Redeemer. Deeply experience the spiritual emotion of awe, which is a signal that tells you Jesus is big, you are small, and you need to let go of your finite, limited perspective to make room for this vast, incomprehensible, mysterious reality, anchored to love.
5. Enhance your worshipful awe of Jesus by thanking him for offering his perfect love on full display by laying down his life for you to relationally reconcile you to God (John 3:16). Allow the emotion of awe to come alive deep within you to feel the vastness and mystery of Jesus right here and now.
6. Conclude the exercise by asking Jesus to reveal his love to you throughout the rest of the day and beyond as you stand in worshipful awe before him as your benevolent King, who lovingly provides.

Upon finishing this exercise, attempt to reflect on the experience by journaling on a separate paper with the following questions:

- What was it like to meditate on Jesus's love for you? How well were you able to focus your attention on him via the selected Bible verse?
- What feelings came up as you engaged in the practice? How well were you able to cultivate awe before Jesus?
- What distractions, if any, got in the way of worshipful awe before Jesus? Thoughts about the self? Others? Things?
- How can you integrate this practice into daily life so you can draw on God's Word to worship him in reverential awe?

EXERCISE: Meditating on Jesus's Resurrection

Ignatius of Loyola was a Spanish priest who lived in the 1500s and wrote *Spiritual Exercises* (mentioned in chap. 4). This famous work is a collection of meditation, prayer, and contemplation practices spread out across a four-week retreat format, to be facilitated by a designated spiritual director.[78] The goal of the various mental and spiritual skills is to help Christian practitioners integrate the mind and heart, cultivate a deeper relationship with the triune God, and elucidate God's will in daily life.[79]

The fourth week's theme involves focusing on Jesus's resurrection. This theme illuminates, among other concepts, Jesus as the Son of God, the apostles' increased boldness and unwavering faith to share the gospel message postresurrection, and Christians' confidence that we, too, will conquer death and be with Jesus in heaven.[80] Most importantly, in heaven, we will be loved by, and love, him for eternity.[81]

Among the various activities of the fourth week is one that is simply titled "Exercise on the Love of God."[82] With this activity, Ignatius asks participants to meditate (that is, think deeply about, ponder, and ruminate on) on three "benefits of God," creation, redemption, and God's providence.[83] With the first, creation, we are to meditate on "all the natural gifts—the soul with its powers, the body with its senses, life with the good things that accompany it."[84] For the second, redemption, we are tasked with meditating on God's grace, or undeserved merit or favor extended to humankind.[85] His grace is displayed via the reconciling act of Jesus's suffering, death, and resurrection.[86] With the third, providence, we are to consider all the ways that God's parental care is displayed in life, including within the context of the cross, which is God's ultimate act of loving reconciliation.[87]

After instructing participants to meditate on these three benefits, Ignatius offers a powerful prayer for us to recite, which fittingly captures the reality that God is big, we are small, and we owe God everything because we "have nothing" on our own:

> Take, O Lord, and receive my entire liberty, my memory, my understanding, and my whole will. All that I am, all that I have, you have given me, and I give it back again to you, to be disposed of according

78. Ignatian Spirituality (n.d.).
79. Ignatius of Loyola (1999).
80. Ignatius of Loyola (1999).
81. Ignatius of Loyola (1999).
82. Ignatius of Loyola (1999), 180.
83. Ignatius of Loyola (1999), 180.
84. Ignatius of Loyola (1999), 180.
85. Ignatius of Loyola (1999).
86. Ignatius of Loyola (1999).
87. Ignatius of Loyola (1999).

to your good pleasure. Give me only your love and your grace: with these I am rich enough.[88]

With these three meditative steps and Ignatius's concluding prayer in mind, let us now turn to a meditation exercise[89] to cultivate worshipful awe of God as *the* Redeemer. Before starting, try to find a quiet location, free from distractions, and sit up straight in a supportive chair. Then, when you are ready, follow along with the steps below.

1. Say a short prayer to God, asking him to reveal the awe-inducing benefits of the cross, both psychological and spiritual, including God's redemptive act to reconcile you to him.
2. Meditate on (i.e., focus all your undivided attention on) the reality that God created you and offered you a body and life itself. Slowly, gently, and internally repeat the passage, "For you created my inmost being; you knit me together in my mother's womb. I praise you because I am fearfully and wonderfully made; your works are wonderful, I know that full well" (Ps. 139:13–14). Then, deepen your worship by saying just the word "creation" a few times. Do so slowly, softly, gently, and internally to capture the awe-inducing reality that God created you and gave you a rich, full, and amazing life.
3. Meditate on the reality that God redeemed you as the ultimate act of grace. He saved you from eternal separation from him. He offered you eternal life via Jesus's loving act on the cross. Slowly, gently, and internally repeat the passage,

> Praise be to the God and Father of our Lord Jesus Christ, who has blessed us in the heavenly realms with every spiritual blessing in Christ. For he chose us in him before the creation of the world to be holy and blameless in his sight. In love he predestined us for adoption to sonship through Jesus Christ, in accordance with his pleasure and will—to the praise of his glorious grace, which he has freely given us in the One he loves. In him we have redemption through his blood, the forgiveness of sins, in accordance with the riches of God's grace that he lavished on us. With all wisdom and understanding, he made known to us the mystery of his will according to his good pleasure, which he purposed in Christ, to be put into effect when the times reach

---

88. Ignatius of Loyola (1999), 181. I have slightly modified the prayer with more contemporary English.
89. Eagle and Amster (2023); Ignatius of Loyola (1999).

their fulfillment—to bring unity to all things in heaven and on earth under Christ. (Eph. 1:3–10)

Then, deepen your worship by saying just the word "redemption" a few times. Do so slowly, softly, gently, and internally to capture the awe-inducing reality that God has saved you and reconciled you to him.

4. Meditate on the reality that God has providentially provided for you daily and will continue to do so. This reality includes the notion that he has reconciled you to him via Jesus's sacrificial act on the cross. Slowly, gently, and internally repeat the passage,

> In him we were also chosen, having been predestined according to the plan of him who works out everything in conformity with the purpose of his will, in order that we, who were the first to put our hope in Christ, might be for the praise of his glory. (Eph. 1:11–12)

Then, deepen your worship by saying just the word "chosen" a few times. Do so slowly, gently, and internally to capture the awe-inducing reality that God has purposefully and providentially selected you to be reconciled to him via the atoning work of his Son, Jesus Christ.

5. Enhance your worshipful awe of God as Redeemer by concluding with Ignatius's prayer. This prayer captures your gratitude to God for redeeming you and reconciling you to him via Jesus's amazing, wondrous work on the cross:

> Take, O Lord, and receive my entire liberty, my memory, my understanding, and my whole will. All that I am, all that I have, you have given me, and I give it back again to you, to be disposed of according to your good pleasure. Give me only your love and your grace: with these I am rich enough.

After concluding this exercise, try to process the experience by journaling on a separate paper with the following questions:

- What was it like to meditate on Jesus's redemptive act? How well were you able to focus your attention on Jesus's redemption via the selected Bible verses?
- What feelings came up as you engaged in the practice? How well were you able to cultivate awe before Jesus?
- What distractions, if any, got in the way of worshipful awe before Jesus? Thoughts about the self? Others? Things?

- How can you integrate this practice into daily life so you can draw on God's Word to worship him in reverential awe?

EXERCISE: Jesus Prayer

The Jesus Prayer (mentioned briefly in chap. 4 in the section on *lectio divina*) is a short prayer, "Lord Jesus Christ, have mercy on me,"[90] which is popular within the Orthodox Church. It slowly developed over the last two millennia, first within a monastic context. It is potentially inspired by Paul's teaching to "pray continually" (1 Thess. 5:17) and the many instances in the Gospels that involve people asking Jesus for mercy (Mark 10:47).[91] Upon calling to Jesus for mercy, practitioners are asking for his compassionate, healing, loving-kindness, not merely petitioning him to withhold punishment and show leniency,[92] as is the case with some definitions of "mercy."[93] Common goals of this classic Christian prayer include (1) asking Jesus for soothing, loving comfort; (2) using the psychological skill of repetition to focus the mind on Jesus (and away from repetitive, distracting, unhelpful thoughts); (3) cultivating an inner peace, concentration, quiet, and stillness; and (4) honoring and calling upon Jesus's holy, awe-inducing name, which is worthy of our worship and adoration.[94]

Within the context of worshipful awe with social/relational triggers, this timeless, concise prayer can help us to, throughout the day, worship God in reverential, thankful awe. We can focus the mind on him with sustained, purposeful attention as we journey through his creation to get to our destination and home—to be face-to-face with him in heaven. For this next exercise, we'll simply be reciting the Jesus Prayer to cultivate worshipful, adoring, thankful awe toward Jesus as our Redeemer. He is the great High Priest who empathizes with our human struggles (Heb. 4:14–16), has reconciled us to God (2 Cor. 5:18–20), and magnificently holds all of creation together (Col. 1:17).

So, for this next exercise,[95] try to, once more, find a quiet location, free from distractions. Sit up straight in a supportive chair with your hands resting in your lap. Then, when you are ready, follow along with the directions below.

---

90. Other versions include a longer form, "Lord Jesus Christ, Son of God, have mercy on me, a sinner," as well as a much shorter one, "Lord Jesus, have mercy," or even the name "Jesus" by itself. Regardless, the most important part is that the name "Jesus" is included. See Gillet (1985).
91. For a history of the Jesus Prayer, see, e.g., Brianchaninov (2006).
92. Ware (2014).
93. Merriam-Webster (n.d.).
94. Ware (2014).
95. Eagle and Amster (2023); Ware (2014).

1. Say a short prayer to God. Ask that he reveal himself to you as your Redeemer in the immediacy of this very moment.
2. Begin to recite the Jesus Prayer, doing so slowly, gently, and internally: "Lord Jesus Christ, have mercy on me." If you'd like, you can pair the first half with the in-breath and second half with the out-breath. Breathe in "Lord Jesus Christ," and breathe out "have mercy on me." Recognize that God is your Redeemer as you worship him.
3. As you continue to repeat the prayer, rest in the reality that Jesus is comforting and loving you right here and now.
4. Enhance your worshipful awe of Jesus by continuing to say his name, embedded in the prayer, with adoration, reverence, and gratitude. Recognize that he has reconciled you to God via his ultimate redemptive act on the cross: Since Jesus has already extended his compassionate, loving-kindness to you—his redemptive act on the cross is "finished" (John 19:30)—rest in this reality, with thankful praise.
5. Conclude with another short prayer to God. Ask that he remind you throughout the day, via the Jesus Prayer, that he is a God of redemption. He offers you compassion, love, kindness, grace, and mercy in each unfolding moment of the day as you walk and talk with him within his wonderful, awe-inducing creation.

Now that you have finished this prayer practice, attempt to further explore the experience by journaling on a separate paper with the following questions:

- What was it like to recite the Jesus Prayer? How well were you able to focus your attention on Jesus's mercy?
- What feelings came up as you engaged in the practice? How well were you able to cultivate awe before Jesus?
- What distractions, if any, got in the way of worshipful awe before Jesus? Thoughts about the self? Others? Things?
- How can you integrate this practice into daily life so you can worship Jesus in reverential awe?

EXERCISE: Admiring a Human Talent

For the last exercise of this chapter, we will be turning to social/relational awe triggers with others. For Christians, this trigger should inevitably point us back to God, who blesses talented humans with their impressive, exemplary, skillful behavioral displays.

Within the psychology literature, again, awe can be triggered when we appreciate someone else's beauty or talent.[96] This may pertain to physical attractiveness or a skill performed by a family member or friend, celebrity, musician, dancer, or athlete.[97] This experience includes goodness, or excellence.[98] It also includes vastness, given the person's skill is perceived to transcend our own individual sense of self and performance level.[99] Finally, it includes mystery and the need to accommodate, since the observed behavior far surpasses our ability to explain how such a talent could be executed.[100]

From a Christian perspective, "No one is good—except God" (Mark 10:18). Yet, God, who is infinitely good/benevolent/loving, offers *all* communities, on at least some level, grace, or undeserved favors. This means he blesses individuals, families, groups, and cultures with a plethora of talents and skills to better society, even though we are all fallen and imperfect and do not necessarily deserve them.[101] What is more, apart from the human influence of sin, what God has created is good, across both Christian and secular communities, and should be "received with thanksgiving" (1 Tim. 4:4).[102] This means that "God has created a wonderful world to be enjoyed—beauty, order, music, fragrance, and form, among many other delights."[103] Therefore, it is inevitable that we will be amazed by our fellow human beings, both religious and nonreligious alike, across a wide variety of life domains, such as family, work, community, church, and entertainment/leisure/hobbies. Still, when we end up worshiping, with excessive adoration and praise, other humans without attributing the talent, skill, or success to God, we may end up engaging in idol worship, which is prohibited within a biblical worldview.[104]

In this exercise,[105] I would like us to practice experiencing awe of another human being. However, we will be praising *God* for generously and graciously offering this person the talents and skills necessary for us to be amazed. Upon doing so, we will be worshiping God, not the imperfect, finite person we are watching. In preparation for this exercise, try to identify some sort of

---

96. Keltner and Haidt (2003).
97. Keltner and Haidt (2003).
98. Güsewell and Ruch (2012).
99. Güsewell and Ruch (2012).
100. Güsewell and Ruch (2012).
101. Grudem (2020); Treier (2017).
102. Although the context for 1 Tim. 4:4 is food and marriage, the general spiritual lesson appears to be, plainly stated, that God created an amazing world for humans to enjoy. In God's world, there are many blessings, rather than humans seeing the physical/natural world (and our embodied existence within it) solely as evil. See Liefeld (1999).
103. Liefeld (1999), 11.
104. Beale (2008).
105. Eagle and Amster (2023); Keltner and Haidt (2003).

talented entertainer to watch, whether it is a singer, dancer, athlete, influencer, or magician. Then, when you are ready, observe this person as you take the following steps:

1. Say a short prayer to God. Ask him to reveal his grace to you as the source for this individual's talent, skill, or other impressive, standout human behavior.
2. Attend to, and focus on, the behavior. Observe how awe inducing it is to watch the individual perform, with their talent clearly rising above and beyond what the "average" person can accomplish. Notice, in the moment, your experience of both vastness (e.g., the performance seems "larger than life") and mystery (e.g., it is hard to understand how this person could perform in such a way) as you appreciate their skill set. As you do so, most importantly, recognize that God is the Creator and Sustainer of this talented individual. Rightfully acknowledge that God has blessed them with the ability to perform in an awe-inspiring manner.
3. Worship God, not the individual. Recognize that the Creator and Sustainer of all has blessed this performer with the talents and skills to entertain and impress a large audience, which includes you, a spectator. To do so, slowly, gently, and internally recite James 1:17 as you watch the entertainer perform: "Every good and perfect gift is from above . . ."
4. Enhance your worshipful awe of God, through watching this entertainer in the immediacy of the moment, by thanking God for blessing imperfect, fallen humans with immense, wonderful talent. Offer gratitude to God for giving you the opportunity to appreciate *all* his creation, which includes the people he has created to impress and entertain. Continuing to watch the event, slowly, gently, and internally recite 1 Timothy 4:4: "For everything God created is good, and nothing is to be rejected if it is received with thanksgiving."
5. Upon finishing watching the performance, say another short prayer. Ask God to help you recognize God as *the* Source of talent and skill in *all* of life so that you can give him all the glory.

Upon completing this exercise, try to further explore the experience by journaling on a separate paper with the following questions:

- What was it like to worship God by appreciating the talents and skills he has blessed humans with? How well were you able to focus your attention on God as you enjoyed the entertainment?

- What feelings came up as you engaged in the practice? How well were you able to cultivate awe before God?
- What distractions, if any, got in the way of worshipful awe before God? Thoughts about the self? Others? Things?
- How can you integrate this practice into daily life so you can worship God in reverential awe?

Prior to concluding both the chapter and book, I would like to offer biblical and psychotherapy examples to enhance our understanding of worshipful awe of God with social/relational triggers.

A Biblical Example

In 1 Chronicles 29, King David gathers his people together to discuss building Israel's future temple under the direction of Solomon, his son. David models to them the importance and necessity of offering, in generosity, personal resources to build the temple, especially since God is the Source of such resources. Then, he prays to God:

> Praise be to you, LORD,
>   the God of our father Israel,
>   from everlasting to everlasting.
> Yours, LORD, is the greatness and the power
>   and the glory and the majesty and the splendor,
>   for everything in heaven and earth is yours.
> Yours, LORD, is the kingdom;
>   you are exalted as head over all.
> Wealth and honor come from you;
>   you are the ruler of all things.
> In your hands are strength and power
>   to exalt and give strength to all.
> Now, our God, we give you thanks,
>   and praise your glorious name. (1 Chron. 29:10–13)

In this prayer, King David captures the major ingredients of worshipful awe before God as Creator and Sustainer, including the acknowledgment of God as vast and infinitely powerful and present. He also captures an inability to fully comprehend just how great God is. We also have a deep appreciation and gratitude for God as ruler over all his creation. Here, thus, King David has modeled for us worshipful awe, extended to all of life, even within the context of the request for resources to build the temple. Let us now turn to a psychotherapy example of worshipful awe of God within the context of social/relational triggers before ending the chapter.

A Psychotherapy Example

Growing up in the foster care system, Benjamin always struggled to feel loved and valued. At the age of two he was taken from his mother, who struggled to find stable income and housing due to an ongoing problem with methamphetamines. By the time Benjamin reached high school, he had been in almost a dozen different foster care home placements. He experienced verbal and physical abuse in some of these homes. Over time, he began to internalize the verbal abuse. He believed about himself the insults he received from others. Common self-criticisms, which led to frequent shame, included the belief that he was "worthless," "stupid," and "unlovable."

At a few of the foster placements, though, Benjamin was exposed to biblical teachings. He sometimes remembered seeing Bibles around the house and would skim through the contents, unsure of what many of the verses he read meant. Yet, he did recall reading and understanding the Psalms, which presented a God who was loving, powerful, and present (see, e.g., Ps. 89). This began to stir in him a longing to have a direct encounter with this mysterious deity of the Bible.

Then, after exiting the foster care system at the age of eighteen, Benjamin met a group of friends who lived in the same apartment complex he moved into. One of them, Nathan, invited Benjamin to a midweek Bible study at Nathan's apartment, just two doors down from Benjamin's humble studio apartment. Eager to make new friends, Benjamin showed up, unsure of what to expect. After some small talk among the half-dozen people in attendance, the topic turned to God's attributes. These attributes were revealed in the very same Psalms that Benjamin had eagerly read as a child. During the next hour or so, Benjamin cautiously listened to the attendees share about God's infinite love and goodness, which he had longed for in his foster care years. Yet, present day, he still struggled to trust that this God of the Psalms could and would love Benjamin, since he still believed he was worthless and stupid.

This constant struggle to reconcile the God of the Bible with his own life experiences led Benjamin to see a psychotherapist, just down the road from where he lived. Upon entering psychotherapy, he shared with his psychotherapist all the psychological pain he had experienced growing up. Benjamin also frequently struggled with shame, which he reluctantly told the psychotherapist about as he wept, with tears rolling down his face.

After about four or five sessions, he shared with the psychotherapist that he wanted to deepen his relationship with God, whom he desired to trust as infinitely good. Therefore, for the next several sessions, Benjamin worked with his psychotherapist on learning to notice his self-criticism and then shift toward worshipful awe of God by meditating on the Psalms, especially those that elucidated God's infinite love and goodness (e.g., Ps. 89:1).[106] Benjamin's psychotherapist shared with him some of the newer theories and research on awe. This literature suggested that awe was a spiritual emotion that conjured up the experience of vastness and incomprehensibility and the need to adjust previous views and mental models, which could even be experienced in a religious context with God.[107] This perspective, for Benjamin, led to a sizeable mental shift, since he recognized for the first time that he could focus on God, not himself, to transcend his relentless self-criticism.

Over time, Benjamin experienced greater dispositional awe, doing so within the context of singing psalms of worship before God that captured God's goodness, love, wisdom, and power (see, e.g., Ps. 139). For Benjamin, worshipful awe, triggered by his burgeoning relationship with God, helped to offer meaning in life. He now had a purpose.[108] In a fallen world, he learned to pivot away from chronic self-criticism and shame and toward the God of love. This led to Benjamin recognizing that he did not need to constantly find evidence he was worthy of love. Instead, he could shift toward worshiping the God of love in the here and now, which brought him comfort, meaning, purpose, and satisfaction in life.

Conclusion

In summation, awe is a God-given spiritual emotion and relational signal that helps us recognize that God is big, we are small, and we need to make room for this reality, through the medium of worship, adoration, and thanksgiving.[109] This reality has profound implications for our psychological and spiritual health. To fully realize this reality, we need to, moment by moment, pivot from being preoccupied with others (and the self and things), including their talents and skills, to focusing on God. Only the triune God of the Bible is the Creator, Sustainer, and Redeemer of all.

---

106. See Knabb (2021) for a model for Christian meditation in psychotherapy.
107. Upenieks and Krause (2024).
108. Consistent with this experience, see Dai et al. (2022). They found that, among a sample of online Chinese adults, awe influenced purpose in life, which influenced life meaning.
109. Keltner and Haidt (2003).

By engaging in Christian psychological and spiritual practices, our relationship with God can become a social/relational (and cognitive and physical/sensory) trigger, which alerts us to the bigness and mysteriousness of the triune God as Father, Son, and Holy Spirit. Upon engaging in such practices, we are moving toward taking the focus off ourselves, others, and things. We are also cultivating greater meaning and purpose in life and, hopefully, ameliorating psychological suffering along the way. Combined with an awareness of cognitive and physical/sensory triggers, which, for Christians, can be tethered to God at the center of existence, our social triggers can help us to appreciate the grace that God extends to us every day.

To end the book, I leave you, a twenty-first-century Christ follower, with a prayer from the nineteenth-century Christian hymnist Sir John Bowring.

> Almighty One! I bend in dust before Thee;
> Even so veiled cherubs bend;
> In calm and still devotion I adore Thee,
> All-wise, all-present Friend!
>
> Thou to the earth its emerald robes hast given,
> Or curtained it in snow;
> And the bright sun, and the soft moon in heaven,
> Before Thy presence bow.
>
> Thou Power sublime! whose throne is firmly seated
> On stars and glowing suns;
> O, could I praise Thee, could my soul, elated,
> Waft Thee seraphic tones,
> Had I the lyres of angels, could I bring Thee
> An offering worthy Thee,
> In what bright notes of glory would I sing Thee,
> Blest notes of ecstasy!
>
> Eternity! Eternity! how solemn,
> How terrible the sound! Here, leaning on thy promises, a column
> Of strength, may I be found,
> O, let my heart be ever Thine, while beating,
> As when twill cease to beat!
> Be Thou my portion, till that awful meeting
> When I my God shall greet![110]

May you continue to, moment by moment and step by step, pivot from self, other, and thing creation worship to Creator worship. May you also recognize

---

110. Tozer (2016), 20–21.

God's presence in the rich array of God-given cognitive, physical/sensory, and relational triggers. These triggers, for Christians, should remind us that God is vast and immense and mysterious and incomprehensible. Our purpose on this planet, in response to this God-centered reality, is to invariably worship him until we see him, face-to-face, for eternity when we fully realize the awesome beatific vision that awaits us.[111]

---

111. Boersma (2018).

Acknowledgments

I would like to, first and foremost, thank my wife, Adrienne, and children, Emory and Rowan, who inspire me on a daily basis to see the wonder and awe in all of life. Next, I would like to acknowledge Anna Moseley Gissing at Baker Academic, who believed in this project and encouraged me along the way. Finally, I would like to give glory to God, the source of all that is awe inducing.

References

Abernethy, A. (Ed.). (2008). *Worship that changes lives: Multidisciplinary and congregational perspectives on spiritual transformation*. Baker Academic.

Abernethy, A. D., Grannum, G. D., Gordon, C. L., Williamson, R., & Currier, J. M. (2016a). The Pastors Empowerment Program: A resilience education intervention to prevent clergy burnout. *Spirituality in Clinical Practice*, 3(3), 175–186. https://doi.org/10.1037/scp0000109

Abernethy, A. D., Kurian, K. R., Brown, S., Uh, M., Rice, B., & Rold, L. (2016b). Varieties of spiritual experience: A study of closeness to God, struggle, transformation, and confession-forgiveness in communal worship. *Journal of Psychology and Christianity*, 35(1), 9–21.

Abernethy, A. D., Rice, B. E., Rold, L., Kurian, K. R., Grannum, G. D., & Jones, H. (2015). Corporate worship and spiritual formation: Insights from worship leaders. *Journal of Psychology & Christianity*, 34(3), 266–279.

American Psychiatric Association. (2022). *Diagnostic and statistical manual of mental disorders* (5th ed., text rev.). https://doi.org/10.1176/appi.books.9780890425787

American Psychological Association. (n.d.a). Awe. In *APA dictionary of psychology*. Retrieved March 26, 2025. https://dictionary.apa.org/awe

American Psychological Association. (n.d.b). Gratitude. In *APA dictionary of psychology*. Retrieved March 26, 2025. https://dictionary.apa.org/gratitude

American Psychological Association. (n.d.c). Materialism. In *APA dictionary of psychology*. Retrieved March 26, 2025. https://dictionary.apa.org/materialism

American Psychological Association. (n.d.d). Narcissism. In *APA dictionary of psychology*. Retrieved March 26, 2025. https://dictionary.apa.org/narcissism

American Psychological Association. (n.d.e). Religion. In *APA dictionary of psychology*. Retrieved March 26, 2025. https://dictionary.apa.org/religion

American Psychological Association. (n.d.f). Spirituality. In *APA dictionary of psychology*. Retrieved March 26, 2025. https://dictionary.apa.org/spirituality

American Psychological Association. (n.d.g). Worship. In *APA dictionary of psychology*. Retrieved March 26, 2025. https://dictionary.apa.org/worship

Anderson, C. L., Monroy, M., & Keltner, D. (2018). Awe in nature heals: Evidence from military veterans, at-risk youth, and college students. *Emotion, 18*(8), 1195–1202. https://doi.org/10.1037/emo0000442

Anderson, T., Clark, W., & Naugle, D. (2017). *An introduction to Christian worldview: Pursuing God's perspective in a pluralistic world*. InterVarsity.

Andreassen, C. S., Pallesen, S., & Griffiths, M. D. (2017). The relationship between addictive use of social media, narcissism, and self-esteem: Findings from a large national survey. *Addictive Behaviors, 64*, 287–293. https://doi.org/10.1016/j.addbeh.2016.03.006

Andresen, J. (1999). Awe and the transforming of awareness. *Contemporary Psychoanalysis, 35*(3), 507–521. http://dx.doi.org/10.1080/00107530.1999.10746397

Aroney-Sine, C. (2019). *The gift of wonder: Creative practices for delighting in God*. InterVarsity.

Ashe, D. D., Maltby, J., & McCutcheon, L. E. (2005). Are celebrity-worshippers more prone to narcissism? A brief report. *North American Journal of Psychology, 7*(2), 239–246.

Bai, Y., Maruskin, L. A., Chen, S., Gordon, A. M., Stellar, J. E., McNeil, G. D., & Keltner, D. (2017). Awe, the diminished self, and collective engagement: Universals and cultural variations in the small self. *Journal of Personality and Social Psychology, 113*(2), 185–209. https://doi.org/10.1037/pspa0000087

Ball, J. (2016). *A treatise of divine meditation*. Puritan Publications.

Ballew, M. T., & Omoto, A. M. (2018). Absorption: How nature experiences promote awe and other positive emotions. *Ecopsychology, 10*(1), 26–35. https://doi.org/10.1089/eco.2017.0044

Barrett, M. (Ed.). (2017). *Reformation theology: A systematic summary*. Crossway.

Bartlett, John. (Ed.). (2003). Self-absorption. *Bartlett's Roget's Thesaurus*. Hachette Book Group.

Baxter, R. (2017). *Walking with God*. Gideon House Books.

Beale, G. K. (2008). *We become what we worship: A biblical theology of idolatry*. IVP Academic.

Beeke, J., & Jones, M. (2012). *A Puritan theology: Doctrine for life*. Reformation Heritage Books.

Beilby, J., & Eddy, P. (Eds.). (2006). *The nature of the atonement: Four views*. IVP Academic.

Bennett, A. (Ed.). (1975). *The valley of vision: A collection of Puritan prayers & devotions*. Banner of Truth.

Bevere, J. (2023). *The awe of God: The astounding way a healthy fear of God transforms your life*. Nelson.

Bishop, S. R., Lau, M., Shapiro, S., Carlson, L., Anderson, N. D., Carmody, J., & Devins, G. (2004). Mindfulness: A proposed operational definition. *Clinical Psychology: Science and Practice, 11*(3), 230–241. https://doi.org/10.1093/clipsy.bph077

Blatchford, F. (2021). *God of wonders: 40 days of awe in the presence of God*. Chosen Books.

Block, D. (2014). *For the glory of God: Recovering a biblical theology of worship*. Baker Academic.

Blomberg, C., & Crenshaw, B. (2021). Worship: A concept study in New Testament Greek. In B. Forrest, W. Kaiser Jr., & V. Whaley (Eds.), *Biblical worship: Theology for God's glory* (pp. 332–349). Kregel Academic.

Boa, K. (2020). *Conformed to his image: Biblical, practical approaches to spiritual formation*. Zondervan.

Boersma, H. (2018). *Seeing God: The beatific vision in Christian tradition*. Eerdmans.

Bonhoeffer, D. (1959). *Creation and fall*. Touchstone.

Bowe, B. (2003). *Biblical foundations of spirituality: Touching a finger to the flame*. Rowman & Littlefield.

Brianchaninov, I. (2006). *On the prayer of Jesus: The classic guide to the practice of unceasing prayer as found in "The Way of a Pilgrim."* New Seeds Books.

Britannica. (n.d.). Worship. In *Encyclopedia Britannica*. Retrieved March 26, 2025. https://www.britannica.com/topic/worship

Brooks, S. K. (2021). FANatics: Systematic literature review of factors associated with celebrity worship, and suggested directions for future research. *Current Psychology, 40*(2), 864–886. https://doi.org/10.1007/s12144-018-9978-4

Brown, S. (1916). The sex worship and symbolism of primitive races. *The Journal of Abnormal Psychology, 10*(6), 418–432. https://doi.org/10.1037/h0073442

Brueggemann, W. (1984). *The message of the Psalms: A theological commentary*. Augsburg.

Burroughs, J. (2018). *Gospel worship: Or, the right manner of sanctifying the name of God in general, in hearing the Word, receiving the Lord's supper, and prayer*. Puritan Publications.

Burton-Christie, D. (1993). *The Word in the desert: Scripture and the quest for holiness in early Christian monasticism*. Oxford University Press.

Büssing, A. (2021). Wondering Awe as a perceptive aspect of spirituality and its relation to indicators of wellbeing: Frequency of perception and underlying triggers. *Frontiers in Psychology, 12*, 738770. https://doi.org/10.3389/fpsyg.2021.738770

Büssing, A., Recchia, D. R., & Baumann, K. (2018). Validation of the gratitude/awe questionnaire and its association with disposition of gratefulness. *Religions, 9*(4), 117. https://doi.org/10.3390/rel9040117

Büssing, A., Rodrigues Recchia, D., Dienberg, T., Surzykiewicz, J., & Baumann, K. (2021). Awe/gratitude as an experiential aspect of spirituality and its association to perceived positive changes during the COVID-19 pandemic. *Frontiers in Psychiatry*, *12*, 642716. https://doi.org/10.3389/fpsyt.2021.642716

Cabot, R. (1914). *What men live by: Work, play, love, worship*. Houghton Mifflin.

Calhoun, A. (2015). *Spiritual disciplines handbook: Practices that transform us*. InterVarsity.

Cavanaugh, W. (2024). *The uses of idolatry*. Oxford University Press.

Chandler, D. (2014). *Christian spiritual formation: An integrated approach for personal and relational wholeness*. InterVarsity.

Cherry, C. (2019). *Worship like Jesus: A guide for every follower*. Abingdon.

Cheung, C. K., & Yue, X. D. (2012). Idol worship as compensation for parental absence. *International Journal of Adolescence and Youth*, *17*(1), 35–46. https://doi.org/10.1080/02673843.2011.649399

Chirico, A., Ferrise, F., Cordella, L., & Gaggioli, A. (2018). Designing awe in virtual reality: An experimental study. *Frontiers in Psychology*, *8*, 2351. https://doi.org/10.3389/fpsyg.2017.02351

Chirico, A., & Gaggioli, A. (2021). The potential role of awe in depression: Reassembling the puzzle. *Frontiers in Psychology*, *12*, 617715. https://doi.org/10.3389/fpsyg.2021.617715

Christopher, A. N., Marek, P., & Carroll, S. M. (2004). Materialism and attitudes toward money: An exploratory investigation. *Individual Differences Research*, *2*(2), 109–117.

Clarke, I. E., Karlov, L., & Neale, N. J. (2015). The many faces of narcissism: Narcissism factors and their predictive utility. *Personality and Individual Differences*, *81*, 90–95. https://doi.org/10.1016/j.paid.2014.11.021

Connors, G. J., Tonigan, J. S., & Miller, W. R. (1996). A measure of religious background and behavior for use in behavior change research. *Psychology of Addictive Behaviors*, *10*(2), 90–96. https://doi.org/10.1037/0893-164X.10.2.90

Cooper, A. (2017). *The cloud: Reflections on selected texts*. St. Paul Publications.

Cordero, A. (2009). Contemporary science and worldview-making. In M. Matthews (Ed.), *Science, worldviews, and education* (pp. 99–116). Springer.

Cottrell, J. (1984). *What the Bible says about God the ruler*. Wipf & Stock.

Dai, Y., Jiang, T., & Miao, M. (2022). Uncovering the effects of awe on meaning in life. *Journal of Happiness Studies*, *23*, 3517–3529. https://doi.org/10.1007/s10902-022-00559-6

Daly, M. (2022). Prevalence of depression among adolescents in the US from 2009 to 2019: Analysis of trends by sex, race/ethnicity, and income. *Journal of Adolescent Health*, *70*(3), 496–499. https://doi.org/10.1016/j.jadohealth.2021.08.026

deClaisse-Walford, N., Jacobson, R., & Laneel Tanner, B. (2014). *The book of Psalms*. Eerdmans.

de Sales, F. (2011). *Treatise on the love of God: Contemporary English edition*. Paraclete.

DeWitt, R. (2018). *Worldviews: An introduction to the history and philosophy of science*. Wiley Blackwell.

Diener, E., Lucas, R. E., & Oishi, S. (2002). Subjective well-being: The science of happiness and life satisfaction. In S. Lopez & C. Snyder (Eds.), *The Oxford handbook of positive psychology* (pp. 63–73). Oxford University Press.

Doehring, C., Clarke, A., Pargament, K., Hayes, A., Hammer, D., Nickolas, M., & Hughes, P. (2009). Perceiving sacredness in life: Correlates and predictors. *Archive for the Psychology of Religion, 31*(1), 55–73. https://doi.org/10.1163/157361209X371492

Dolezal, J. (2011). *God without parts: Divine simplicity and the metaphysics of God's absoluteness*. Wipf & Stock.

Dong, X., & Geng, L. (2023). The role of mindfulness and meaning in life in adolescents' dispositional awe and life satisfaction: The broaden-and-build theory perspective. *Current Psychology, 42*(33), 28911–28924. https://doi.org/10.1007/s12144-022-03924-z

Eagle, J., & Amster, M. (2023). *The power of awe: Overcome burnout & anxiety, ease chronic pain, find clarity & purpose—in less than 1 minute per day*. Hachette.

Ellens, J. H. (1973). Psychological dynamics in Christian worship: A beginning inquiry. *Journal of Psychology and Theology, 1*(4), 10–19. https://doi.org/10.1177/009164717300100402

Elmer, R. (Ed.). (2019). *Piercing heaven: Prayers of the Puritans*. Lexham.

Elwell, W., & Comfort, P. (Eds.). (2001). *Tyndale Bible dictionary*. Tyndale.

Endean, P. (1990). The Ignatian prayer of the senses. *Heythrop Journal, 31*(4), 391–418. https://doi.org/10.1111/j.1468-2265.1990.tb00145.x

Entwistle, D. (2015). *Integrative approaches to psychology and Christianity: An introduction to worldview issues, philosophical foundations, and models of integration* (3rd ed.). Wipf & Stock.

Evagrius of Ponticus. (2009). *Talking back: A monastic handbook for combating demons*. Cistercian Publications.

Fairbairn, D., & Reeves, R. (2019). *The story of creeds and confessions: Tracing the development of the Christian faith*. Baker Academic.

Feldman, G., Hayes, A., Kumar, S., Greeson, J., & Laurenceau, J. P. (2007). Mindfulness and emotion regulation: The development and initial validation of the Cognitive and Affective Mindfulness Scale-Revised (CAMS-R). *Journal of Psychopathology and Behavioral Assessment, 29*, 177–190. https://doi.org/10.1007/s10862-006-9035-8

Flavel, J. (2011). *The mystery of providence*. GLH Publishing.

Forrest, B., Kaiser, W., Jr., & Whaley, V. (Eds.). (2021). *Biblical worship: Theology for God's glory*. Kregel Academic.

Foster, R. (1992). *Prayer: Finding the heart's true home*. HarperCollins.

Foster, R. (2008). *Celebration of discipline: The path to spiritual growth*. Hodder & Stoughton.

Fredrickson, B. L., Cohn, M. A., Coffey, K. A., Pek, J., & Finkel, S. M. (2008). Open hearts build lives: Positive emotions, induced through loving-kindness meditation, build consequential personal resources. *Journal of Personality and Social Psychology, 95*(5), 1045–1062. https://doi.org/10.1037/a0013262

Gallagher, T. (2008). *Meditation and contemplation: An Ignatian guide to praying with Scripture*. Crossway.

Garber, K., & Lustig, R. (2011). Is fast food addictive? *Current Drug Abuse Reviews, 4*(3), 146–162. https://www.ingentaconnect.com/content/ben/cdar/2011/00000004/00000003/art00004

Gillet, L. (1985). *On the invocation of the name of Jesus*. Templegate.

Goggin, J., & Strobel, K. (Eds.). (2013). *Reading the Christian spiritual classics: A guide for Evangelicals*. InterVarsity.

Goldingay, J. (2006). *Psalms 1–41* (vol. 1). Baker Academic.

Goodwin, R. (1999). *Give us this day: The story of prayer*. Lindisfarne Books.

Gray, T. (2009). *Lectio divina: Praying Scripture for a change*. Ascension.

Graziosi, M., & Yaden, D. (2021). Interpersonal awe: Exploring the social domain of awe elicitors. *Journal of Positive Psychology, 16*(2), 263–271. https://doi.org/10.1080/17439760.2019.1689422

Greenacre, P. (1956). Experiences of awe in childhood. *Psychoanalytic Study of the Child, 11*(1), 9–30. https://doi.org/10.1080/00797308.1956.11822780

Grenz, S. (2001). *The social God and the relational self: A trinitarian theology of the imago Dei*. Westminster John Knox.

Grudem, W. (2020). *Systematic theology: An introduction to biblical doctrine* (2nd ed.). Zondervan Academic.

Guigo II. (2012). *The ladder of monks*. Sr. Pascale Dominique Nau.

Güsewell, A., & Ruch, W. (2012). Are there multiple channels through which we connect with beauty and excellence? *Journal of Positive Psychology, 7*(6), 516–529. https://doi.org/10.1080/17439760.2012.726636

Hagner, D. (1990). *Hebrews*. Baker.

Hall, J. (2007). *The art of divine meditation* [Kindle version]. Amazon.com

Hall, T. W., & Edwards, K. J. (2002). The Spiritual Assessment Inventory: A theistic model and measure for assessing spiritual development. *Journal for the Scientific Study of Religion, 41*(2), 341–357. https://doi.org/10.1111/1468-5906.00121

Hansen, G. (2012). *Kneeling with giants: Learning to pray with history's best teachers*. InterVarsity.

Harrison, I. B. (1975). On the maternal origins of awe. *Psychoanalytic Study of the Child, 30*(1), 181–195. https://doi.org/10.1080/00797308.1975.11823305

Hayes, S., Strosahl, K., & Wilson, K. (2012). *Acceptance and commitment therapy: The process and practice of mindful change* (2nd ed.). Guilford.

Hayes, S. C., Wilson, K. G., Gifford, E. V., Follette, V. M., & Strosahl, K. (1996). Experiential avoidance and behavioral disorders: A functional dimensional approach to diagnosis and treatment. *Journal of Consulting and Clinical Psychology, 64*(6), 1152–1168. https://doi.org/10.1037/0022-006X.64.6.1152

Henttonen, P., Salmi, J., Peräkylä, A., & Krusemark, E. A. (2022). Grandiosity, vulnerability, and narcissistic fluctuation: Examining reliability, measurement invariance, and construct validity of four brief narcissism measures. *Frontiers in Psychology, 13*, 993663. https://doi.org/10.3389/fpsyg.2022.993663

Hill, P., & Hood, R. (Eds.). (1999). *Measures of religiosity*. Religious Education Press.

Hindson, E. (2021). Hallelujah, what a Savior! Worship in the Apocalypse. In B. Forrest, W. Kaiser Jr., & V. Whaley (Eds.), *Biblical worship: Theology for God's glory* (pp. 503–514). Kregel Academic.

Holman. (2004a). Awe. In *Holman Bible Dictionary*. Holman Bible Publishers.

Holman. (2004b). Holy. In *Holman Bible Dictionary*. Holman Bible Publishers.

Holman. (2004c). Image of God. In *Holman Bible Dictionary*. Holman Bible Publishers.

Holman. (2004d). Worship. In *Holman Bible Dictionary*. Holman Bible Publishers.

Horton, M. (2011). *The Christian faith: A systematic theology for pilgrims on the way*. Zondervan.

Hylan, J. (1901). *Public worship: A study in the psychology of religion*. Open Court.

Ignatian Spirituality. (n.d.). *Spiritual exercises*. Retrieved March 26, 2025. https://www.ignatianspirituality.com/ignatian-prayer/the-spiritual-exercises/

Ignatius of Loyola. (1999). *The spiritual exercises*. TAN Books.

Iodice, J. A., Malouff, J. M., & Schutte, N. S. (2021). The association between gratitude and depression: A meta-analysis. *International Journal of Depression and Anxiety, 4*(1), 1–12. https://doi.org/10.23937/2643-4059/1710024

Ivens, M. (1998). *Understanding the Spiritual Exercises: Text and commentary—A handbook for retreat directors*. Cromwell.

Janz, D. (Ed.). (2008). *A reformation reader: Primary texts and introductions*. Fortress.

Ji, Q., Janicke-Bowles, S. H., De Leeuw, R. N., & Oliver, M. B. (2021). The melody to inspiration: The effects of awe-eliciting music on approach motivation and positive well-being. *Media Psychology, 24*(3), 305–331. https://doi.org/10.1080/15213269.2019.1693402

Jiao, L., & Luo, L. (2022). Dispositional awe positively predicts prosocial tendencies: The multiple mediation effects of connectedness and empathy. *International Journal of Environmental Research and Public Health*, 19(24), 16605. https://doi.org/10.3390/ijerph192416605

Johnson, C. (2010a). *The globalization of hesychasm and the Jesus prayer: Contesting contemplation*. Continuum.

Johnson, E. (Ed.). (2010b). *Psychology and Christianity: Five views* (2nd ed.). InterVarsity.

Johnston, R. (2014). *God's wider presence: Reconsidering general revelation*. Baker Academic.

Johnston, W. (Ed.). (1973). *The cloud of unknowing and the book of privy counseling*. Image Books.

Kabat-Zinn, J. (2016). *Mindfulness for beginners: Reclaiming the present moment—and your life*. Jaico.

Kaiser, W., Jr., VanGemeren, W., & Moore, E. (2021). The context of worship in the psalter. In B. Forrest, W. Kaiser Jr., & V. Whaley (Eds.), *Biblical worship: Theology for God's glory* (pp. 155–162). Kregel Academic.

Kasser, T., & Ryan, R. M. (1993). A dark side of the American dream: Correlates of financial success as a central life aspiration. *Journal of Personality and Social Psychology*, 65(2), 410–422. https://doi.org/10.1037/0022-3514.65.2.410

Kaufman, G. (1996). *The psychology of shame: Theory and treatment of shame-based syndromes* (2nd ed.). Springer.

Kearns, P. O., & Tyler, J. M. (2022). Examining the relationship between awe, spirituality, and religiosity. *Psychology of Religion and Spirituality*, 14(4), 436–444. https://doi.org/10.1037/rel0000365

Keltner, D. (2023). *Awe: The new science of everyday wonder and how it can transform your life*. Penguin.

Keltner, D., & Haidt, J. (2003). Approaching awe, a moral, spiritual, and aesthetic emotion. *Cognition and Emotion*, 17(2), 297–314. https://doi.org/10.1080/02699930302297

King, D., Viney, W., & Woody, W. (2013). *A history of psychology: Ideas & context* (5th ed.). Pearson Education.

Klapp, O. E. (1949). Hero worship in America. *American Sociological Review*, 14(1), 53–62. https://doi.org/10.2307/2086446

Knabb, J. (2021). *Christian meditation in clinical practice: A four-step model and workbook for therapists and clients*. IVP Academic.

Knabb, J., & Bates, M. (2020). "Holy desire" within the "Cloud of Unknowing": The psychological contributions of medieval apophatic contemplation to Christian mental health in the 21st century. *Journal of Psychology and Christianity*, 39(1), 24–39.

Knabb, J., Frederick, T., & Cumming, G. (2017). Surrendering to God's providence: A three-part study on providence-focused therapy for recurrent worry (PFT-RW). *Psychology of Religion and Spirituality, 9*(2), 180–196. https://doi.org/10.1037/rel0000081

Knabb, J., Johnson, E., Bates, T., & Sisemore, T. (2019). *Christian psychotherapy in context: Theoretical and empirical explorations in faith-based mental health.* Routledge.

Knabb, J., Pate, R., Sullivan, S., Salley, E., Miller, A., & Boyer, W. (2020). "Walking with God": Developing and pilot testing a manualized four-week program combining Christian meditation and light-to-moderate physical activity for daily stress. *Mental Health, Religion & Culture, 23*(9), 756–776. https://doi.org/10.1080/13674676.2020.1819221

Knabb, J., & Vazquez, V. (2018). A randomized controlled trial of a two-week internet-based contemplative prayer program for Christians with daily stress. *Spirituality in Clinical Practice, 5*(1), 37–53. https://doi.org/10.1037/scp0000154

Knabb, J. J., & Vazquez, V. E. (2023). Decentering mindfulness: Toward greater meditative diversity in global public health. *Mindfulness*. Advance online publication. https://doi.org/10.1007/s12671-023-02203-7

Knabb, J. J., Vazquez, V. E., Garzon, F. L., Ford, K. M., Wang, K. T., Conner, K. W., & Weston, D. M. (2020). Christian meditation for repetitive negative thinking: A multisite randomized trial examining the effects of a 4-week preventative program. *Spirituality in Clinical Practice, 7*(1), 34–50. https://doi.org/10.1037/scp0000206

Knabb, J., Vazquez, V., Pate, R., Garzon, F., Wang, K., Edison-Riley, D., Slick, A., Smith, R., & Weber, S. (2022). Christian meditation for trauma-based rumination: A two-part study examining the effects of an internet-based four-week program. *Spirituality in Clinical Practice, 9*(4), 253–271. https://doi.org/10.1037/scp0000255

Knabb, J., Vazquez, V., Pate, R., Wang, K., Lowell, J., De Leeuw, T., Dominguez, A., Duvall, K., Esperante, J., Gonzalez, Y., Nagel, G., Novasel, C., Pelaez, A., Strickland, S., & Park, J. (2022). Lectio divina for trauma symptoms: A two-part study. *Spirituality in Clinical Practice, 9*(4), 232–252. https://doi.org/10.1037/scp0000303

Knabb, J. J., Vazquez, V. E., Wang, K. T., & Pate, R. A. (2023). The Christian Gratitude Scale: An emic approach to measuring thankfulness in every season of life. *Spirituality in Clinical Practice, 10*(4), 304–315. http://dx.doi.org/10.1037/scp0000278

Knabb, J. J., Wang, K. T., Hall, M. E. L., & Vazquez, V. E. (2025). The Christian Worldview Scale: An emic measure for assessing a comprehensive view of life within the Christian tradition. *Spirituality in Clinical Practice, 12*(1), 1–19. https://dx.doi.org/10.1037/scp0000306

Knox, J. (2018). *True worship and the consequences of idolatry.* Puritan Publications.

Koltko-Rivera, M. E. (2004). The psychology of worldviews. *Review of General Psychology, 8*(1), 3–58. https://doi.org/10.1037/1089-2680.8.1.3

Krause, N., & Hayward, R. D. (2015a). Assessing whether practical wisdom and awe of God are associated with life satisfaction. *Psychology of Religion and Spirituality*, 7(1), 51–59. https://doi.org/10.1037/a0037694

Krause, N., & Hayward, R. D. (2015b). Awe of God, congregational embeddedness, and religious meaning in life. *Review of Religious Research*, 57(2), 219–238. https://doi.org/10.1007/s13644-014-0195-9

Kuster, F., Orth, U., & Meier, L. L. (2012). Rumination mediates the prospective effect of low self-esteem on depression: A five-wave longitudinal study. *Personality and Social Psychology Bulletin*, 38(6), 747–759. https://doi.org/10.1177/0146167212437250

Kuyper, A. (2010). *Lectures on Calvinism*. Sovereign Grace.

Lawrence, B. (1993). *Writings and conversations on the practice of the presence of God*. ISC Publications.

Lee, P. (2021). Worship: A concept study in biblical Hebrew. In B. Forrest, W. Kaiser Jr., & V. Whaley (Eds.), *Biblical worship: Theology for God's glory* (pp. 23–36). Kregel Academic.

Lewis, C. S. (1958). *Reflections on the Psalms*. Harcourt.

Lewis, C. S. (1994). *The great divorce*. HarperOne.

Lewis, C. S. (1996). *The Screwtape letters*. Scribner.

Liefeld, W. (1999). *The NIV application commentary: 1 & 2 Timothy, Titus*. Zondervan.

Lin, Y., & Lin, C. (2007). Impetus for worship: An exploratory study of adolescents' idol adoration behaviors. *Adolescence*, 42(167), 575–588.

Linehan, M. (2015). *DBT skills training manual* (2nd ed.). Guilford.

Liu, J., Huo, Y., Wang, J., Bai, Y., Zhao, M., & Di, M. (2023). Awe of nature and well-being: Roles of nature connectedness and powerlessness. *Personality and Individual Differences*, 201, 111946. https://doi.org/10.1016/j.paid.2022.111946

Longman, T. (2014). *Psalms: An introduction and commentary*. InterVarsity.

Luo, L., Mao, J., Gao, W., & Yuan, J. (2021). Psychological research of awe: Definition, functions, and application in psychotherapy. *Stress and Brain*, 1(1), 59–75. https://doi.org/10.26599/SAB.2020.9060003

Luo, L., Zou, R., Yang, D., & Yuan, J. (2023). Awe experience triggered by fighting against COVID-19 promotes prosociality through increased feeling of connectedness and empathy. *Journal of Positive Psychology*, 18(6), 866–882. https://doi.org/10.1080/17439760.2022.2131607

Macchia, F. (2023). *Introduction to theology: Declaring the wonders of God*. Baker Academic.

Males, M. (2018). Racial implications of the narcissistic personality inventory reinterpreting popular depictions of narcissism trends. *Journal of Psychology and Psychiatry*, 2, 1–4. https://doi.org/10.15761/JPP.1000106

Maltby, J., Day, L., McCutcheon, L. E., Martin, M. M., & Cayanus, J. L. (2004). Celebrity worship, cognitive flexibility, and social complexity. *Personality and Individual Differences*, *37*(7), 1475–1482. https://doi.org/10.1016/j.paid.2004.02.004

Maltby, J., Houran, J., Lange, R., Ashe, D., & McCutcheon, L. E. (2002). Thou shalt worship no other gods—unless they are celebrities: The relationship between celebrity worship and religious orientation. *Personality and Individual Differences*, *32*(7), 1157–1172. https://doi.org/10.1016/S0191-8869(01)00059-9

Marčinko, D., Jakšić, N., Ivezić, E., Skočić, M., Surányi, Z., Lončar, M., & Jakovljević, M. (2014). Pathological narcissism and depressive symptoms in psychiatric outpatients: Mediating role of dysfunctional attitudes. *Journal of Clinical Psychology*, *70*(4), 341–352. https://doi.org/10.1002/jclp.22033

Mathers, D., Miller, M., & Ando, O. (Eds.). (2009). *Self and no-self: Continuing the dialogue between Buddhism and psychotherapy*. Routledge.

McConnell, W. (2021). *How majestic is your name: An introduction to biblical worship*. Wipf & Stock.

McCutcheon, L. E., & Aruguete, M. S. (2021). Is celebrity worship increasing over time? *Journal of Studies in Social Sciences and Humanities*, *7*(1), 66–75.

McCutcheon, L. E., Lange, R., & Houran, J. (2002). Conceptualization and measurement of celebrity worship. *British Journal of Psychology*, *93*(1), 67–87. https://doi.org/10.1348/000712602162454

McCutcheon, L., Lowinger, R., Wong, M., & Jenkins, W. (2013). Celebrity worship and religion revisited. *Implicit Religion*, *16*(3), 319–328. https://journal.equinoxpub.com/IR/article/view/3383

McGowin, E. H. (2022). Wonder and theology. In J. Barbeau & E. Hunter McGowin (Eds.), *God and wonder: Theology, imagination, and the arts* (pp. 3–10). Cascade Books.

McGrath, A. (2011). *Christian theology: An introduction* (5th ed.). Wiley-Blackwell.

McGuckin, J. (Ed.). (2010). *The encyclopedia of Eastern Orthodox Christianity*. Wiley & Sons.

McKim, D. (1996). *Westminster dictionary of theological terms*. Westminster John Knox.

Merriam-Webster. (n.d.). Mercy. In *Merriam Webster Dictionary*. Retrieved March 26, 2025. https://www.merriam-webster.com/dictionary/mercy

Meyer, S. G. (1975). Neuropsychology and worship. *Journal of Psychology and Theology*, *3*(4), 281–289. https://doi.org/10.1177/009164717500300407

Middleton, J. (2005). *The liberating image: The imago Dei in Genesis 1*. Brazos.

Miller, A., & Worthington, E. (2012). Connection between personality and religion and spirituality. In J. Aten, K. O'Grady, & E. Worthington (Eds.), *The psychology of religion and spirituality for clinicians: Using research in your practice* (pp. 101–130). Routledge.

Miller, D. K. (2011). Responsible relationship: *Imago Dei* and the moral distinction between humans and other animals. *International Journal of Systematic Theology*, *13*(3), 323–339. https://doi.org/10.1111/j.1468-2400.2011.00561.x

Miller, J. D., Back, M. D., Lynam, D. R., & Wright, A. G. (2021). Narcissism today: What we know and what we need to learn. *Current Directions in Psychological Science*, *30*(6), 519–525. https://doi.org/10.1177/09637214211044109

Monroy, M., & Keltner, D. (2023). Awe as a pathway to mental and physical health. *Perspectives on Psychological Science*, *18*(2), 309–320. https://doi.org/10.1177/17456916221094856

Moore, E. (2021). Covenant hope in the king regardless of circumstances: Worship in book (1–41) of the Psalter. In B. Forrest, W. Kaiser Jr., & V. Whaley (Eds.), *Biblical worship: Theology for God's glory* (pp. 163–175). Kregel Academic.

Morgan, C., & Peterson, R. (2020). *Christian theology: The biblical story and our faith*. B&H Academic.

Morris, L. (1992). *The Gospel according to Matthew*. Eerdmans.

Mouw, R. (2001). *He shines in all that's fair: Culture and common grace*. Eerdmans.

Muñiz-Velázquez, J. A., Gomez-Baya, D., & Lopez-Casquete, M. (2017). Implicit and explicit assessment of materialism: Associations with happiness and depression. *Personality and Individual Differences*, *116*, 123–132. https://doi.org/10.1016/j.paid.2017.04.033

Olsen, J. (2022). From teleology to psychology. *Human Arenas*, *5*(2), 359–368. https://doi.org/10.1007/s42087-020-00137-3

Osborne, W. (2021). Royal priests created to worship: Worship in the garden and beyond. In B. Forrest, W. Kaiser Jr., & V. Whaley (Eds.), *Biblical worship: Theology for God's glory* (pp. 37–50). Kregel Academic.

Owen, J. (2018). *The glory of evangelical worship*. Puritan Publications.

Packer, J. (2010). *A quest for godliness: The Puritan vision of the Christian life*. Crossway.

Pérez, K. A., Lench, H. C., Thompson, C. G., & North, S. (2023). Experimental elicitations of awe: A meta-analysis. *Cognition and Emotion*, *37*(1), 18–33. https://doi.org/10.1080/02699931.2022.2140126

Peterson, D. (1992). *Engaging with God: A biblical theology of worship*. InterVarsity.

Pierce, T. (2008). *Enthroned on your praise: An Old Testament theology of worship*. B&H.

Pieters, R. (2013). Bidirectional dynamics of materialism and loneliness: Not just a vicious cycle. *Journal of Consumer Research*, *40*(4), 615–631. https://doi.org/10.1086/671564

Piff, P. K., Dietze, P., Feinberg, M., Stancato, D. M., & Keltner, D. (2015). Awe, the small self, and prosocial behavior. *Journal of Personality and Social Psychology*, *108*(6), 883–899. https://doi.org/10.1037/pspi0000018

Pilgrim, L., Norris, J. I., & Hackathorn, J. (2017). Music is awesome: Influences of emotion, personality, and preference on experienced awe. *Journal of Consumer Behaviour, 16*(5), 442–451. https://doi.org/10.1002/cb.1645

Piper, J. (2011). *Desiring God*. Multnomah Books.

Piper, J. (2020). *Providence*. Crossway.

Preston, J. L., & Shin, F. (2017). Spiritual experiences evoke awe through the small self in both religious and non-religious individuals. *Journal of Experimental Social Psychology, 70*, 212–221. https://doi.org/10.1016/j.jesp.2016.11.006

Protestant Reformed Churches in America. (n.d.). *Belgic confession*. Retrieved March 26, 2025. http://www.prca.org/about/official-standards/creeds/three-forms-of-unity/belgic-confession

Rice, H., & Huffstutler, J. (2001). *Reformed worship*. Geneva Press.

Richins, M. L. (2017). Materialism pathways: The processes that create and perpetuate materialism. *Journal of Consumer Psychology, 27*(4), 480–499. https://doi.org/10.1016/j.jcps.2017.07.006

Robertson, D. (2011). *Lectio divina: The medieval experience of reading*. Liturgical Press.

Ross, A. (2006). *Recalling the hope of glory: Biblical worship from the garden to the new creation*. Kregel Academic.

Ross, A. (2011). *A commentary on the Psalms: Volume 1 (1–41)*. Kregel Academic.

Ross, J. (2021). Deteriorating devotion among God's people: Worship in the book of Judges. In B. Forrest, W. Kaiser Jr., & V. Whaley (Eds.), *Biblical worship: Theology for God's glory* (pp. 97–119). Kregel Academic.

Rudd, M., Vohs, K. D., & Aaker, J. (2012). Awe expands people's perception of time, alters decision making, and enhances well-being. *Psychological Science, 23*(10), 1130–1136. https://doi.org/10.1177/0956797612438731

Ryrie, C. (1999). *Basic theology: A popular systematic guide to understanding biblical truth*. Moody.

Sandage, S. J., & Moe, S. P. (2011). Narcissism and spirituality. In W. Campbell & J. Miller (Eds.), *The handbook of narcissism and narcissistic personality disorder: Theoretical approaches, empirical findings, and treatments* (pp. 410–419). Wiley & Sons.

Sansone, R. A., & Sansone, L. A. (2014). "I'm Your Number One Fan"—A clinical look at celebrity worship. *Innovations in Clinical Neuroscience, 11*(1–2), 39–43. https://www.ncbi.nlm.nih.gov/pmc/articles/PMC3960781/

Schneider, K. J. (1990). The worship of food: An existential perspective. *Psychotherapy: Theory, Research, Practice, Training, 27*(1), 95–97. https://doi.org/10.1037/0033-3204.27.1.95

Schneider, K. (2004). *Rediscovery of awe: Splendor, mystery, and the fluid center of life*. Paragon House.

Schneider, K. (2009). *Awakening to awe: Personal stories of profound transformation*. Jason Aronson.

Schneider, K. (2017). The resurgence of awe in psychology: Promise, hope, and perils. *The Humanistic Psychologist*, 45(2), 103–108. https://doi.org/10.1037/hum0000060

Schoenleber, M., Roche, M. J., Wetzel, E., Pincus, A. L., & Roberts, B. W. (2015). Development of a brief version of the Pathological Narcissism Inventory. *Psychological assessment*, 27(4), 1520–1526. https://doi.org/10.1037/pas0000158

Seaward, B. (2023). *Managing stress: Skills for anxiety reduction, self-care, & personal resiliency*. Jones & Bartlett Learning.

Sesini, G., & Lozza, E. (2023). Understanding individual attitude to money: A systematic scoping review and research agenda. *Collabra: Psychology*, 9(1), 77305. https://doi.org/10.1525/collabra.77305

Shiota, M. N., Keltner, D., & Mossman, A. (2007). The nature of awe: Elicitors, appraisals, and effects on self-concept. *Cognition and Emotion*, 21(5), 944–963. https://doi.org/10.1080/02699930600923668

Shiota, M. N., Thrash, T. M., Danvers, A., & Dombrowski, J. T. (2014). Transcending the self: Awe, elevation, and inspiration. In M. Tugade, M. Shiota, & L. Kirby (Eds.), *Handbook of positive emotions* (pp. 362–377). Guilford.

Slife, B., O'Grady, K., & Kosits, R. (Eds.). (2017). *The hidden worldviews of psychology's theory, research, and practice*. Routledge.

Smith, J. (2021). The psychology of relaxation, meditation, and mindfulness: An introduction to RMM theory, practice, and assessment. In P. Lehrer & R. Woolfolk (Eds.), *Principles and practice of stress management* (4th ed., pp. 39–57). Guilford.

Smith, J. K. A. (2009). *Desiring the kingdom: Worship, worldview, and cultural formation*. Baker Academic.

Smith, J. K. A. (2016). *You are what you love: The spiritual power of habit*. Brazos.

Spilka, B., & Ladd, K. (2013). *The psychology of prayer: A scientific approach*. Guilford.

Sproul, R. C. (1997). *What is Reformed theology? Understanding the basics*. Baker.

Stellar, J. E., Gordon, A., Anderson, C. L., Piff, P. K., McNeil, G. D., & Keltner, D. (2018). Awe and humility. *Journal of Personality and Social Psychology*, 114(2), 258–269. https://doi.org/10.1037/pspi0000109

Strawn, B. D., & Brown, W. S. (2013). Liturgical animals: What psychology and neuroscience tell us about formation and worship. *Liturgy*, 28(4), 3–14. https://doi.org/10.1080/0458063X.2013.803838

Strong's Lexicon. (n.d.a). *Deos*. Bible Hub. https://biblehub.com/greek/1190a.htm

Strong's Lexicon. (n.d.b). *Hagah*. Bible Hub. https://biblehub.com/hebrew/1898.htm

Strong's Lexicon. (n.d.c). *Phobeó*. Bible Hub. https://biblehub.com/greek/5399.htm

Sturm, V. E., Datta, S., Roy, A. R. K., Sible, I. J., Kosik, E. L., Veziris, C. R., Chow, T. E., Morris, N. A., Neuhaus, J., Kramer, J. H., Miller, B. L., Holley, S. R., & Keltner, D.

(2022). Big smile, small self: Awe walks promote prosocial positive emotions in older adults. *Emotion*, 22(5), 1044–1058. https://doi.org/10.1037/emo0000876

Sundararajan, L. (2002). Religious awe: Potential contributions of negative theology to psychology, "positive" or otherwise. *Journal of Theoretical and Philosophical Psychology*, 22(2), 174–197. https://doi.org/10.1037/h0091221

Sung, B., & Yih, J. (2016). Does interest broaden or narrow attentional scope? *Cognition and Emotion*, 30(8), 1485–1494. https://doi.org/10.1080/02699931.2015.1071241

Tabb, B. (2021). Life together in the last days: Worship in the Acts of the Apostles. In B. Forrest, W. Kaiser Jr., & V. Whaley (Eds.), *Biblical worship: Theology for God's glory* (pp. 377–396). Kregel Academic.

Taylor, C. (2007). *A secular age*. Harvard University Press.

Taylor, S., & Workman, L. (2022). *Cognitive psychology: The basics*. Routledge.

Thompson, J. (2022). Awe narratives: A mindfulness practice to enhance resilience and wellbeing. *Frontiers in Psychology*, 13, 840944. https://doi.org/10.3389/fpsyg.2022.840944

Tillich, P. (1980). *The courage to be*. Yale University Press.

Tirch, D., Silberstein, L., & Kolts, R. (2016). *Buddhist psychology and cognitive-behavioral therapy: A clinician's guide*. Guilford.

Tozer, A. W. (2009). *The purpose of man: Designed to worship*. Bethany House.

Tozer, A. W. (2016). *The Christian book of mystical verse: A collection of poems, hymns, and prayers for devotional reading*. Moody.

Treier, D. (Ed.). (2017). *Evangelical dictionary of theology* (3rd ed.). Baker Academic.

Tripp, P. (2015). *Awe: Why it matters for everything we think, say, and do*. Crossway.

Twenge, J. (2014). *Generation me: Why today's young Americans are more confident, assertive, entitled—and more miserable than ever before*. Atria.

Twenge, J. (2018). *iGen: Why today's super-connected kids are growing up less rebellious, more tolerant, less happy—and completely unprepared for adulthood—and what that means for the rest of us*. Atria.

Twenge, J. M., Konrath, S. H., Cooper, A. B., Foster, J. D., Campbell, W. K., & McAllister, C. (2021). Egos deflating with the Great Recession: A cross-temporal meta-analysis and within-campus analysis of the Narcissistic Personality Inventory, 1982–2016. *Personality and Individual Differences*, 179, 110947. https://doi.org/10.1016/j.paid.2021.110947

Underwood, L. G., & Teresi, J. A. (2002). The daily spiritual experience scale: Development, theoretical description, reliability, exploratory factor analysis, and preliminary construct validity using health-related data. *Annals of Behavioral Medicine*, 24(1), 22–33. https://doi.org/10.1207/S15324796ABM2401_04

Upenieks, L., & Krause, N. (2024). Transcendental awe of God and dimensions of well-being: Exploring the mediating role of meaning in life. *Journal of Religion, Spirituality & Aging 36*, 5–25. https://doi.org/10.1080/15528030.2022.2114575

Upper Room. (n.d.). *Visio divina*. Retrieved March 26, 2025. https://www.upperroom.org/resources/visio-divina

Upper Room. (2003a). Awe. In *Upper Room Dictionary of Christian Spiritual Formation*. Upper Room Books.

Upper Room. (2003b). Contemplation. In *Upper Room Dictionary of Christian Spiritual Formation*. Upper Room Books.

Upper Room. (2003c). Discipline. In *Upper Room Dictionary of Christian Spiritual Formation*. Upper Room Books.

Upper Room. (2003d). Labyrinth. In *Upper Room Dictionary of Christian Spiritual Formation*. Upper Room Books.

Upper Room. (2003e). Meditation. In *Upper Room Dictionary of Christian Spiritual Formation*. Upper Room Books.

Upper Room. (2003f). Negative way. In *Upper Room Dictionary of Christian Spiritual Formation*. Upper Room Books.

Upper Room. (2003g). Positive way. In *Upper Room Dictionary of Christian Spiritual Formation*. Upper Room Books.

Upper Room. (2003h). Prayer. In *Upper Room Dictionary of Christian Spiritual Formation*. Upper Room Books.

Upper Room. (2003i). Worship. In *Upper Room Dictionary of Christian Spiritual Formation*. Upper Room Books.

Van Cappellen, P., Edwards, M. E., & Fredrickson, B. L. (2021). Upward spirals of positive emotions and religious behaviors. *Current Opinion in Psychology, 40*, 92–98. https://doi.org/10.1016/j.copsyc.2020.09.004

Van Cappellen, P., & Saroglou, V. (2012). Awe activates religious and spiritual feelings and behavioral intentions. *Psychology of Religion and Spirituality, 4*(3), 223–236. https://doi.org/10.1037/a0025986

Van Cappellen, P., Toth-Gauthier, M., Saroglou, V., & Fredrickson, B. L. (2016). Religion and well-being: The mediating role of positive emotions. *Journal of Happiness Studies, 17*, 485–505. https://doi.org/10.1007/s10902-014-9605-5

Van Engen, A. (2015). *Sympathetic Puritans: Calvinist fellow feeling in early New England*. Oxford University Press.

van Mulukom, V., Patterson, R. E., & van Elk, M. (2020). Broadening your mind to include others: The relationship between serotonergic psychedelic experiences and maladaptive narcissism. *Psychopharmacology, 237*, 2725–2737. https://doi.org/10.1007/s00213-020-05568-y

Vitz, P. (1994). *Psychology as religion: The cult of self-worship* (2nd ed.). Eerdmans.

Vocabulary.com. (n.d.). *Reverence*. Retrieved March 26, 2025. https://www.vocabulary.com/dictionary/reverence

Wang, G., Liu, L., Tan, X., & Zheng, W. (2017). The moderating effect of dispositional mindfulness on the relationship between materialism and mental health. *Personality and Individual Differences*, *107*, 131–136. https://doi.org/10.1016/j.paid.2016.11.041

Ware, K. (2014). *The Jesus prayer*. Catholic Truth Society.

Warner, L. (2010). *Journey with Jesus: Discovering the spiritual exercises of Saint Ignatius*. InterVarsity.

Watson, J. (1999). *The English hymn: A critical and historical study*. Oxford University Press.

Watson, P. J., Hood, R. W., Jr., & Morris, R. J. (1984). Religious orientation, humanistic values, and narcissism. *Review of Religious Research*, *25*(3), 257–264. https://www.jstor.org/stable/3511123

Watson, P. J., Jones, N. D., & Morris, R. J. (2004). Religious orientation and attitudes toward money: Relationships with narcissism and the influence of gender. *Mental Health, Religion & Culture*, *7*(4), 277–288. https://doi.org/10.1080/13674670310001606478

Watson, T. (2014). *A treatise concerning meditation*. Waxkeep.

Weidmann, R., Chopik, W. J., Ackerman, R. A., Allroggen, M., Bianchi, E. C., Brecheen, C., Campbell, W. K., Gerlach, T. M., Geukes, K., Grijalva, E., Grossmann, I., Hopwood, C. J., Hutteman, R., Konrath, S., Küfner, A. C. P., Leckelt, M., Miller, J. D., Penke, L., Pincus, A. L., & Back, M. D. (2023). Age and gender differences in narcissism: A comprehensive study across eight measures and over 250,000 participants. *Journal of Personality and Social Psychology*, *124*(6), 1277–1298. https://doi.org/10.1037/pspp0000463

Welch, S. (2014). *A labyrinth prayer handbook: Creative resources for worship and reflection*. Canterbury.

Welsh, R., & Knabb, J. (2009). Renunciation of the self in psychotherapy. *Mental Health, Religion & Culture*, *12*(4), 401–414. https://doi.org/10.1080/13674670902752946

Westminster Shorter Catechism. (n.d.). What is the chief end of man? Retrieved March 21, 2025. https://prts.edu/wp-content/uploads/2016/12/Shorter_Catechism.pdf

Whaley, V. (2009). *Called to worship: The biblical foundations of our response to God's call*. Nelson.

Whitney, D. (2014). *Spiritual disciplines for the Christian life*. NavPress.

Wilhoit, J., & Howard, E. (2012). *Discovering lectio divina: Bringing Scripture into ordinary life*. InterVarsity.

Williams, K., & Lamport, M. (Eds.). (2021). *Theological foundations of worship: Biblical, systematic, and practical perspectives*. Baker Academic.

Wilson, A. (2021). *God of all things: Rediscovering the sacred in an everyday world.* Zondervan.

Wilson, J. (2018). *The simplicity of holy worship.* Puritan Publications.

Wolters, A. (2005). *Creation regained: Biblical basics for a reformational worldview.* Eerdmans.

Wolterstorff, N. (2021). Series introduction. In K. Williams & M. Lamport (Eds.), *Theological foundations of worship: Biblical, systematic, and practical perspectives.* Baker Academic.

Wright, C. (2013). *The mission of God: Unlocking the Bible's grand narrative.* InterVarsity.

Wright, C. (2017). *Cultivating the fruit of the Spirit: Growing in Christlikeness.* InterVarsity.

Wright, N. T. (2014). *For all God's worth: True worship and the calling of the church.* Eerdmans.

Yaden, D., Kaufman, S., Hyde, E., Chirico, A., Gaggioli, A., Zhang, J., & Keltner, D. (2019). The development of the Awe Experience Scale (AWE-S): A multifactorial measure for a complex emotion. *Journal of Positive Psychology, 14*(4), 474–488. https://doi.org/10.1080/17439760.2018.1484940

Yakeley, J. (2018). Current understanding of narcissism and narcissistic personality disorder. *BJPsych Advances, 24*(5), 305–315. https://doi.org/10.1192/bja.2018.20

Yousaf, O., Love, S., Hampson, P., Hedderly, J., & Rogers, M. (2022). Conceptualising and measuring mindfulness during worship and prayer: Scale development and initial validation of the Mindfulness during Worship Scale (MWS). *Personality and Individual Differences, 196,* 111683. https://doi.org/10.1016/j.paid.2022.111683

Zaleski, I. (2011). *Living the Jesus prayer.* Canterbury.

Zhao, H., Zhang, H., Xu, Y., He, W., & Lu, J. (2019). Why are people high in dispositional awe happier? The roles of meaning in life and materialism. *Frontiers in Psychology, 10,* 1208. https://doi.org/10.3389/fpsyg.2019.01208

Index

Abernethy, Alexis, 73, 84
abuse, 162, 197
acceptance and commitment therapy (ACT), xv*n*7, 68
accommodating new reality, 12, 57, 64, 136, 173, 174, 177
Adam and Eve
 banishment from Eden, 4
 rebellion of, 30
 worship of self, 44
admiring human talent exercise, 193–96
adoration, 75, 139
 prayers of, 102
adoration and thanksgiving, prayers of, 101
affections, 185
"all-knowing adolescent," 89–91
altruism, 61–62, 88
Amster, Michael, 136
Andresen, Jeffry J., 56
anxiety, 8, 17, 24–25, 64–65, 71, 78, 83, 88, 175
apophatic theology, 40–41, 43, 52
architecture, 136
Aroney-Sine, Christine, 47
arrow prayers, 102
Aruguete, Mara, 79
atheism, 3, 5–7, 9
atonement, 144–45
attend, attention (*AWE* exercise), 14, 22, 108, 121, 136
Augustine, 78n129
avoidance, 162
awe
 and altruism, 61–62
 in Christian worship, 38–42
 and connection, 62

 as construct, 60–62
 distinctively biblical form of, 97
 drives worship, 10, 17
 as emotion, 17, 57, 172–73
 of God, 70
 and gratitude, 12n54, 15, 62, 65
 as an intervention, 62–63
 and mental and spiritual health, 12–14, 61, 63–68
 psychological perspective on, 12–15, 56–63, 105–6
 and spirituality, 68–70
 and widening of attention, 64–65
Awe Experience Scale (AWE-S), 60
awe interventions, 13, 55
awe literature, 9, 55, 68, 133
AWE technique (attending, worshiping, enhancing), 14, 20, 22, 87, 107, 108–9, 120–21
awe triggers, xvii, 15, 55, 57, 58, 59, 71. *See also* cognitive/conceptual triggers; physical/sensory triggers; social/relational triggers
"awe walks," 13, 138

Baxter, Richard, 6–7
Beale, G. K., 27, 29
beginner's mind, xiii, 66–68
behaviors. *See* physical/sensory triggers
Belgic Confession, 181–82, 183
Bevere, John, 38–39
Bible
 on behaviors, 128–34
 grand narrative of, 171–72, 173, 174
 on relationships, 168–74
 on thoughts and images, 96–105
 on worship and awe, 10–12

221

Bible reading, 97, 118
Blatchford, Faith, 47–48
blessings of God, 122, 186
Block, Daniel, 1, 32
Bonhoeffer, Dietrich, 96
Book of Privy Counseling, 104
Bowring, John, 199
breathing in, 22
"breath of life," 48
Brooks, Samantha, 81
Brother Lawrence, 19–20, 22, 107, 150, 152
Brown, Warren, 73
Buddhist meditation, 106, 125
Buddhist mindfulness, xiv, 14, 16, 18, 20, 21, 66, 68, 85, 88n193, 107, 139
Buddhist psychology, 66, 67
Burroughs, Jeremiah, 33, 100, 111
Büssing, Arndt, 12n54, 69

Cabot, Richard, 72
Cain and Abel, 131
Calhoun, Adele, 21, 48, 144
Cappeau, Placide, 27
celebrity worship, 8, 44, 73–74, 79–81, 86
Celebrity Worship Scale, 80
childlike awe and wonder, 47, 49, 50, 56, 67, 68, 90
chills, 58, 59
Christian life
  importance of worship and awe in, 27
  telos of, 5
Christian meditation, 88n193, 99, 106, 198
Christian psychology, xvi
Christian spiritual disciplines, xvi, 16, 19, 21
Cloud of Unknowing, 104, 116
cognitive/conceptual triggers, xvii, 13, 15, 59, 71, 95–96, 105, 106, 108, 168, 199
cognitive flexibility, 81
common grace, 129, 134, 164, 172, 175, 178
Communion, 157–59
contemplation, 21, 46, 52, 88n193, 97, 103–5, 118
corporate worship, 18, 21, 76
covenant, 169
creation
  beauty of, 134
  vastness and mysteriousness of, 128, 135, 137
creation worship, 18, 87, 89, 174
Creator-creation distinction, 93
Creator worship, 18, 87, 89
Crosby, Fanny, 155
curiosity, 22, 66–67

daily log, 109–11, 140–41, 179–80
Daily Spiritual Experiences Scale (DSES), 76
Daly, M., xivn5
David (model of worshipful awe), 196
Davis, John Jefferson, 95
delight in God, 122
depression, 17, 64–65, 71, 78, 88, 175, 176
  and materialism, 8–9, 83
  and narcissism, 8
de Sales, Francis, 104
desert Christians, 102
desert monks, 99
disenchantment, 5–7, 9, 25, 174
dispositional awe, 65, 67, 68, 88, 137

eating, 7, 45, 98, 136
egocentrism, 3, 77
Einstein, Albert, 55, 71
Ellens, Harold, 72
El Olam, 48
El Shaddai, 48
empathy, 60, 61–62
empty self, 80, 85
enchantment, 9–10
enhance (AWE technique), 14, 22, 108, 121, 137
environmental distractions, 143, 145, 148, 150, 152, 154, 157, 159
esher, 122
Evagrius, 99
expand. *See* enhance (AWE technique)
experiential triggers. *See* social/relational triggers

false gods, 10
fear of God, 34, 39
fellowship with God, 10
fruit of the Holy Spirit, 132

gambling disorder, 91–93
general revelation, 30–31, 40, 42, 106, 129, 134
God
  attributes of, 43, 59, 100–101, 185, 197
  center of Christian life, 27, 52, 173
  at center of creation, 20, 22, 30, 130, 164
  goodness of, 100, 170
  holiness of, 101, 131
  incomprehensibility of, 174, 178
  love of, 40–41, 77
  names of, 48
  power of, 101, 170
  presence of, 101
  simplicity of, 178

sovereignty of, 10, 27
vastness and mysteriousness of, 16, 61, 159, 163, 173, 199
wisdom of, 100, 170
goosebumps, 58, 59
grand narrative of Scripture, 4, 31, 139, 171–72
gratitude, 12n54, 15, 58, 62, 65, 107, 139
Great Pyramid of Giza, 58
Greenacre, Phyllis, 56
Guigo II (Carthusian monk), 45, 98

hagah, 99, 122
Haidt, Jonathan, 57, 105
Harrison, Irvin, 56
Hayward, R. D., 70
Henry, Matthew, 112–13, 153–54
Hindu mantra meditation, 106
human beauty, 176
humans, humanity
  created in image of God, 11, 29
  designed to worship God, 10–12, 28–29
  purpose to glorify God and enjoy him forever, 31–32
  rebellion against God, 4
  as relational beings, 172
human talent, 176, 193–96
human virtue, 176
humility, 65, 88
Hylan, John, 71
hymn meditation, 119–20
hypervigilance, 162

idolatry, 4, 29, 42, 44, 45, 73, 78n129, 93, 139
  psychological and spiritual consequences of, 45
idol worship, 73–74, 86, 108, 172
Ignatian spirituality, 20, 103, 113–16
Ignatius of Loyola, 103, 113, 188–91
image of God, 44, 168–69, 178
imaginative contemplation, 103
"imaging creatures," 29–30
incomprehensibility, experience of, 58, 87, 198.
  See also God, incomprehensibility of
industrialization, 3
inside-to-outside worship, 133
integrative perspective, on worship and awe, 15–23
intimacy with God, 47
intrusive memories, 123, 162
Israel, sacrificial system, 34

Jesuits, 102–3
Jesus Christ
  as awe-inspiring neighbor, 23
  crucifixion of, 144–45
  deserves our worship, 11
  as exemplar for worship of God, 171
  love of, 187–88
Jesus Prayer, 102, 192–93
justification, 4

kataphatic theology, 40–41, 43, 52
Kearns, P. O., 68
Keltner, Dacher, 57, 105, 167
Klapp, Orrin, 72
Knox, John, 29, 44
Krause, N., 70
Kuyper, Abraham, 55

labyrinth exercise, 145–48
labyrinth prayer, 133
lectio divina, 45–46, 51, 52, 97, 99, 103, 104, 118–19, 124, 181
Lewis, C. S., 2–3, 19, 27, 36
life, as gift of God, 49
Lin, Chien-Hsin, 73
Lin, Ying-Ching, 73
listening to a hymn exercise, 155–57
loneliness, 82, 86, 88, 93
Lozza, Edoardo, 82
Luo, Li, 62
Luther, Martin, 29, 43

Macchia, Frank, 39
mantra, 99
materialism, 3, 8–9, 81–84, 86, 92, 174
McCutcheon, Lynn, 79–81
McGowin, Emily Hunter, 39
medieval contemplation, 116–18
meditating on creation exercise, 181–82
meditating on God's gifts exercise, 184–86
meditating on God's providence exercise, 182–84
meditating on Jesus's love exercise, 187–88
meditating on Jesus's resurrection exercise, 188–91
meditation, 21, 40, 45–46, 52, 98–101, 118, 133
meditative walking exercise, 148–50
mental disorders, xiv, xv, xvi, 14, 65
mental health, xiv, 63–68
  and materialism, 83–84
  and worship, 85–86, 88
Meyer, Stephen, 72

"microdosing mindfulness," 14, 20
mindfulness, xiii–xiv, 14, 16–17, 67, 77, 83
mirror metaphor exercise, 142–43
money, 82, 86, 92
monologic prayer, 101, 102
music, 136
mysteriousness, 75, 90, 135, 163, 177. *See also* God, vastness and mysteriousness of; vastness, experience of

narcissism, 3, 7–8, 77–79, 86
narcissistic personality disorder (NPD), 78
nature
  induces awe, 137–38
  worshipful experiences in, 135, 137
nature hike, 163
neuropsychology, and worship, 72
New Testament
  on awe, 40
  on worship, 37–38
Newton, John, 155
non-Christian worship and awe, 44–45
"no-self," 66, 67, 68. *See* also "small self"

"O Holy Night" (hymn), 50
Old Testament
  on awe, 39
  on God, 130–31
  on worship, 33–36, 134
ordinariness, of life, 2–4
other-focused, 65
others, as social/relational trigger, 175, 176
other worship, 79–81, 86
Owen, John, 33

participation in communion exercise, 157–59
Peterson, David, 32
petition and intercession, prayers of, 101
physical/sensory triggers, xv, 13, 15, 105, 127–29, 135–36, 138–39, 164
Pieters, Rik, 82
pilgrimages, 145–46
Piper, John, 185
pivoting from self, other, and thing worship to God worship, xv, 25, 45, 47, 66, 85, 88, 89, 93, 96, 134, 139, 198–99
play deprivation, 47
post-traumatic stress disorders (PTSD), 162–63
practicing the presence of God exercise, 150–52
prayer, 21, 46, 97, 101–3, 118
"praying with the eyes," 144
Preston, Jesse, 69

providence, 30, 169–71, 173, 174, 178, 182–84
Psalms
  meditation on, 198
  orientation, disorientation, and new orientation, 35–36
psychology
  perspective on cognitive/conceptual triggers, 105–6
  perspective on physical/sensory triggers, 134–35
  perspective on social/relational triggers, 174–76
Puritan prayer of praise exercise, 153–54
Puritans
  on meditation, 111–12, 184–86
  prayers of, 102, 112–13
  spirituality of, 20
  on worship, 33

rainbow, 90–91
reading, 45–46
re-enchantment, 7, 9
relationships. *See* social/relational triggers
relationship with God, 173, 175, 176–79
religion, as organized system, 75
Religious Background and Behavior questionnaire (RBB), 77
reverence, 75, 79
reverential awe, xiv, 17, 75–76, 96–97
  Baxter on, 6–7
  Brother Lawrence on, 21
  Christian form of, 20
  for creation, 128
Richins, Marsha, 83
Robison, Robert, 155
Ross, Allen, 169
Rudd, Melanie, 61
rumination. *See* self-rumination

Saint-Jure, Jean Baptiste, 167
sanctification, 4
Sansone, Lori, 81
Sansone, Randy, 81
Saroglou, V., 68
Schneider, K., 84
Screwtape Letters, The, 2–3
Scripture. *See* Bible
secular awe, 17
secularization, 3
self, not at center, 30. *See* also "small self"
self-aggrandizement, 82
self-centeredness, 3, 8

self-criticism, 197, 198
self-denial, 68
self-entitlement, 79
self-esteem, 64
self-importance, 108
self-preoccupation, xv, 9, 13, 62, 97, 162–63, 164, 175, 177
self-rumination, xvi, 14, 17, 62, 63–64, 88, 124, 137, 162–63
self-worship, 4, 5, 30, 56, 77–79, 86
Sesini, Giulua, 82
Shin, Faith, 69
"small self," 66, 69, 70, 175, 177
social/relational triggers, xvii, 15, 59, 71, 105, 164, 167, 168, 174–77, 199
special revelation, 31, 40, 42, 106
Spiritual Assessment Inventory (SAI), 76–77
spiritual disciplines, 131–36
spirituality
  and awe, 68–70, 105–6
  and fewer symptoms of narcissism, 7
  and well-being, 101
  and worship, 74–75
spiritual transformation, 84–85
Strawn, Brad, 73
stress, xvi, 71
supernatural causality, 175

tabernacle, 35
Taylor, Charles, 5–7, 174
technology, 3
telos, teleology of life, 3, 28, 29, 42, 52
temple, 35
Ten Commandments, 10, 29
theism, 9
thing worship, 81–84, 86
"This Is My Father's World" (hymn), 119–20
thoughts and images. *See* cognitive/conceptual triggers
Tozer, A. W., 1, 29, 32, 44, 127
trauma, xvi, 65, 71, 123–24, 162, 175
Treatise on the Love of God, 104
tree of life, 96
tree of the knowledge of good and evil, 96–97
trinitarian worship, 37
Tripp, Paul, 38
Twenge, Jean, xivn5, 78
Tyler, J. M., 68

union with Christ, 37–38

Valley of Vision, 102, 153
Van Cappellen, P., 68

vastness, experience of, 58, 59, 60, 66, 71, 75, 87, 90, 128, 137, 163, 177, 198
verbalized rumination, 122
virtual reality (VR), 63, 138
visio divina, 133
visio divina exercise, 144–45
Vitz, Paul, 78n129

wait. *See* worship (AWE technique)
walking, 133
walking with God, 6
Wang, Gouzhou, 83
Watson, Thomas, 184–86
Watts, Isaac, 155
Westminster Shorter Catechism, 5
"When I Survey the Wondrous Cross" (hymn), 155–56
Whitney, Donald, 21, 132, 142
Wilson, John, 33
wonder, 66–67, 70
worldview, 28–29
World-Wide Labyrinth Locator, 146
worry, xvi
worship, 16, 87
  as celebration, 72, 169
  of Creator or his creation, 75
  definition of, 32
  as foundational, 31
  integrative perspective on, 86–93
  mechanism through which awe is pursued, 56
  and mental and spiritual health, 17, 25, 85–86
  in the Old Testament, 131
  psychological perspective on, 12–15, 71–84
  of self. *See* self-worship
  as spiritual discipline, 48, 128
  and spirituality, 74–75, 84–85
  as telos of Christian life, 42
worship (AWE technique), 14, 22, 108, 121, 136–37
worship and awe
  biblical perspective, 10–12
  integrative perspective, 15–23
  psychological perspective, 12–15, 76–84
  in psychotherapy, 50–52, 91–93
  as telos for humanity, 11
worshipfulness, xiii–xiv, 5, 13, 16, 38, 107, 146
worshiping creation. *See* creation worship
Wright, N. T., 32

yare, 39
Yousaf, Omar, 86

Zhao, Huanhuan, 61